WALK
CORI

G000230097

With Friends,
Flowers and Food

John Waller

YIANNIS BOOKS
England

YIANNIS BOOKS

WALKING THE CORFU TRAIL
Copyright © 2010 by John Waller

Published in 2010 by YIANNIS BOOKS
101 Strawberry Vale, Twickenham, TW1 4SJ UK

Layout and typesetting by Mike Cooper,
25 Orchard Rd, Sutton SM1 2QA

Printed by CPI Antony Rowe, Chippenham, Wiltshire, UK

288 pp
ISBN 978-0954-7887-6-6

Walking the Corfu Trail

To Hilary Whitton Paipeti
who loves her island so much

Acknowledgements

I thank Hilary Whitton Paipeti, the co-founder of the Corfu Trail, who has been in the forefront of so many campaigns to keep Corfu the unspoilt treasure that so many love. Her essential guide to walking the Trail can be obtained from www.corfutrailguide.com.

To the cast of characters, I also give thanks. Without their support my walk would not have been possible. In particular, my team mate Sydney Fremantle has put in many hours identifying the flowers I photographed.

The maps showing the Corfu Trail are published by Freytag & Berndt and are useful guides to the journey and to planning future walks.

My daughter has worked late hours in editing my manuscript. It is proof of her love for Corfu.

The numerous quotations from Edward Lear's letters have been taken from *Edward Lear – the Corfu Years* by Denise Harvey and Company of Athens and Dedham.

The characters

In order of appearance.

The team:

JANNIE WALLER, in charge of transport

JOHN WALLER, always last on the walk

CHARLES HENDERSON CB, ex Head of Energy Directorate, Department of Trade and Industry, ex Chairman of Total UK

SYDNEY FREMANTLE CBE, ex Head of International Energy Policy, Department of Trade and Industry

The friends and guest walkers:

NIKOS PAPAVLASSOPOULOS, Civil Engineer

'HARRY' VASSILAKIS, waymarker of Corfu Trail

DIMITRIS CHARITOS, President of Corfu Travel Agents

MITCH and DENISE CONYARD, Heating Engineer and Interior designer

BILL and BARBARA POPE, both retired teachers

FOTIS DOUKAKIS, co-owner of Theodoros Taverna, Ag. Gordis

HILARY WHITTON PAIPETI, co-founder of Corfu Trail and editor of the *Corfiot*

ROGER and PAT HUNSTONE, retired Travel Consultant

DIERK and CHRISTINE HOGE, retired European Space Agency and Eurobus respectively

PATRICIA COOKSON, founder of Corfu Villas, now CV Travel

KEITH MILLER, NBC News Senior Foreign Correspondent

JIM POTTS OBE, author and retired director British Council in Sweden etc

PETER and PAM JENKINS, retired photographers

JUDY MACKREL, involved in Corfu Tourism since 1970

FRIED AUMANN, co-founder of Corfu Trail

The plan is taking shape

Today is Easter Saturday 2009 – Orthodox Easter. I'm sad. For the ten years since I retired, we have celebrated Easter with around one hundred thousand Greeks on the Esplanade of Corfu Town, the largest square in the Balkans and the cricket ground of the British for the 50 years of their rule in the 19th century. Today we will miss this unique experience and walk in the mountains.

At 11 this morning high up on Mt. Pantokrator, Corfu's highest point at 915 metres, I look towards the Town and imagine the scene. At the sound of a gun, enormous clay pots are pushed off the balconies of the beautiful six-storey buildings in the historic centre – now a World Heritage Site – and crash to the ground. This ancient custom is said to represent the betrayal of Judas. Jannie and I would then break through the crowd and jog around the magnificent Garitsa Bay to claim a table in *Nautilus* next to the windmill, share a small *Poikilia Thalassinon*, the local *fruit de mer*, drink a half-litre of chilled white wine and gaze across the bay to the Venetian Old Fort and, in the distance, Mt. Pantokrator.

The Old Fort's twin peaks, *Koryphai* in Greek, give us the name of the island. Legend has it they are the testicles of Uranus, petrified after he had been emasculated by his son Kronos!

Legend also tells us that Mt. Pantokrator was the final battleground of the ancient Corcyraeans. The oligarchic party entrenched itself half-way up the mountain. There, for two years, they defied the democrats of the town. Then they were wiped out in a terrible internecine massacre.

For lunch today we are sitting in the square of the last village before the summit of Mt. Pantokrator, beside the great elm tree which shelters the centre of Strinilas from the summer heat.

Hilary Paipeti, co-founder of the Corfu Trail and organiser of the Saturday walks on the island, has just led us across the wild karst plateau below the peak of Mt. Pantokrator to a scramble down the almost sheer rock wall to Spartilas.

No plate of fried fish today, just eggs and chips – but what eggs! They are fresh and full of flavour from the chickens that run free behind Stamatis' little taverna. This is simple country food to follow a glorious hike.

Standard fare it might be, but special: white *taramasalata*, not the usual red smoked roe paste of tourist tables; a plate of *nouboulo*, Corfu's unique pork filet or tenderloin, salted for a week and then smoked over scented wood in a traditional oven; dry and smoked local salamis; the ever present *horiatiki*, the Greek salad plus a extra plate of local *feta*. This is not the cheese found on supermarket shelves; it is kept under the counter for special customers. It is neither dry nor damp, but smooth and succulent; not sharp but sweet – a creamy treasure from Petalia, the village one passes before approaching the karst plateau.

"I hear you are writing another book, John," someone says.

We are a few loyal walkers today; most of the usual crowd of Greeks, British, French, Germans and Dutch that, each Saturday, follow the goat tracks through the olive groves and mountain maquis are celebrating Easter with friends in their villages or in town. We dozen instead enjoy the tranquillity of the countryside.

"Another book? What about?"

"The Corfu Trail."

Eyes turn to Hilary, the co-founder of Corfu's long-distance footpath. With a substantial EU grant, she and Fried Aumann set up the Trail in 2001 and have waymarked and maintained it ever since.

"But it's Hilary's Trail."

Hilary laughs. "It's everyone's. John's book will bring

other walkers to the island and that will be good for Corfu."

"You are going to walk it?" questions someone in disbelief. My Danish wife Jannie and I are usually the rearguard in Hilary's expeditions. Jannie has problems going downhill – there are few hills in Denmark – and I have difficulty on the ascents.

"I've just bought a walking stick in Metsovo," I boast, as if this would make the difference. Beautiful Metsovo is high in the Pindus Mountains on the mainland and home to the Vlachs, the transhumant shepherds who once roamed with their enormous flocks throughout the south Balkans, from the valleys in the winter to the mountain pastures in the summer.

"You'll get lost," chipped in another fellow.

On a recent walk, the rearguard had fallen so far behind that we had indeed got lost. Today, although the yellow waymarks had guided us through myrtle thickets that linked the small green fields of the rugged limestone karst plateau and down the tunnel of holm oak to the cliff above Spartillas, I would not have had full confidence of finding my way if Hilary and Fried had not been leading.

"But the stick has a compass on it. I will look at my Freytag & Berndt map, which shows the Trail and well – just map-read!"

"John will be fine. He'll follow my guide," encourages Hilary. Hilary's *The Companion Guide to the Corfu Trail* is in fact essential for serious walkers. Her instructions are precise and the maps are drawn from the most detailed available. "If they get lost, they can phone me and I will drive to the rescue."

"In the famous yellow Suzuki 4x4," someone chips in. "It'll go anywhere, won't it, Hilary?"

"If a donkey can go along a *kalderimi*, the cobbled path will be no problem for the Suzuki."

"We'll be setting out in ten days time. On each day we'll be inviting a different friend to join us: a guest who knows the area we are walking through," I add. "We'll ask them about their Corfu and talk about the island's future."

"Who are we then?"

"Two long-distance walkers, both ex-senior civil servants from England – average age over 70. One's an amateur botanist; so we'll take photos of flowers. The book will be called *Walking the Corfu Trail with Friends, Flowers and Food* – a taste of the countryside for independent walkers – expert or novice."

"The subtitle should be *Turn Left at the Olive Tree*." Everyone laughs. There are over three million olive trees on the island.

"Like the walking guide that said 'Turn left at the cow!'" quips Hilary. "My guide gives detailed instructions. John, I prefer *Walking over Olives* as a title."

"But search engines looking for 'Corfu' find the four books I published in the top seven titles, with *Greek Walls, an Odyssey in Corfu* at number one ahead of Gerald Durrell."

"Then add a sub-title *From Kavos to Agni*," suggests Hilary referring to Corfu's infamous and famous resorts.

"*In eight days*." I add.

"You're mad. All the way from Kavos …"

"You mean *Chavos*," chips in one of the walkers; by now the wine is flowing. Kavos is the sin city of the south, the bacchanalian haunt of the 18-30s.

"… to Agni?" Agni is at the other end of the social scale. On Corfu's north-east coast, it is nick-named *Kensington-on-Sea*, and in summer 2008 the area hit the headlines over *Yachtgate*. Labour peer and ex-European Commissioner Lord Mandelson, Tory shadow chancellor George Osborne and Russian oligarch Oleg Deripaska were reported to have had 'conversations' there: the first two about Prime Minister Gordon Brown; the latter two about contributions to Conservative Party coffers. Local resident Lord Rothschild then became involved.

The general incredulity persists. "John, are you walking for charity, then?"

People had indeed offered me money for the walk, but I was worried I wouldn't finish. My past record of long-distance trips was a catalogue of failure: because of the weather, the Alpine guide refused to take us along the *Haute Route*; the boat accompanying us on a round-Corfu windsurf refused to go to sea, and we got only a quarter of the way before the wind died; and I have still not finished my punt trip down the Thames from source to sea.

Still walking for charity is an excellent idea – maybe one of my readers will walk the Trail and raise money for some worthy cause and have a great holiday as well.

"No, I'm doing it because I'm angry – very angry. People write such lies about our island; I want to tell everyone the truth."

"Did you read what Simon Jenkins wrote?" interjects Hilary, brandishing a crumpled copy of *The Times*. She gets even more irate than me when journalists slag off her beloved home of nearly 30 years.

I read from his article: "'The ruination of Corfu by developers cannot be regarded as a gain for civilisation, or even really for the visitors. Spain now regrets the desecration of the Costa Brava, its towns reduced to such ugliness as to be deserted by package tours. Few countries seem able to link their planning system to some concept of beauty, at least until it is too late.'"

"That's wrong for a start," explains Hilary, "as planning laws in Corfu restrict building to seven metres tall. That's no Spanish-style ruination! He obviously knows *nothing* about Corfu. The patches that have been 'spoilt' are tiny. Vast tracts of the island are completely unspoiled, and there are innumerable viewpoints with *no sight* of human activity."

Now I am a great admirer of Simon Jenkins: I fully support

his long-running opposition to the war in Afghanistan. But surely Corfu is nothing like Simon Jenkins' description of the Costa Brava. I hope my walk will illustrate the truth.

Even today's short section of the Trail has given me a foretaste of future discoveries. Standing on the edge of the almost vertical wall of the Mt. Pantokrator massif, beside the ruins of the once beautiful Taxiachis Chapel, I had looked down on Ipsos beach nine hundred metres below. From this vantage point, I saw that, driving along the sea front, any visiting journalist would be saddened by the rather tatty two-storey tourist shops and restaurants. However, I could also see that less than a hundred metres behind the strip development the olive groves which cover the island begin. If the journalists chose to deviate inland, then Corfu's treasures would reappear.

Indeed, Hilary had planned her final walk of the season to start from this same Ipsos beach and to finish, within twenty minutes, in virgin countryside for the traditional end-of-season picnic.

My thoughts had triggered an idea for other ex-pats on the island to take up. Just as my A5 guides *Corfu Town Walks* will encourage people to wander off the Tourist Trail in town, a similar small guide might lead tourists off the beach to the little villages inland. The *Ipsos Walks* would take them to Agios Markos and Ano Korakiana, where they could wander through narrow alleys under beautiful gateways and rest at the café-bars. They would witness scenes of village life and people, similar to those Theresa Nicholas has recorded in her book *Corfu Sketches*: the old widow in black riding past on her donkey and the elderly men playing backgammon at a table beside the road.

I join in the conversation again. "It's not only *The Times* that infuriates me; it's the *Guardian*, the paper I have read all my life." I too unfold my evidence and read: 'Mon Repos, one-time palace of Prince Philip, the Duke of Edinburgh, had been allowed to fall into disrepair.'"

"That's not true," says someone; "it was beautifully renovated a few years ago. The *Guardian* should write about its museum which illustrates Corfu's history – it's great. The photos there from 1857 by John Shakespear are unbelievable. He bought, what he called 'the photographic machine' from Edward Lear for fifteen shillings!"

I read on: "'Corfu Town, a protected UNESCO heritage site, had been left to rot.' This makes me so furious. I remember it back in 1966, a Balkan backwater – though with some fine buildings – with baby Fiats and donkeys passing through grubby streets. It's pedestrianised now. My friend Nikos, who's the engineer on the refurbishment project, told me that over six years €45 million is being spent on 76 different projects. He'll be my first guest on the walk. I checked his figures out with the mayor, who gave me a full list with 218 items totalling €77 million."

"I reckon the *Guardian's* Greek correspondent has got it in for us," says Hilary. "She couldn't have even been to look at Corfu Town. Major renovation work started in 1994 when the European Summit was held in Corfu. At that time they said we would never be ready for the summit; and they were wrong."

I continue. "They even quote that 'we still don't have a hospital and new born babies die as a result'. At least the *Guardian* published a correction on this."

"But they should check up on the facts before they publish such lies," says someone in defence of the local doctors.

"I want visitors who came here in the past to come back to Corfu and love our town and countryside," I conclude.

"Then let's talk about the Trail," suggests Hilary. "You say you will walk it in eight days – but my *Guide* says strong hikers will take ten days for its 220 kilometre length." She pauses, then with a sweet smile adds: "And you are not a strong walker, are you John?"

"Well, I'll walk the last section from Agni to the end of the Trail in the cool of autumn."

"When the cyclamen cover the island and the *Sternbergia* hide in the mountains – our second Spring. I like that."

"Now we'll take a one-day short cut along the west coast via Agios Gordis, so missing out the two-day loop in the middle of the island. I'll do the loop in October as well. I want visitors to be able to walk the Trail in a week's holiday, plus the weekends, if they are really keen."

"And where will you stay?"

"Jannie will take us back to Agios Gordis every night, but hikers have a number of options. One is to use Anna Aperghi's travel office which arranges accommodation and transports luggage from starting point to end point each day. Or they could stay in town and get a bus to the start point and back from the end point each morning and evening. Finally they could do as we are doing, staying near the centre of the island and organise their own transport."

"Or they could walk parts of the Trail over a number of visits to the island," suggests Hilary, "and join us on our Saturday walks." Now, there's an invitation worth taking up.

That night we attend midnight Mass in Corfu Town. Whereas Catholics bring lighted candles to their service, Greeks assemble on the Esplanade holding their candles unlit. In the darkness, beside the priests on their podium, one central candle is lit and the flame is passed from person to person until a hundred thousand little glimmers create a brightness that illuminates us all. On the stroke of midnight, the magic words *Xristos Anesti*, 'Christ is risen', light up under the cross on the Old Fort, and the sky bursts into flames as an immense fireworks display commences. At this point we normally break our Easter fast with a meal which lasts well into the early morning and tomorrow there will be more religious parades in Town and families will lunch on lamb, which has been turning on the spit all morning, and break red painted hard boiled eggs, as we do with conkers in Britain.

But this year we have serious business to attend to: we join the Sunday walkers. These are mainly British residents, who live in the centre of the island. They walk with Hilary's group if she ventures south from the magnificent, mountainous, but for them, remote north of the island.

Not only do I confirm that some friends will join me on my eight day walk, but I can also continue the serious training I need for the journey ahead. Like Hilary's Saturday walks, the Sunday group uses a clever ploy: the weaker walkers, including Jannie, are persuaded to be 'Wimps' for the day and concentrate on the extra pleasures in life, the coffee and scones, as well as a short amble amongst the olive trees down to the beach. The rest walk fast.

The Sunday walkers today start at Paramonas on the west coast and follow the Corfu Trail on its first serious ascent, the 300-metre climb up onto the west coast ridge and over to Ano Pavliana. If all goes to plan, this will actually form the last part of our third day – the first two-thirds being across the gentle rolling countryside of the south of the island. At the top of the climb, we gaze in awe north to Paleokastritsa, two days away on our journey. This part of the island, overlooking the open sea to the west, is so underdeveloped, yet less than half-an-hour by car from Corfu Town, that I am certain that this view would be able to win what has become locally known as the 'Simon Jenkins challenge'.

In the centre of picturesque Ano Pavliana, which I remember from the early 1970s, when 'Colonels' ruled in Greece, as having a well-dressed young 'policeman' watching over everyone, I join up with a tall, athletic Greek, whom everyone calls Harry but I have never met before.

We stride out ahead of the rest on our return to Paramonas. We pass through the lovely village square and then walk round the back of the ridge to meet up with Jannie and the other 'Wimps' who are sitting in an olive grove beside the bridge over the little stream from Agios Mattheos. Harry turns out to be the answer to the missing link in my journey – Day 2 from Lefkimmi to St. George of the South. He, with Hilary and Fried, waymarks the Corfu Trail (his signs are all high up, while Hilary, a whole foot shorter, puts her waymarks way down!) and he is happy to guide us as long as we can finish in time for him to get back to Town to open up his café bar. Jannie assures him that she will drive him back from St. George to Lefkimmi, where he will leave his car.

The Sunday walkers, now gathered into one group, drive to Pentati for an excellent lunch at Chris's Place overlooking our bay of Agios Gordis. Sitting out with friends, and eating and drinking too much, is one of the major pleasures of the walking on Corfu. But today Jannie and I leave early to reconnoitre the southern half of our journey as she has the key role of transport manager. Our daughter thinks that Jannie cannot read a map and is never certain in which compass direction she is pointing, but I am confident she can find her way round the island after 40 years.

We start by making our way to the end of the Lefkimmi bypass. The road to the right goes to our starting point Kavos, straight ahead is Lefkimmi Port and to the left is the back entrance into the town. We decide to turn left and just before the bridge over the river we turn right to arrange for our first meal to be ready at the end of our first day. Charles, the leader of the team, has requested fish.

Bourdetto and *Bianco* are Corfu's two most special fish dishes: one red, one white; one hot, one garlicky. *Bourdetto* comes from the pan-Adriatic word *brodetto*, meaning stew with tomato sauce and hot red pepper. Traditionally it was eaten in Corfu by fisherman in winter when they returned cold and wet from a night's fishing. We will, we hope, be neither cold nor wet. So *Bianco* it will be.

Having carefully pre-booked our lunch, we carry on to Kavos, where Jannie will drop us off at the start of our epic journey. Day 1 looks fine so we check out Day 2. I am already getting nervous, as Harry, who is rather larger than me, had been adamant that we finish on time so he can open up in town.

The good news is that the original Day 2 of the Trail has been changed. The Freytag & Berndt map shows it going along the coast from Lefkimmi and across the Alikes saltpans, which in Venetian times generated 3% of the island's income – the other 97% coming from the olive oil for the lamps of Venice! But a beach-side hotelier took against the hikers and kept on removing the Trail signs, so now the Trail goes through the town, across the bypass and down to the west coast; thus saving an hour's walk.

By missing out the section of the walk through the rather lovely old town of Lefkimmi, with its beautiful churches, which Hilary documents in her *Companion Guide*, we can start on the bypass, the first unasphalted road south of the Lidl supermarket, further reducing the walk to four hours; so Harry will be back in town well before three.

As a final contingency, in case of delay Jannie checks out the side roads leading down from the main road to the beaches we will pass on our walk. She can always pick him up if we are running late. These precautions seem sensible.

Day 3 will be easy for her as she knows the start and the end; so all we need to do is to check out our lunch-time restaurant. Day 4 is home territory.

Jannie and I feel well pleased with our day: we have a full guest-list and half the route reconnoitred. The plan is taking shape.

With ten days to go, I just need to confirm our guests, arrange the remaining meals on route – *and carry on training*.

The team arrives

Today I have to finalise the arrangements for our first day's walk and confirm our first guest walker – Nikos, my building engineer – and then pick up the team from the airport.

I phone Nikos' mobile. I can just imagine him: hands free, on his Honda moped, stuck in traffic in Corfu Town. Engineers buy mopeds and lawyers buy classic motorcycles to beat the jams. Their choice matches their status. His phone continues to ring.

Maybe he's not in town, but down south near Lefkimmi, or even Kavos.

He finally answers.

"*Nai?*"

"Niko?"

"Hello, my friend. How are you?"

"Good, very good."

"What's news?" he asks.

"Maria's closing down," I reply sadly.

"Maria?"

"You told me she would make the *Bianco*, but she's stopping work this year. You didn't tell me she's nearly 80. But she took me next door to *Stis Basilos*; they can make some. And, oh yes! Jannie went down to the River Taverna, where we've been before. They are going to make some too!"

"Let me ask Maria. She makes the best in Lefkimmi. I always go there."

"No, don't worry, I will cancel *Stis Basilos*. They are a nice family but we'll go to the River Taverna – Hilary recommends them. Are you still on for Saturday?"

There is a long pause. I knew it.

"I'm shooting. You said you would remind me. I have to go to Saloniki; everyone's there." Nikos is in the Greek National shooting squad.

"But, Niko, you promised me you'd come! I don't know the far south. I'll only forgive you if you get to London in 2012."

I have to forgive Nikos. Eight years ago, I had vowed he would be my friend for life – if he finished the access road up to our house on time. The builder had proposed an eight-metre high retaining wall with foundations on the main road below. Nikos agreed with me that our beautiful island must be saved from concrete and our olive trees must be retained, so we needed to find an alternative solution.

"We will build the road across the contours of the land and save the olive trees. The road will be very steep and the corner up to the house will be very sharp," he warned, "but it will work."

Nikos' career has progressed rapidly over recent years. He was appointed one of the engineers for Corfu Town's World Heritage Site. I am looking forward to hearing his comments on the *Guardian* article, but this will have to wait to the meal we will have after the walk is over. Instead I will rely on my walking team to pass judgement. As retired senior civil servants, they would definitely be unbiased.

I am an optimist; I always look for the silver lining. Without our local 'guide' we will have to depend on Hilary's *Companion Guide*. If we lose our way we will blame Hilary. If we don't we will congratulate Charles, our chief navigator. But first I must sort out the issue of the *Bianco*, the Corfiot fish speciality. I phone the River Taverna.

"Hello, Spiro. I'm the Englishman. We came Sunday before last and said we wanted *Bianco* for five this Saturday."

"No problem. What time?"

"About three, but we will pop by and confirm our plans earlier in the day, before we walk from Kavos."

That was easy. Now the difficult one – *Stis Basilos*.

"Hello, I'm the Englishman. We came Sunday before last

19

and said we wanted *Bianco* for five this Saturday." There is silence. "I'm the English walker, do you remember?"

"Yes, of course, but we made the *Bianco* last Saturday."

I apologise. I grovel – I'm used to grovelling.

"Plan the dive and dive the plan," my son and scuba buddy always used to say. Already my plans are going astray – even before we have started walking.

Now it is time to get to the airport; easyJet is punctual. Charles Henderson is serious and immaculately turned out in well-pressed trousers. He is pushing his wife Rachel, who suffers from MS and is in her wheelchair but is still cheerful. Sydney Fremantle, with an immense grin, follows along behind. Our botanist, he is dressed for the key role he will play on the expedition: he is in his shorts – his knees are white. My team looks tired and bedraggled, having left Gatwick at some unearthly hour of the morning. Charles picks up his hired car, a small Susuki jeep.

Sydney's enthusiasm is catching: "It looks such a green island!" Appropriately the sun, with perfect timing, has just come out. I cannot dishearten him by telling him that we have just had four days rain and that the flowers are on strike. Jannie and Sydney set off in the Land Rover.

As I leave the airport with Charles and Rachel I get the *Guardian* article off my chest. I mention the final two quotes from the leader of the new self-rule party for Corfu: "The island's heartland resembled a war zone of discarded cars and rubbish and the roads have become pot-holed death traps with more tourists dying on them every year."

"Sounds like a Liberal to me – a pavement politician," suggests Charles, knowing that I had been, for 17 years, a Liberal councillor on Richmond Council. What a wit!

"Charles, one of your jobs on the walk is to comment on the *Guardian's* points," I explain.

Ten minutes from the airport, we are climbing out of the

valley; the flowers are smiling, the olive trees show their silver and green, and towards Agii Deka, the cypresses stand tall in a great forest. Charles and Rachel are enchanted.

"I haven't seen any rubbish yet, just a couple of pieces of litter," says Charles. "It must be because of all the large wheelie-bins along the road – you even have blue ones for recycling. That politician should drive round the Oxford bypass if he wants real rubbish."

We drive over the pass above Sinarades, our local village, and start to descend. I decide to stop at our famous viewpoint to show my guests the little island of Ortholithi at the end of the great bay, which is surrounded by olive-clad mountains. Way below, Agios Gordis is recovering from the previous day's storm. The visibility is perfect.

"So where do you live, John?" asks Charles.

"One hundred metres – straight down!"

He looks over the cliff's edge. "I can't see any house below – so how do you know where it is?" A typical civil service question!

"Because someone drove over the cliff last week. The driver survived the fall – but bits of his car are still beside the road, just above the house."

They are not amused.

"Charles, do you think our resort is a 'ruination'?"

"No."

"Would you describe it as a 'descration'?"

"No way. Why do you ask?"

"Because Simon Jenkins wrote about the ruination of Corfu by developers and desecration like the Costa Brava."

"John, he'd better come here and see how wrong he is."

(The *Guardian* article to which I objected can be found on: http://www.guardian.co.uk/world/2008/sep/26/greece. It contains a photograph of Agios Gordis, from where we are standing.)

We drive home in silence. Charles stops his Suzuki on the main road and I suggest he drives up the very steep access road.

"But the ramp up to your drive is nearly vertical!" he exclaims.

"Our original ramp was removed when the main road disappeared down a 60-metre long pot-hole," I explain.

They get out of the car and inspect the new six-metre-high retaining wall and the destruction caused to our friend's hotel below when an underground river washed away the road and the old wall – the same river that in 1971 moved our own retaining wall down the mountain.

"Some pot-hole!" jokes Charles nervously.

"I'm an expert on pot-holes!" I volunteer. "We have a problem on the island – the weather. In winter, it rains so much that roads can become like rivers, washing away the surface if it is in poor repair."

"So how do we get up to the house?" asks Rachel in alarm. She has difficulty walking even a short distance.

"Charles, put the car in its lowest gear and four-wheel drive and go for it."

He looks up to see the road disappear around another retaining wall. "And when I get to the corner?"

"Keep going, you should get round without stopping, even if we can't in the Land Rover."

We get back in the car and Charles gets out the manual. After much pulling and shoving, the gear stick arrives at the right place and, with tyres screeching and wheels spinning, we are off. Round the corner we creep to the top.

"That's the last time I do that," says Rachel, shaking as she gets out.

"But I told Charles to order you a Suzuki to get you up to the house."

"Then I'll walk," she replies. After a pause, she adds, "somehow."

We sit down to fine food and cheap wine under the warm spring sun with a beautiful view of the bay below and the olive-covered mountains ahead, and then we retire for a long siesta. The team is now happy.

"What's on the agenda, John?" asks Charles, after a nap, in his best civil service manner.

I can almost imagine him calling me 'Minister', which makes me grin. "We are going to inspect the World Heritage Site and then we'll take a short training walk to a good restaurant."

"With good wine?" asks Sydney, perhaps as a comment on my cheap plonk.

"Ignore him," says Charles. "On all our walks together, he always says the same."

"Charles, your job is to use one of the laminated guides from my *Corfu Town Walks* and lead us round the Tourist Trail."

"He'll get us lost," interjects Sydney. "He can't read a map!"

"Rubbish, Sydney. I'll just check the accuracy of John's guide."

"And then tell me if you think the World Heritage Site has been left to rot – as suggested by the *Guardian*."

"Rotten paper," comments Charles, "I read the *FT*."

"And I read *The Times*," adds Sydney.

I decide not to fall for the bait.

We make for Town – all five of us in our Land Rover. Parking is always a problem right in the centre, but Rachel pulls out her Disabled Person's Parking Card as if it is a magic wand. It is. I'm impressed that it should work in Corfu, but on inspection of the card I find the blue European symbol with its twelve stars.

We are admitted to the car park on the outfield of the cricket square and sent to the parking place next to the British Palace of St. Michael and St. George and nearest to the French-built

Liston, Corfu's 'Rue de Rivoli' – for free!

Reading from his laminated guide to the first walk, 'Along the Tourist Trail', Charles gives a running commentary:

"Number 1 – the Old Fort, yes, I can see it. Number 2 – the Palace, that's obvious. Number 3 – the Liston, the arches. You see, Sydney, I can read a map."

"Must be a good map," Sydney replies.

"Number 4 – the Square of the Saints, that's correct." He starts striding out. "You say 100 metres to Number 5 – the centre of the World Heritage Site. It's only 80 metres."

He has long legs. "Lovely sketch isn't it? It was drawn thirty years ago. The tobacconist and the fruit and vegetable are still there," I comment.

"Oh, all right. We'll miss out Numbers 6 and 7, and look for 8. Let's try another walk. Which one, John?"

"Let's go on the last walk 'To Campielo, the Old Town'."

We go down Filellinon, a narrow alley with washing hanging across it high above us. We pass the Durrell School of Corfu and a beautiful Renaissance doorway and turn right to a sign pointing to the Venetian Well. Faced with steps, we leave Rachel in her wheelchair and admire the glorious Kremasti Square and the 17th-century well.

"Whoever said that the town has been left to rot is, well, talking rot. It's beautiful," says Charles.

"And lived in, not like Venice, where sadly the population is falling. You are seeing it at the best time of day, in the evening when most of the tourists have gone and the café bars are full of locals. I remember visiting San Gimignano many years ago. George, our great Greek friend, told us to arrive after all the tourist buses had left and stay in the Hotel Cisterna, right on the town's beautiful 14th-century central square. He was so right. I hope visitors to Corfu will stay in town, perhaps at the Hotel Kavalieri on the Esplanade or the Hotel Konstantinopolis overlooking the harbour, and then wander around our old town as Jannie and I have done for so many years."

We wheel Rachel back towards the Number 8 on the first walk, Agios Spiridonas, the main tourist shopping street. I notice she is wincing. The pavements in the Old Town are covered in old stones. I fear it has not the best disabled access.

Tourist shops all over the world sell plastic objects made in China. In Corfu, they also sell some great local products: olive wood dishes, kumquat liqueurs and crystalline fruits, silver jewellery made in the town and lace made in the villages. We are near the end of the day; I am impressed to see a couple of shopkeepers sweeping up cigarette-ends from the alleyways.

Before returning to the car park, we turn left through the Palace of St. Michael and St. George and come to *Mourayia*, the sea walls. The view to the north across the great bay to Mt. Pantokrator and the end of our trail is spectacular, particularly in the evening sunset.

Edward Lear – the inventor of the Limerick rhyming form, but also a magnificent landscape painter – looked out on 'Salvador', as he called Mt. Pantokrator, from his apartment on the *Mourayia*. He wrote in February 1863: 'The gorgeousness of the mountains has been daily most wonderful.' Later he commented: 'The same perfect weather. Hardly a cloud in the sky: every crag & wrinkle of Salvador, every gull & goose, every sail & boat, reflected clear & calm in the bright sea from 7.30 to 6 p.m. It is not possible to imagine greater beauty of nature.'

Getting back to the car park, the men leave Jannie and Rachel to drive to one of our favourite restaurants. We walk the length of the Esplanade, past the bandstand, a reminder of our colonial days which is used on Easter Saturday for midnight Mass.

At the south end of the Esplanade is the recently-restored Maitland Rotunda built as a memorial by Ionian well-wishers to the first Lord High Commissioner of the British Protectorate and Governor of Malta, Sir Thomas Maitland. 'King Tom' was an autocrat and was described at the time as 'insufferably rude and abrupt, particularly dirty in person, constantly drunk and surrounded by sycophants'. Maitland did, however, bring the finances of the island under control and started the road-building programme, one of the legacies of British rule. From 1818 to 1823, he supervised the building of the Palace of St. Michael and St. George, which became the headquarters of the Order of the same name, with honours being distributed to local worthies. The Palace, and particularly its Museum of Asiatic Art, is well worth a visit.

We continue over what were once the outer walls of the town down to the sea. This has been the battleground for a more recent vehicular skirmish. I have always found fallacious the argument by the anti-Europeans that the Union destroys national characteristics, particularly when it comes to parking. Socially-aware Danes display a clock on the dashboard to show how long they have been parking. The financially-motivated British buy a parking ticket, which is checked by income-generating traffic wardens. The Greeks unsuccessfully used parking fines against anarchic offenders. Then, to my personal annoyance, particularly as it was when I was visiting the mayor to discuss the *Guardian* article, they started to remove licence plates as a deterrent! Now they have decided to clear narrow streets by erecting the bollards we see placed on the hill.

Our short training walk proceeds round the length of Garitsa Bay, once described to me as 'the road to recovery'. It seems that doctors prescribe easy exercise to patients with heart problems: a gentle amble beside the sea on the promenade south of town. Sketches and watercolours from the first half of the eighteenth century show the British similarly taking their constitutionals.

I look at the team and decide which category we fall into: invalid or military? Charles, at over six-foot and slim, could have been an army man. Sydney Fremantle is descended from Admiral Fremantle and was in the navy during his national service. I feel like the recuperating medical case.

Today a few fishermen are dangling their lines off the sea wall. In all the years we have been in Corfu, I cannot remember a fish being caught; but I do recollect an octopus being hauled in and then smashed on the sea wall to tenderise it for the pot.

Each year when we arrive in Corfu in March, Jannie and I can check how stormy the winter has been. A huge bank of seaweed remains at the water's edge, the result of strong north-easterlies driving in this dead *Posidonio* from the underwater forests which lie between Corfu and the mainland. They shelter an extensive marine life, and have been rewarded by a *Natura 2000* listing, the European equivalent of our Sites of Special Scientific Interest.

Instead of continuing round to the windmill at the end of the bay at Anemomilos, we follow the road towards Kanoni, the 'One Gun Battery', so often mentioned by Edward Lear on his stays on the island over the winters from 1848 to 1864, the year when the British passed the Ionian Island into union with Greece.

After a hundred metres we bear left past the 10th-century Church of Saints Jason and Sosipatros, who brought Christianity to the island in 70AD. Corfu's only cross-shaped Byzantine church with a beautiful dome, it is a little gem and always worth a visit.

A few metres on, we arrive at *O Yiannis*, the best restaurant on the island, according to reports in the Travel sections of UK papers. For once, I agree with the British press.

In Greece, there are three main types of cooking: the grill, the *meze* of many starters, and the pots. There is a fourth, the gastra from the mountains of Epirus, but that is very rare. *O Yiannis* is the best pot place on the island and its proprietor, Costas, is carrying on a long tradition. In the early 1970s, we used to visit the original owner, Yiannis Kremonis, but as he got old the restaurant became scruffy, though the food stayed the same. Yiannis owned the plot of land next to us in Agios Gordis, but we never saw him there. After retirement he would still visit *O Yiannis*. One day, he came round and had a few too many. On his way home on his scooter, 'a building came out and hit him', or so he claimed.

Costas has dramatically upgraded the kitchens, though he blamed this on EU regulations. The décor inside the restaurant is particularly comforting. On one wall, there are old photographs of 19th-century Corfiot workers. Elsewhere, there are scenes of Corfu from the past. I have pestered poor Costas for a picture of fishermen bringing in their nets in Benitses, with an uncompleted Hotel San Stephano in the background. I have dated it at 1971, when my great friend George Manessis and I were struggling with our different building projects. But Costas is loath to part with a picture of such a well recognized location. Perhaps as compensation he gave me a photo of a boy with his dog taken in Perama in front of Mouse Island. I treasure it at home in England.

We are welcomed by Costas, his English wife Sarah, their daughter and their son, Will, who, dressed like his father in chef's outfit, helps with the cooking.

The main change to the cuisine is that there is now also a charcoal grill – for the Italians so Costas says. Otherwise the casseroles have changed little over the forty years since it originally opened.

The five of us enter the kitchen to inspect the *meze* and casseroles. This is standard procedure in Greece. Tonight, we choose:

Imam, the team's favourite starter: aubergine sliced in half and baked until soft, then an onion and tomato sauce poured over, rebaked and finally sprinkled with feta.

Bourdetto: the fish fan's choice: huge rock salmon steaks in onion, garlic, cayenne pepper and fresh tomato sauce based on a stone fish stock. Costas' special ingredient is a generous addition of sun-dried tomatoes.

Large, long, yellowy-green sweet peppers slowly baked.

Slow-cooked pork in beer sauce: the carnivore's favourite.

Meat balls in cumin sauce.

Gigantes, a standard classic: giant butter beans in a tomato sauce.

Beef in a red wine sauce.

Tsigarelli: greens, such as white beets and sorrel, in a cayenne sauce.

Slow-cooked lamb with prunes: another favourite, which I have tried to copy.

Sofrito, the Corfiot classic: slow-stewed veal steak in almost overpowering garlic sauce.

Sardines with sun-dried tomatoes, slow cooked in the oven: so soft I eat heads and all.

Oven-baked *Potates Fournou*, or rice or just bread accompany each main course.

We leave for another day the rabbit *stifado*, which has been slowly cooked with shallots; the oven-baked octopus; the *kleftiko*, very slowly-cooked lamb shoulder; *moussaka*; and the rooster in a white wine and mushroom sauce. At other times, Costas has snails and mussels.

We also missed out on Costas' *taramasalata* which Jannie says is the best she's ever tasted, even better than her own, which is made from smoked cod's roe ideally from a Danish smokery, bread, crushed garlic, lemon juice and olive oil. She hand-mixes the ingredients to give a slightly rougher texture; others prefer using a food mixer, with the oil added slowly at the end.

Two half-kilo red tin jugs of wine are brought to the table. Sydney, whom we have elected as team wine-taster, gives his verdict: "The red excellent, the white OK." We order a further litre of red wine.

Every dish is savoured and enjoyed.

"Summarise the plan, John," orders Charles, once eating and drinking have slowed down.

"Jannie takes us in the Land Rover to the start of each day's walk and picks us up at the end. We walk for eight days – simple. Agreed?"

"Not agreed," replies Charles. "I think I should drive you to the start in the Suzuki, and at the end of the day Jannie and Rachel should pick us up and take us back to the start for us to pick up the Suzuki."

I hesitate as Jannie and I had trial-run the week with great success and I am not going to reduce her vital role until she has had her say. "Let's discuss it tomorrow," I reply diplomatically, stalling for time.

"Any other rules, John?"

"Just one," I reply. Before driving down to Bath to meet Sydney last year for the first time, I had asked Charles about Sydney's politics. As a good civil servant he said he didn't know. Sydney welcomed me with the perfect words: 'I voted for you in Twickenham!' Lunch went very well, his home-made wine was excellent and his company delightful. His parting words triggered a warning: 'Let's conspire against Charles!'

"Charles, there will be no politics talked on the trip. I want to avoid rows. Edward Lear put it perfectly. He said: 'It was one of the most lovely of afternoons, & the colour & the scenery were enough to delight a dead man. These 2 live ones however never once looked at or spoke of it: their talk was of money & politics only, & made me sick for 3 hours.'"

"Then we will make up for it after each day's walk. Any other instructions, John?"

"You must write a one paragraph comment on the *Guardian* article – in best civil service lingo."

"Which you won't edit?"

"Of course not, Charles."

This is Charles' first comment:

'Corfu Old Town still preserves the hallmarks of its varied past, with a fine range of grand buildings overlooking the cricket ground and beyond that the sea front. Behind these imposing imperial-era buildings is a network of streets, squares and alleyways (all pedestrianised) populated by small shops, restaurants and cafés, housed in period buildings of great variety and styles, but all well maintained and brightly painted. Surprisingly little new building is in evidence, suggesting that the town is very careful to preserve the appearance and atmosphere of what is now a World Heritage Site, and one of the key attractions for tourist visitors to the island.'

Sydney has not become involved in setting the rules; he just clears up each unfinished plate. "What a marvellous meal!"

I checked later why he was unable to leave any food uneaten. I knew what his answer would be: we both came from the generation which grew up in the Second World War, when sometimes one was lucky to get any food at all.

We say our goodbyes to Costas and his family and then wander through the old suburb of Anemomilos, looking up into the first-floor rooms with their beautiful wooden ceilings. We finish at *Nautilus*, which is right on the water front, for a coffee and some background history, with a gorgeous view of the town, now twinkling across Garitsa Bay.

1966 Corfu – no roads
2009 Corfu Trail – off road

In 1966, my Danish wife Jannie and I visited Corfu and fell in love with this heaven on earth. We explored the island using the map printed opposite. As can be seen, few of the roads had been asphalted.

The Corfu Trail, according to Hilary Paipeti's *Companion Guide*, was created 'to both avoid heavily developed areas and also, in passing through all the island's rural regions, to take in as many of its finest locations – obscure spots as well as familiar ones'. It also avoids the roads shown on the 1966 map.

In fact the Trail follows many of the tracks that were built by the British from 1814 to 1864. Back in 1859, these roads were praised by the French traveller M. About in his *Grèce Contemporaine: 'La pays est traversé en tous sens par des routes admirables'*.

Corfu has enchanted many visitors and authors in the past, perhaps the best known being Gerald and Lawrence Durrell. The lover of Corfu who will delight you on many occasions on our journey and from whom I quote is Edward Lear, who spent winters on the island from 1855 to 1864 and wrote many letters to his sister and his friends. He said: "I think no place on Earth can be lovelier than this."

His description of the places we visit is delightful but also interesting as little has changed since his time once one gets off-road.

I wish you well in your walk and hope you will also fall in love with our island.

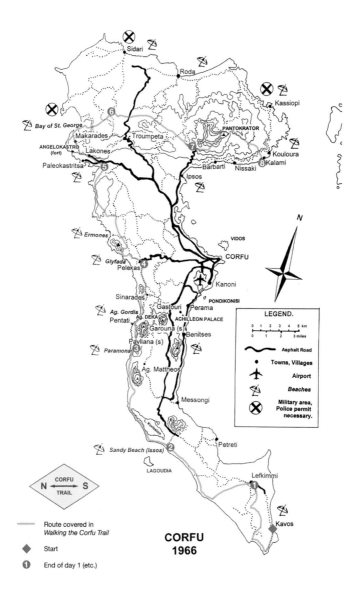

Sidari

Roda

Kassiopi

Bay of St. George

PANTOKRATOR

Makarades   Troumpeta

ANGELOKASTRO
(fort)   Lakones

Kouloura

Paleokastritsa

Barbarti   Nissaki   Kalami

Ipsos

Ermones

VIDOS

N

Glyfada
Pelekas

CORFU

Kanoni

Sinarades

PONDIKONISI

Gastouri   Perama

Ag. Gordis

Ag. DEKA   ACHILLEON PALACE

Pentati

Garouna (s)

Pavliana (s)

Benitses

Paramona

Ag. Mattheos

Messongi

Sandy Beach (Issos)

Petreti

LAGOUDIA

Lefkimmi

CORFU
N ⟷ S
TRAIL

Kavos

CORFU
1966

Route covered in
Walking the Corfu Trail

◆   Start

❶   End of day 1 (etc.)

LEGEND.

0 1 2 3 4 5 km
0   1   2   3 miles

Asphalt Road

•   Towns, Villages

✈   Airport

Beaches

⊗   Military area,
Police permit
necessary.

33

Day 1: from Kavos to Lefkimmi
Day 2: from Lefkimmi to St. George (Ag. Georgios)

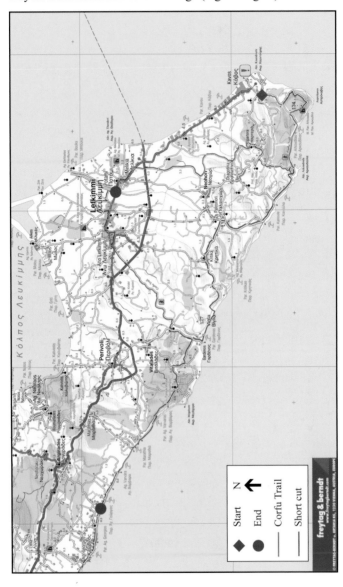

Day 3: from St. George to Ano Pavliana

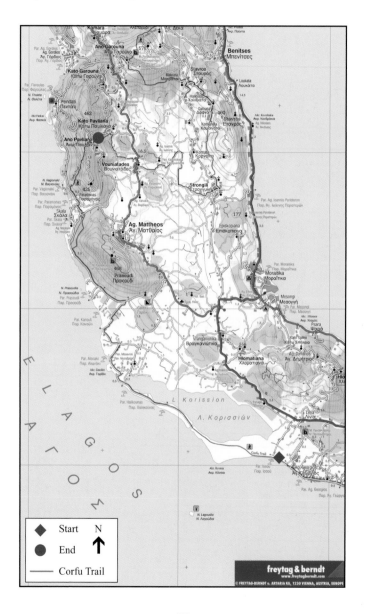

Day 4: from Ano Pavliana to Pelekas
Autumn: from Ano Pavliana to Stavros and Sinarades

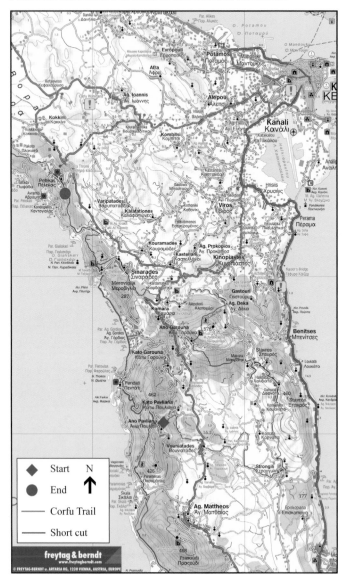

Day 5: from Pelekas to Paleokastritsa

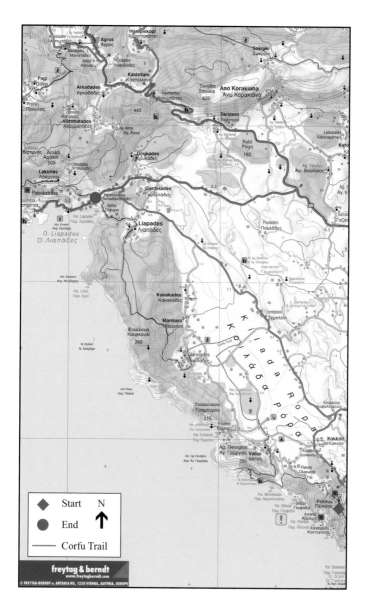

Day 6: from Paleokastritsa to Agros
Day 7: from Agros to Spartilas

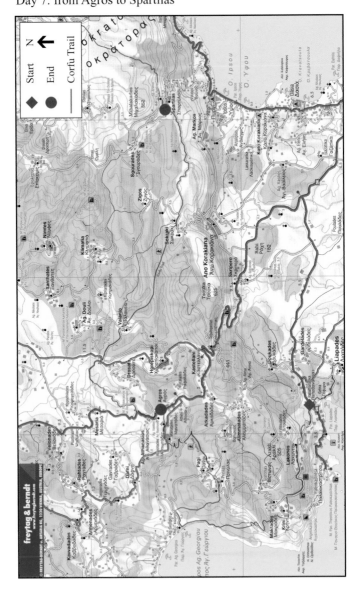

Day 8: from Spartilas to Agni
Autumn: from Agni via Old Perithia to the Trail's end

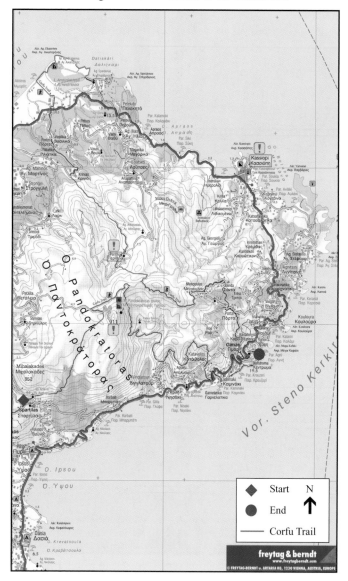

Sydney, Charles, Fotis and John   Jannie and Nikos

Dierk, Hilary, Fried and Christine
plus Lulu, Bruni and Valentino

Harry, Bill and Barbara (front) and Denise and Mitch (right)

Arkoudilas Beach

Lefkimmi River

Lake Korission fish traps

Pentati to Myrtiotissa

Agios Gordis Beach

Sinarades at Easter

Villages of the west coast
(by Theresa Nicholas from *Corfu Sketches*)

Kalafationes

Liapedes

Lakones

Pelekas

Olive grove in bloom

Olive grove in harvest

North east Corfu in 1970!

North east Corfu now – overdeveloped?

Houses of Lords and Commons v. Corfu

Potholes after the winter –
day 3

Potholes after the winter –
day 6

Day 1: from Kavos to Lefkimmi
We get lost

Flowers 4, Scenery 7, Underdeveloped 9, Challenge 4, Hrs 5
See map on page 34.

On our first day Charles, Sydney and I will follow the Corfu Trail from Kavos, Corfu's most notorious resort, to Lefkimmi, the largest town in the south of the island. This bland statement would suggest overdevelopment and ugliness. In fact the opposite is true. For walkers it is an easy, beautiful stroll away from the tourist bustle, a perfect start of our long walk. For the energetic, it is possible to walk Days 1 and 2 of our trip in a single day. But we oldies will pace ourselves wisely. Details are given at the end of this chapter.

At the end of each day the committee is reconvened and we debate our day, giving marks up to 10 for the four key characteristics of our walk. I have also given an indication on how long it will take to walk the day's section. Hilary's Guide gives a detailed breakdown for each part of the walk.

The great adventure starts with a meeting: one of those 'Yes, Minister' ones. I am in the chair; Charles, as senior civil servant, is in command; Sydney is eating his breakfast.

"John, why is Jannie taking us to Kavos?" Charles enquires brusquely.

"Because it's in the plan," I reply, nearly calling him Sir Humphrey.

Rachel enters and decides she would prefer coffee to tea. Mug, spoon, Nescafé and boiled water: I am the perfect host.

"But she'll have to come back here and return to Lefkimmi later. Now if I drive to Kavos, Rachel and Jannie can go into town and see some museums. What do you think, Sydney?"

"You'll get lost," he snipes, mouth full of delicious fresh bread.

"Haven't you any proper coffee?" asks Rachel, obviously delighted that she is involved in the planning.

"Jannie has bought some." I look at her with pleading eyes: filter coffee and hot milk takes time to make and is too complicated in the morning. "OK, Charles, I agree. You drive."

With Sydney squashed in the back next to the rucksacks, I navigate: down into the resort of Agios Gordis and up to charming Kato Garouna, with its local sandstone buildings; down into the bowl between west coast and east coast mountains; through quaint Vouniatades, where the loop of the Corfu Trail which we will miss out crosses the valley; and on to Agios Mattheos, the largest village in the south-centre of the island.

"Charles, turn left. Let's try the new bypass."

A minute later, we stop in the square in front of the football ground.

"Which way?" asks the driver.

I consult my Freytag & Berndt map. "The bypass is not on the map. Let's go straight ahead."

"But that's into the country," replies Charles. "The road to the right looks wider."

It soon gets narrower. We stop and I try out my appalling Greek on an old lady, who obviously is against the bypass. She points in the direction we are going. Charles is pleased. The road is now a village alley. We have another consultation.

"I told you he would get lost," says Sydney.

"Then I'll turn round," Charles replies at last.

Half-way through a seventeen-point turn another car arrives to block the road.

Greek drivers normally believe that they are the only ones on the road, but today we have found a delightful local, who prefers to watch Charles in amazement. He then backs down the road to let us get back to the square and continue round the bypass. This is no British road but a narrow piece of tarmac which meanders through the olive groves.

Once past the village and its guardian mountain, nearly 500 metres high, we enter the flatter lands of the south of the island. On we hurtle at 50 miles per hour to Kavos.

"It's like a run-down, one-street, American town in the mid-west," volunteers Charles, when we get there.

He has a point: diners offering full British breakfasts and bars selling the 'cheapest beer in town' line the main street. However, the liberal use of the word 'sex' and its derivatives would probably not be tolerated in conservative USA.

We turn right at the junction at the end of town, fork left where the road carries on to Spartera and then stop at a sign to the 'Monastery of the Blessed Virgin Arkoudilas 1700'. I'm not sure she would be happy with modern-day Kavos.

Above the yellow diamond on which is printed 'Corfu Trail', there is a sign 'To the most beautiful beach in the world'. Now everyone knows that Lawrence Durrell coined this expression for Myrtiotissa, which we pass on Day 5. I wonder who has had such cheek to question one of Corfu's most famous writers. (Hilary later admits to writing an article about the beach which apparently inspired locals to instal the sign.)

Dismounting from the little jeep, we get ready for the long journey ahead. Charles is smart and colour-coordinated: dark-blue sweater over lighter blue T-shirt; the same dark-blue outer socks and even darker-blue trousers, tucked plus-two style into red inner socks. He extends an elegant walking stick. With his short shorts and short socks, Sydney is not fashion conscious; his black knee support almost hides one white leg. His white floppy cotton hat suggests a recent holiday on Brighton beach. He grips two walking sticks which he will use throughout the trek, in the mountains and on the flat, as an extra pair of legs.

This unlikely band sets off and follows the gently-climbing track 'avoiding minor tracks either side' as instructed in Hilary's *Companion Guide*. The countryside is deserted but slightly scruffy: to the right, tall ivy-clad trees drop down to a stream; to the left the olive-groves have been left unattended, some even with the tell-tale evidence of brambles. Tall asphodels, no longer blooming here in the south of the island, watch us pass. Everything is blissfully peaceful. (Nikos later tells me that the villagers of Kavos no longer need the olives as the tourist income, the largest on the whole island, has made them rich.)

After a kilometre we turn left at the sign to the monastery. Sydney sits down on a rock and takes out his camera. I continue almost out of sight and also sit down. Charles joins me.

"We've been going only 15 minutes and he's having a rest already," I exclaim.

Charles goes back to Sydney and then returns.

"He's got his flower books out and is checking up the name of what he describes as 'an interesting one'."

"If he's going to stop every time he sees a flower we'll never get to Lefkimmi tonight, and as for getting to Agni; well, that's a joke."

Charles goes back to Sydney. I look across the track and see a 'dump'. I inspect it. The villagers have collected the seaweed from the beach and flattened it across a large area of land. It is slowly decomposing into earth. Beside roads all over the island, one finds similar dumps and also builders' rubble, ugly at first, but useful as what we might call 'pre-foundations' when a house is eventually built. Here though other villagers have added a mattress and some plastic chairs. I am unhappy, as I have to concede a point to the 'rubbish critics'.

Charles returns.

"Sydney has agreed to stop, for water, at the end of each hour; but you must help by taking photos of the flowers." I am impressed with his diplomacy.

I walk down to see Sydney struggling with his camera. Click, click, click, I capture the flower for posterity with my new camera and its excellent 'macro', whatever that means, and off we go. I pass the *Guide* to Charles who is now in the lead.

"We'll get lost," warns Sydney, with alarm. He should know; they've been on many hiking holidays before. I ignore this jibe as I am now engrossed in my new job of expedition photographer.

500 metres on, we come to another flattened seaweed and furniture dump. (Some friends, who will remain nameless, confessed that they had found there a perfect chest of drawers for their kitchen – but sadly it was too big for their car!)

I rather like this dump: it has a couple of poles rising high above it. Both have solar cells attached and one has wind-cups hurtling round on its top. Alternative energy has arrived in Corfu! Perhaps the dry seaweed could be burnt, with the heat powering a generator?

Charles and Sydney are looking out to sea across to the mainland, temptingly close. They then peer over the edge of the dump down to the sea below.

We are not far from the beach where my son, his friend and I had started our round-Corfu windsurfing expedition in 1986. Within ten minutes, Peter's friend had been forced to retire: a force seven north-westerly had 'wiped' her out. Maybe the idea of some wind turbines on this southernmost tip of the island isn't such a bad idea after all.

We continue along the track, pausing to look over the cliff again towards Paxos, almost within touch. Charles strides out; Sydney, insect-like with professional walking sticks in each hand, flits from flower to flower; the photographer is in the rear, eagerly awaiting instruction. We are a happy band.

The trail narrows from car-width (two tracks) to motorcycle-width (one track) to footpath (no tracks) as the trees encroach on our way. Finally we slide down a slippery gully down which a raging torrent will rush after a storm. We pass our Blessed Virgin Arkoudilas: no time to pay respects as we have 168 kilometres to go and her monastery is in ruins, though Hilary says a fine arch remains.

We descend deeper into the forest; this must be what the Amazon jungle looks like. Finally we come to a small stream and clamber up the other side onto the now concreted road from Kavos. I check on the map. We have taken a 2km detour round a half a kilometre road. Bless you Hilary, you make my life difficult. I will concede however that the yellow waymarks on trees and rocks along our scenic route have been excellent.

A further half a kilometre on, we come to 'the most beautiful beach in the world'. The west of Ireland it isn't; the Bahamas it isn't; but it is lovely – and totally deserted. Sandstone cliffs fall down onto a golden stretch of sand. It is clean – locals have gathered driftwood into piles for bonfires perhaps. The water is clear and the view to Paxos is thrilling. I like beaches. This is my terrain: flat, firm and fast.

We stride out together and only stop when we get to an impassable boulder, some three metres high.

"This must be the wrong way, Charles," suggests Sydney. Charles consults the guide. "It says we have to go over an outcrop of rocks." Faced by a sheer wall of sandstone, we simultaneously and in silence start removing boots and socks. We paddle round; the water is cool but refreshing.

"We must speed up," announces our leader. We do so. Walking along a sandy beach with water squelching between one's toes is one of nature's delights. At the end of the beach, we put on our socks and boots. I find I have only three socks. "Where the heck did I drop the fourth?" I ask myself. So this is why walkers wear two socks on each foot: they have a couple of spares! I go back to the rocky outcrop. No sock to be found. I return to my companions in disgrace.

We walk up from the beach and arrive at a junction. I

check my Freytag & Berndt map: straight on up the coast is the logical way forward; up the hill to the right is the Corfu Trail to Lefkimmi. I promise to return in the autumn and see if we can cut out this trip inland and then back across to the west coast, and so reduce our Trail to seven days. [We found it and instructions for this short cut are described at the end of this chapter.]

Charles is progressing ahead of us. Sydney finds flowers and I photograph them; we slowly move uphill. I stop again to take a picture of the beach (with the missing sock somewhere); it is a stupendous view, as can be seen in the photo on page 41, and I have a moment to regain my breath. I inspect the gully beside the track: there appear to be dried-up mini-waterfalls. The amateur geologist in me says that the cliffs are stratified, perhaps between soft sand and slippery clay.

"Keep going," says Charles enthusiastically. "Hilary's *Guide* tells us 'we have a 20–25 minute steep climb, with dangerous edges to the track and great views'. I can't agree that it's steep; I call this nicely graded."

I'm on Hilary's side of the argument. Charles believes he is right as we reach the brow in 20 minutes, though the photographer has tried to slow down the march. Sydney is also getting me interested in flowers.

"Slap your arse!" he exclaims. Well, that's what I think he called the flower *serapias*.

From now on, I can communicate with our tame botanist. "Any more slap your arses, Sydney?"

Over the hill, we arrive in another world: beautifully maintained olive groves; well-ploughed fields; vegetables growing profusely; flower-covered verges, and no humans in sight. Along a long-hairpin bend, ewes watch us suspiciously as we go past. I never realised they have such elastic necks: they stand still yet keep their eyes on us for 360°. Donkeys nibble grass under the olive trees – they ignore us. This landscape is truly idyllic.

An hour after we have left the beach, Sydney gets irritable. It's time for Sydney's second water stop of the day. We come to a main road and follow the sign: 'Taverna Paradiso 200m. Mythos.'

"Sydney, let's stop for a beer," I suggest.

"Not when we are walking," he replies. This professional hiking can be a bit of a bore.

We continue along the road, on which has been painted KALO AEXA XSTOANEH, which I cannot translate. I'm more used to KALO PASKA (Happy Easter) and XRISTOS ANESTI (Christ has arisen).

Charles stops after a few minutes in the centre of the village of Spartera and reads out of Hilary's *Guide*: 'Where the main road bends right, you take the downhill road to the left.' We do as we are told and arrive at the beautiful bell-tower of Ag. Martinas. There is a stupendous view north to Lefkimmi. "Time for Sydney's stop," he says.

I phone Jannie on my mobile. "All's well; we'll be in Lefkimmi in just over two hours time." We linger long; it's a perfect place at a perfect time: half-way through day one. After 20 minutes, Charles orders us on. I immediately see a scooter hidden in the undergrowth; then another and yet one more. These ancient two-wheelers take me back to my youth when I drove my Lambretta to Switzerland and then over the Alps to Turin. I had watched with amazement a youngster on his scooter driving up to the Basilica of Superga, then down the mountain and up and down again; what a wonderful way to spend a day. On the way home, I chose the Col de l'Iseran, Europe's highest pass at over 2,700 metres high. Tragically, I fell asleep and we came off the road as we descended. My friend was slightly injured and I escaped unharmed.

As Charles disappears into the distance, I inspect my find and think about bidding for all three; but they are Vespas not

Lambrettas. At last I catch up with Sydney and glance ahead at Charles. Before I can shout a warning, his foot is trapped under a cable crossing the road. He hurtles through the air and falls with great skill. We pick him up. Nothing is broken. I then realise the obvious: we are on a road, not on a track as Hilary had suggested in her *Guide*. Which road are we on? I check the compass at the end of my walking stick.

"Charles, we are going due east, back on the main road to Kavos," I quietly suggest. "We should be going north to Lefkimmi."

"I told you he would get us lost," adds Sydney.

"It's Hilary's lousy instructions," pleads our leader. In his defence, he reads from the *Guide*. "'You take the downhill road to the left. Past a little church, you keep going downhill to a T-junction, where you turn left.'"

I decide this is a slur against the author of our guide. I read on: "'Still downhill, the track leads through a forest.' Charles, this isn't a track; it's a bloody road and we are going through olive groves."

I check the road: it is bloody. Poor Charles. We return to the village and Vespa corner. I'm rather pleased with my walking stick.

I didn't question whether he had seen a yellow waymark – he hadn't, and neither had I as I was more interested in the Vespas. Nor had I been checking my Freytag & Berndt map which clearly showed we should be going north after the church rather than south.

"Haven't you been following the map in the back of Hilary's *Guide*?"

He hadn't, but arguing isn't getting us anywhere.

I phone Jannie again. "Small hitch, according to Hilary's *Guide*, we'll be in Lefkimmi in 2¼ to 2½ hours."

With empty stomachs urging us on – our fish lunch would soon be on the table – we stride out. The track leads us through the forest then reaches olive groves – just as the *Guide* says. It cannot, however, describe the tranquillity and the beauty. Not a soul is to be seen; there is just no development.

Somewhere here, though, could be the future site of the new island refuse tip; the present one has reached capacity. Battles with the police were recently fought over the proposal, and tragically a young mother was killed defending this virgin countryside. From the early days of my love for the island, I had despaired of the way Greeks resort to bloodshed in resolving a dispute. They have been fearless in the fight for right, be it against the Italian invader in 1940, the Colonels in the early 70s, and now against desecration of the environment. As individuals they can still randomly discard their rubbish (and old Vespas) but collectively they will fight against the authorities dumping in their backyard. Perhaps if the community could see an advantage from the proposal, such as free energy from processing the waste, their anger would subside.

On the hour, we reach a main road. We are confused. Hilary's instructions mentions a junction 'easy to miss'. Further on we are instructed to 'cross the Lefkimmi bypass with great care and continue along a track opposite'.

"Charles, where are we?" Sydney asks.

Silence.

"The by-pass goes west-east," I suggest. "This road goes south-north. Let's turn left."

I decide my plan to get a local guide had been the right one. We can blame Nikos, unless he has succeeded in the shooting competition.

Now, before the start of the season, the Kavos to Lefkimmi road carries little traffic. On our right, there are small family-run guest houses, backing onto the shallow beach I remember from nearly 40 years ago. Sadly, for many, the proximity of Kavos must have hit their trade. If they could rebrand their accommodation as 'family-run for families, between a deserted beach and glorious undeveloped countryside ideal for walking', perhaps they could have a better future. With Hilary's help, I am sure they could produce local guides for their guests.

With the finishing line in sight, we speed up. We go through the little villages of Melikia and Potami, both beautiful even though linked into Greater Lefkimmi. At last, we reach the bridge over the Lefkimmi River and turn right along the nearside quay to collapse at 'The River Taverna', only an hour and a half after leaving the village of Spartera.

In 1862, Edward Lear made a round trip from Lefkimmi, visiting the places we have seen today. He said: 'From Lefkimi, inland to Ag. Prokopios – a picturesque little monastery, beautiful olives. Hills near sea, Cape Lefkimi solitary, fine ravine, then Monastery of Arkoudilas. Wonderful grove of cypresses. Walked down the hill by beautiful zigzags to Ag. Prokopios – a wonderfully pretty specimen of rural Greek monastery. To the sea thence, & bathed, & so by sand & hilly modulations, back to Melikia'. Three days later, on his fiftieth birthday, he returned to Spartera: 'From Dragontina, great groups of vast olives higher up, we arrive at Spartero. There is superb scenery all about the place. We took a boy to guide us to Ag. Prokopios (the best place to pass the rest of the day in) – ever-winding paths thro' thickets, a few scared cattle, a church (in a wilderness), & thus we reached the grove of Holy Prokopios. Nothing but a very elaborate study of this wood could convey an idea of this beautiful place: the quiet, warmth, & semi-shade are delightful. In these Prokopian holy glades are but 3 very manifold colours: the warm pale green of the floor, with long shades, the gray uniform freckle-shimmer of the roof, with dark brown gray of the supporting pillartrux'.

Some say that the best hole on a golf course is the nineteenth. I decide that the same can apply to walking. Sitting under an umbrella on a warm afternoon, drinking a beer, whilst watching a fishing dinghy chugging up the canal to be moored just opposite, is bliss.

Wouldn't it be great to put one's feet up and stay overnight? I notice a sign, 'www.holidaysincorfu.gr 2662022958', offering rooms to let. But Jannie, the transport manager who will take us back to Kavos to pick up the Suzuki, will want to go home and watch the sunset sink over the sea. She also has a great story to tell about taking the wrong exit from the bypass, driving round the narrow one-way streets of the town and finally arriving at the gorgeous church she remembered from the 1970s. There she met a handsome Greek electrician who told her the river was just 200 metres down the hill. I think it made Charles happy that others can get 'lost'.

It is time to meet our hosts. Spiros Pandis has retired after working for 25 years on ships all over the world. His wife Andrianoula has decided that it is time for her to retire as well. As with so many Greek families, the next generation will inherit the restaurant. Their beautiful daughter Irini – I ask myself how can she have three old children? – is ready to take over. Their son, Yiannis, is married in Italy.

Thanks to walkers of the Corfu Trail and the extension of the holiday season by the early arrival of EasyJet, they now open on April 1st. I am told that the taverna next door, Stis Basilos (2662024616), may be open all year round. Near the bridge on the northern quayside, Cheeky Face, a pot place, is also open all year round.

Lovers of Greece will know that inspection and discussion of the food in the kitchen compliment the chef and excite the guest. Menus have changed from the 1960s, when every dish was listed but nearly all were 'off today'. I had ordered *Bianco*, for us and sure enough a lid was removed from a pot to reveal small fish in a white sauce. Its garlic aroma nearly knocked us out of the kitchen.

"What's the fish, John?" asks Charles. "I thought it would

be a larger fish."

I do not rise to the bait. I want to ask him whether he had expected 'Cod and chips', 'Haddock and chips' or 'Plaice and chips'. "Whatever was caught this morning," I reply. He is not so keen now. He is happy, though, to choose either chicken from the oven or *Sofrito*, veal in a garlic sauce. Modern Greek cuisine, with its small choice of excellent fresh dishes, is my type of food.

We start with home-made white *taramasalata* and *fasolia*, excellent broad beans in tomato sauce. My *Bianco* is mouth-watering, but breath-destroying. I justify my extra portion to its medicinal qualities: *Bianco* for high blood pressure rather than *Bourdetto* for low pressure.

We drink to our absent guest walker, Nikos, who has contributed to our adventures by his absence. A few nights later we meet him. He tells us he was seventh out of 120 in the shooting competition, which we decide is an excellent result and thus we forgive him for not being our guide. But he claims it is not good enough for a place in the Olympic team. Here is his story.

Raised by his grandfather – Nikos' father died before he was ten – he must have been one of the local lads. His friends could all get their hands on guns to shoot the birds that flew in from Africa on their voyage north. But Nikos never had a gun – until he 'borrowed' his grandfather's when he was out of the house. Nikos was caught, of course, when he was returning it to its hiding place.

"Papa, I only borrowed your gun," he said.

"Boy, you stole it. Why didn't you ask me?"

"Because I was afraid."

"Afraid of a good thrashing if you were caught?" Nikos was silent. "How many did you shoot?"

"Three, Papa. I was the best."

"Then I forgive you, but next time, ask me!"

As years went by, he moved from shooting live birds to shooting clay pigeons. He competed in Corfu, then Epirus and finally nationally. He made the Greek team and looked an outside bet to shoot in the 2004 Olympics. After the first day of the Olympic trials, Nikos was leading. It was cold in Crete and he felt he had caught something so he went to the coach, who gave him some pills. Next morning his vision was blurred; he could barely see the clays when they were fired. He dropped down the rankings and failed to make the team for Athens. Now that's a mystery!

Disillusioned, he packed up shooting and turned to dancing. Anna, his wife, is an accomplished ballet dancer. I shall never forget the show we were invited to in the Theatre in Corfu Town. Nikos was the star.

But I must go back to 2001, the summer of the 'great project': building a road up to our little summer-house and extending it; then erecting a pool in front of the long veranda to reflect the sun as it set out to sea. As a reward for their efforts in delivering the work on time, we held a party for engineer and workers. My present to him was a gun – a plastic one – to be used if we had another dispute; our only major blow-up had been over the pool. Nikos had wanted a concrete one; I chose a pre-fabricated one. 'The plastic pool', he called it.

Over a meal at Taverna Max on the Lefkimmi National Road, I started on one of my favourite subjects.

"How is the World Heritage Site progressing?" I ask.

"Well, I'm told. But I am now working on one of your other favourite issues: energy conservation."

"In Greece?" I exclaim, surprised that an island which leaves all its lights on year round has even heard of the words.

As with all engineers, he takes out his pen, clears the table of plates and starts sketching on the paper tablecloth. He starts: "To build your wall, we erected wooden shuttering, inserted rods between and then poured in the concrete."

"The shuttering was the mould, which we removed once the concrete was dry," I confirm.

"Exactly. Now we are using a pioneering method of house construction called Quad-Lock. We assemble 57mm thick polystyrene panels, each 300mm by 1200mm block firmly fitting into its neighbouring panels using the 'stud' into 'hole' principle." He illustrates it on the tablecloth.

"Like Lego," suggests Jannie.

"Ties keep inside and outside panels, which form the mould, tight, straight and parallel and have slots into which steel rods are inserted before the concrete is poured. The panels become the inside and outside surface of the wall."

"Bravo, Niko. You've made a plastic house!"

He laughs. "Like your pool, it's quick to assemble; we built a house in a week. Everything comes from Austria in a container. The polystyrene is easily cut to insert pipes and wires. At €1000 per square metre for a completed building, excluding the cost of planning and foundations, we are cheaper than standard construction. Insulation is two to four times better and you use a third less energy: heat the house for fifteen minutes and the temperature stays stable for five hours."

"But it's made of polystyrene, which emits toxic gases if it catches fire," I suggest.

"Wrong, John. That's chemically expanded polystyrene; this had 98% air blown into the mould. It's completely safe."

"You are talking about new houses. What if I want to renovate an old house?"

"We assemble the panels inside with special ties to the old walls: no more dampness and fantastic insulation."

"We'll call you Mr. Eco soon," I quip.

"How about installing solar PV panels? In Greece, we are introducing a 'feed-in' tariff similar to Germany's. You are paid for any electricity you generate but don't use. Your investment is paid back in seven to eight years, and the EU-sponsored scheme guarantees your income for 25 years."

"I'll be 95 by then!"

"We've also installed what I call a 'summer-storage' heating system. We dug a 30 cubic metre hole, filled it with rocks and pipes which are connected to a solar water heating circuit. After four summer months, the rocks are hot enough to provide four months heating in the winter."

"Niko, please come to England; we need engineers like you. We'll convert all the multi-storey car parks in city centres to storage heaters. But seriously, if you are so keen on saving energy, why are the authorities planning to build an airport on the salt-pans by Lefkimmi? For the Green Corfu you would like to create, how can you justify the energy used in constructing it and needed for building a new road to Corfu, plus the extra fuel used to carry tourists the length of the island?"

"Don't worry, John. They won't finish it in 50 years. The plan is to build a tunnel from Benitses to a new road parallel to the current runway and then bypass the town to continue to the north of the island, bypassing Skripero. But they will run out of money in 2013."

"So what's going to happen to Kavos?"

"It's already changing. The season lasts only four months now, with the British youngsters here for about a month. Greeks and Bulgarians come by the new motorway from Saloniki for the rest of the season."

[We checked in October. He was right. Ironically, only the clinics have had a good summer. As the doctor said, "the British, depressed by unemployment at home, seemed to compensate for their reduced numbers by the increased intake of alcohol which resulted in excellent business for us".]

The reader will be surprised that we found the area round Kavos so underdeveloped. The views above the west coast beach and those across rolling countryside to the east side of the island were enchanting. The flowers in the verges and olive groves were as we would expect in the spring and our five-hour walk had been a comfortable start to our journey.

* * * * *

In the autumn Jannie and I follow the road from Arkoudilas Beach to the village of Kritika. Where the road goes right to Lefkimmi and the church is on the left, we go along the main street for 100 metres to where the road widens into a square. We bear left at the sign to 'Secret Paradise Café – Snack Bar'. After 200 metres we turn left between two breeze block sheds. (Going on would take us to a church with a cemetery). We then continue for one kilometre (past a turning to the right) to a three-way fork. We ignore the left and right forks and continue straight on. A further kilometre on, after going over a hill, the road zigzags past the Secret Paradise Café down into a beautiful gorge and finishes at the south end of the deserted Gardenos beach, at the end of which is a footbridge over the river if it is in full flow. 500 metres along the Vitalades road we are on Day 2's route.

Day 2: from Lefkimmi to St. George
A race against time

Flowers 6, Scenery 5, Underdeveloped 7, Challenge 1, Hrs 4
See map on page 34.

*Today the team will follow the Corfu Trail from the Lefkimmi
bypass. This misses out a wander through this extremely
picturesque town, which contains a number of beautiful
churches. At the end of the day we will arrive in the long-low
rise tourist development of Agios Georgios, otherwise known
as St. George of the South. The scenery will be slightly less
dramatic and we will spend the last half-hour walking along
an unspoilt sandy beach. For me, the flowers are as delightful
as on the first day, but Sydney is extremely excited by a 'find',
so we accept his higher marks. Other than the fact we are in a
race against time, it is not a challenging walk.*

Charles proposes we repeat the transport arrangements, so I
phone Harry at his café/bar and suggest we meet on the main
road, inland from our destination, St. George of the South. I
sense concern as he has to be back in Corfu Town to open up at
three o'clock.

At 9.30 we are waiting on the road as suggested. Harry
arrives in his very old and small car; it's so full that it is doubtful
if he could take more than one passenger, so scuppering my
plan for him to take us to the start of our walk. He looks at
my two companions. As one would expect from a senior civil
servant, Charles is wearing creased long trousers, smart enough
for the office; Sydney has knobbly knees. Harry is shocked.

"Where's Jannie?" he asks.

"Slight change of plan: we'll drive now to the end of the
walk and drop your car off. Then we'll go with Charles to the

start of the walk."

He looks again at the team.

"There is no way I can get back to Town to open up at two."

I was certain he had said three o'clock. "We'll start on the Lefkimmi bypass, that will save the best part of an hour."

"It is still over four hours from there to St. George!"

"Yesterday, we walked from Spartera to Lefkimmi in an hour and a half. We should easily finish in three hours," I claim. I could see trouble ahead; we wouldn't be able to do any flower-spotting and I doubted whether Sydney would get his hourly water breaks.

Reluctantly, Harry agrees and we follow him to the southern end of the St. George's resort, where he leaves his car. I clamber into the back of the Suzuki with Sydney and the rucksacks and off we go to Lefkimmi. As navigator, I have a couple of problems: I cannot unfold the Freytag map and I can barely see out of the front to see where we are going. Rather than retrace our journey to where we met Harry, I decide it would be quicker to cut across country to Argirades. Harry mutters something in Greek, which I don't understand. We enter this beautiful old village along a six-foot wide alleyway.

"The car's too wide," says Charles. His voice barely hides the fear that he will have to reverse out.

Harry opens his windows and pulls in the mirror. "OK?"

Charles, honour at stake, does the same. We creep forward. Thank goodness we are not in the Discovery. Ahead we see an old lady on a donkey, its panniers almost touching the walls either side, confirming the Corfiot rule that a track is a road if it is wider than an animal plus its baskets. Beast and rider have obviously met stupid tourists before, and they move down a side alley. Above us a room connects the buildings on each side. We slowly move forward and finally arrive on the main road south.

Nine kilometres and eight minutes later, we join the

Lefkimmi bypass where the old road turns left into the town and the supermarket *Dimitra* is on the right. One kilometre on, past Lidl Supermarket and a small furniture store with a large sign *KENTRO EPIPLO*, we stop. Our track, still not asphalted, leads off to the right.

Harry and I set off at a cracking pace across the fallow landscape. I look back; Charles and Sydney are falling behind. I bend down to do up my laces, so they can catch up.

"Harry," starts Charles. "It's beautiful; the fields are so yellow."

"We saw all these flowers yesterday," I say, hoping that I could dampen Sydney's enthusiasm.

"No we didn't," he replies. "There are loads of flowers."

"What flowers?" asks Harry angrily. He wants to walk and then open up in town.

"I'm sorry, Sydney, but today I don't think I'll be able to take any pictures," I quietly suggest.

Charles can see trouble; he has walked with Sydney before. He had warned me that Sydney could often slow up the walk but, faced by a challenge to get to the top of a mountain, would pass everyone on the way. Sadly, we didn't have any mountains today. "Why don't you record in your dictaphone all the flowers you see?" Charles proposes.

On our first day, Sydney would natter away to his machine: "John is taking a photo of a *cistus*. We have already seen two different types. I think this is a third. That leaves us one more to find and then we will have seen all the ones there are on Corfu."

Sydney agrees; he wants to avoid an international incident. We are now all happy.

I had met Harry for the first time a couple of weeks before. He had agreed to come as it was obvious that I could walk fast downhill. Now it was time to prove my speed along the flat. When I was ten, my eldest brother and I played three rounds of golf every day throughout the summer. As a man of the links, I have no problems keeping up with Harry. I had been told that he swims the crawl in Garitsa Bay for two hours every day of the year. At over six feet tall, with close cut hair, he is the modern-day version of an ancient Greek Olympian. I had been warned that some of the Sunday walkers call him the 'Land Rover' as he carries on uphill as fast as he goes on the flat. I decide that when we reach the hills I will let Charles walk with him. He leaps over the puddles from last night's rain, I walk through them. I ask myself if age is catching up on me. No, it's just that Harry is really a Range Rover Sport.

After half-an-hour walking across grassland and then through olive groves, we come to an asphalted road. Harry, who has waymarked this part of the Trail, points to the yellow mark on an olive tree, turns right, and continues over a bridge to meet the main road from Vitalades to Gardenos beach. We follow the road towards the beach and just before Alexandros Taverna we turn up a concrete ramp to the right. The taverna would make an ideal stop as it is an hour from our start, though, chasing Harry, we have taken just 40 minutes. Whilst we wait for Charles and Sydney, who has been gabbling away into his dictaphone, I look at my Freytag & Berndt map. Yesterday, we had gone inland from Arkoudilas Beach. I show Harry an alternative route along the coast and then inland through Paleohori and Kritika, which misses out our trip to Lefkimmi and would enable us to walk from Kavos to St. George in one day.

"Kritika is over those hills," answers Harry, pointing to the south-east. "There must be a track down to the far end of Gardenos Beach."

[Jannie and I checked this out in the autumn and indeed the short-cut exists. Details are at the end of the previous chapter.]

With Sydney happy and Charles egging him on, Harry and I set off up the hill and into the olive groves. Only two- and four-legged animals could tackle the climb. Tied to the trees are poles, planks, sticks and twigs. It is a mystery what these are. I guess it must be some ancient remedy against the dreaded *Dakos* or fruit-fly, which lays its eggs in the olives, so rendering them useless for eating or pressing into good-quality oil. I have even heard of bottles containing the pheromone of the female fly hanging from trees to attract and then entrap the males.

Further on in front of a remote house, I see an old car with German number plates. "I am 100% certain it was brought to Corfu by a worker from Germany," claims Harry. The claim that cars are dumped all over the island has a ring of truth.

It's not long before Harry the Range Rover Sport moves ahead. My legs are really beginning to ache. As he disappears out of sight, I hear Sydney, perhaps a quarter of a mile down the hill, crying out for help. I ignore him as this might make him think we are a mile ahead. He calls again. I carry on uphill, with views of the west coast appearing. At the top, I collapse. Sydney arrives, not best pleased with me.

"Hello, Sydney. The hour is up. We've stopped for your water break," I lie.

"Didn't you hear me?"

"What's that? Are you OK?"

"No!"

"Are we going too fast?"

"No, I found a flower I have never seen before," explains our botanist. "Let's go down and take a photo of it."

I look at Harry, who doesn't need to sit down.

"Sorry, Sydney. We've got to get Harry home."

"Then we'll come back later in the week," he threatens.

Sydney gets out his flower books, to look for his major discovery. He is in no hurry; he is punishing me. I check my watch – he has only a couple of minutes left of his water break. Harry is fidgeting as if he wants to get started. To delay our departure I stand up to admire the view to the east.

Pointing to the villages and the olive groves far below, Harry says "Just look down there: Vitalades and Perivoli and what wonderful countryside! Then the bay of Lefkimmi, and the whole length of the east side of the island. And we can see the mountains of Albania in the distance. Corfiots always complain about how the island has changed. They should come up here and see how lovely it is." He shakes his head sadly and shrugs his shoulders in resignation.

Harry's love for his island makes me like him, though I had my doubts when he raced ahead of me during our last climb. But now we are at the top of the hill, so it should be downhill all the way home.

Charles glances at Sydney and senses our predicament. After so many walks together, Charles recognises the signs of a friend on strike. The perfect diplomat turns to our impatient guest.

"I must congratulate you, Harry. You have done a wonderful job marking the Trail. I usually walk in Italy. Terrible problems: waymarks missing, no maps and even when we have them the trail disappears."

"Thank you, Charles." Harry is slightly placated. "We are making good time. I think we could get to St. George's in time for me to get to Town."

"Then I'll walk with you," concludes our leader and gets to his feet. Off they go.

Sydney is packing up his books and bottle. Thankfully, his camera is still in his rucksack. Ahead, Charles turns round to check we are following. We haven't yet started. Moments later he stops at a junction to look for something. Now Harry stops. He retraces his steps and then rubs the grit off the track to expose a yellow mark.

"Look, it's there."

"Sorry, missed it," says Charles now happier that the rearguard is on the way down the hill.

Sydney and I reach the T-junction and walk a short distance along the main road and then bear right to start climbing. Sydney moves slightly ahead; he is still smarting at my refusal to clamber back down to see his flower.

Soon enough we reach the top of the west coast ridge. Today's walk has been through a totally undeveloped landscape, and now the views north are awesome and inspiring. Sandy beaches follow sandy beaches, all deserted at this time of year. The resort of St. George is in the middle distance, with the great Lake Korission, a site of outstanding natural beauty, behind; and in the far distance the volcano-shaped mountain above Agios Mattheos rises up from the plain.

Alone at the back, I guiltily bring out my camera and stand on the sheer cliffs snapping away. As I stroll down the long path to the beach, I reflect on how important the sea has been in my life. My Irish father met my English mother in the Canaries, having sailed his 26-foot yacht single-handed from Limerick. In the war, we were evacuated from East Kent to Cornwall, where he worked as a coastguard above Perranporth and saw me, his youngest son, disappear into a whirlpool on the beach far below, only to be pulled out by my eldest brother. I learnt my golf at Littlestone on the Kent coast and went to school in Sandwich. Jannie's father gave his consent to our marriage during the early morning swim in the Skagerrak off North Jutland. For nearly 40 years we had spent much time on the west coast of Corfu. The sea has sculpted my life if not seeped into my blood.

After the steep descent to the beach, I see the first sign of tourism, a shack above which the Union Jack and the German, Czech and Greek flags are flying. It tells me who their clients are in the summer. We stop on St. Barbara beach in front of the Sunset Café; sadly it is closed. One day, I will come back and see if the sunset is as good as from my own beach, still two days ahead.

As we set off on our last leg to Marathia Beach and home, Harry points to a pallet in a stream crossing the beach. The makeshift bridge is 'for the English'; he grins and promptly leaps the rivulet. I watch our leaders stride ahead: Harry always follows the hard sand; the English seem to get into slower 'quicksand'. Charles is now leading by 50 metres, followed by Harry, with the 'flower-power boys' trailing by a further 50 metres. I watch as Charles takes off his sweater and Harry surges ahead; he is enjoying the competition as well as wanting to get back to Town.

An outcrop of the cliff has been eroded by the sea, pitting the surface and making walking more difficult. Charles claims mountain walkers cope best on the rocks, but who cares? I think the rock is limestone, so I take a sample for analysis back in England.

We come to a bamboo thicket growing on the edge of the beach; a sure sign that water comes down the cliffs after heavy rain. At the bottom is a bamboo shelter; has Robinson Crusoe been this way?

I see a large black crab scuttling off into a shallow pool; my grandchildren would love this place. By now I'm the slowest, but probably the happiest. Determined not to be left behind, I make a superhuman effort to catch up with Sydney.

"Sorry, Sydney. There are no flowers on the beach."

"Don't worry, I can still think about flowers. I'm working out which 20 photographs we will use."

Feeling in an excellent mood as the finishing line is in sight and Sydney has forgiven me, I suggest we could select maybe 48 photos. He gives me a big grin, my previous misdemeanour forgotten.

In the distance, Harry suddenly disappears up off the beach, closely followed by Charles. I check my watch; we've walked just 2½ hours. This is far less than Hilary's estimate of 4 hours – not bad for three old men!

Harry is clearing the passenger seat. There's tension in the air: it seems that Harry had wanted to drive straight back to town, but Charles has insisted on a lift back to Lefkimmi to pick his Suzuki from the start of the walk.

"Thank you, Harry. You were a great leader. I'll see you in Town for a talk," I propose.

He smiles. "That was a very good walk, John. We go fast; I like that. See you some time."

Harry and Charles drive off leaving Sydney and me to wait hopefully for Charles' return.

Across the road, is our 'oasis', a bar on stilts called *Kafesas* ('Your Café'). "Let's have that beer you promised me," says Sydney with a big grin. I have been forgiven for the mad race.

The botanist and his assistant climb the wooden stairs and enter an Aladdin's cave. Beyond a pile of fresh vegetables from the garden, a supermarket chill cabinet displays a remarkable variety of meze: anchovy filets in garlic, anchovy filets in chilli, *dolmades* (stuffed wine leaves), red peppers, octopus salad, beetroot & garlic, olives, *gigantes* (large butter beans in tomato sauce), *skordalia* (a garlic and potato mash), *tirokafteri* (a peppery cheese spread), *tsatsiki*, *tarama*, rough *melitsanosalata* (aubergine dip, home made like everything else), cheese croquettes (made with four cheeses including parmesan), mushroom croquettes, aubergine croquettes and a whole octopus ready to be barbecued. Hanging from a bar attached to the ceiling are *avgotaraho* (smoked fish roes from Petriti on the east coast), home-made *nouboulo* and *pastourmas* (home-dried beef).

"Sydney, why on earth didn't we get Jannie to come and collect us like yesterday?"

"Because we changed the plans," replies my friend.

"In October she and I will come back and stuff ourselves silly."

We finish our beer and are settling down to a second when

Charles arrives having collected his car. It is time go home to our patient wives.

A week after the rest of the team has returned to England, I visit Harry in the café he has run for five years. Situated between the airport and Garitsa Bay, it is the focal point for locals, who sit inside, and passing tourists who prefer the smoke free open air. A green sign on the door indicates 'smokers' are allowed in the café. There is also a black-and-blue government health warning sign, which is ignored by all.

A group of foreign students is sitting at the outermost table, paying for their coffees. Harry is teaching them a few words of Greek.

"*Ola mazi?*" giving his all-together wave.

"No, how much?"

"*Ena euro missi,*" which is less than the two euros paid in the tourist areas. "*Siga, siga,*" Harry says, almost overwhelmed by the change proffered by each. It takes me back to my days as a bus conductor in Folkestone. I would stand at the bottom of the stairs, collecting 10-shilling notes from hordes of French students rushing out in fear of missing their stop. On honest days, I would suggest that one note equalled five passengers. My life as an entrepreneur had started. I decide Harry is more honest than I was.

"*Pose lene?*" He asks the girls their names; what a charmer! "*Me lene Harry. Hairo poli.*"

Inside, his clients are all men, mostly over 60. On the walls there are photos of football teams dating back to 1949 and joke family groups, dressed as actors with full make-up. Harry is too busy to talk. Leon, a local, half-French and half-Greek, tells me that Corfu resorts have been destroyed.

"Greeks and Bulgarians can get from Saloniki to Igoumenitsa in two hours now." A slight exaggeration, but I take his point that the island is now facing a new invasion from visitors from the Balkans. "But they then wait three hours for a ferry," he suggests in despair.

He angrily continues. "I've just been on holiday to Rhodes. The old town is clean and stays open until midnight. In Corfu, everything closes at eight."

"But what about our lovely countryside and villages?" I suggest.

He concedes my point. Eventually Harry stops and asks me what I would like to know.

"I wanted to find out what you think about Corfu and its future. But you are too busy."

"I think you must go and see Dimitris Charitos. He is the expert."

I have met Dimitris before, so Jannie and I pop into his office on the way home. He is President of the Corfu Travel Agents and a busy man, but he agrees to a meeting the next day.

For half an hour the following morning he tells me his thoughts. "We want better quality tourists. Therefore we must improve what we offer and avoid what they don't like."

"Like Kavos," I suggest.

"No. Let Kavos and Sidari remain, as their visitors spend money which goes into our local communities." Angrily he raises his hands. "British papers write such bad things about them; therefore we must keep the resorts safe and fully under control, which means extra police on foot patrol," he suggests.

"The British love Corfu and they keep our economy going. 60% of all tourists were previously from Britain: that is 650,000, but now it is down to 450,000. The Germans are the next largest group with 200,000. Because of the financial crisis, tourists look for cheaper holidays and bigger discounts which only the all-inclusive large hotels can offer. Smaller hotels just cannot compete. This is not good for other parts of our small tourist industry such as restaurants. All the tourists stay in their

I am cheered that one of the leading figures on the island is so positive and determined to bring improvements for tourists to Corfu.

In October we return to St. George and have a fantastic lunch at *Kafesas*. It is more of a French bistro than a Greek taverna. There are fishing nets and lights in baskets hanging from the ceiling. The tables are covered with blue gingham tablecloths.

Our hostess, Miriam, arrived from Nelson in New Zealand at the end of the 1980s and married moustachioed Akis, who is the creative genius in the kitchen.

In typical Greek-style, she takes me into the kitchen. Olive wood is burning, the embers ready to barbecue the fish that lies in a cabinet in the pantry. "It's from our little harbour, fresh every day of the year. But phone first to check what we have."

I start taking the lids off the pots, which is much more exciting. Warm starters include *horta* (local wild vegetables), *tsigarelli* (spinach or chard in a hot sauce) and fresh boiled courgette and french beans, which will be served with oil and lemon. There is also fish soup; but I am faithful to my favourite breakfast food, which we eat with my son in the Bahamas, stewed fish (grouper in a thick spicy brown sauce into which one squeezes lime and chilli to taste).

Today we are also offered *margeiritsa* (sheep's innards) which is normally eaten at Easter, but is an all-year round speciality of the house. Finally I see *bourdetto* made from *skorpio*, a bony fish which my Jamaican daughter-in-law would suck clean of meat. She always chooses the head of the grouper in her stewed fish; I prefer the body.

Plate after plate arrives. Akis joins us and asks for our views on his food. Jannie has fallen in a big way for the anchovy filets in garlic; she says they are as good as those we had eaten in Vigo where we had stopped off on our trip researching my father's Atlantic journey.

"The croquettes are wonderful." She compliments the chef. "How do you make them?"

"I use four cheeses, the main one being freshly grated parmesan," replies Akis.

I have survived the *margiritsa*, which actually tasted excellent, but I am fascinated by the *bourdetto*. It is very, very hot.

"I make it like the fisherman did in the old days. If they were hungry during the night, they would make a meal only of fish, oil, chilli and onions. They couldn't take tomatoes on board. The red of the dish came only from the chilli – *kokkino piperi*, it was called," explains Akis.

"And if they didn't catch any fish?" I asked.

"Then they would use just potatoes. The hotter the sauce, the more wine they would drink."

Miriam comes over. I want to know about her early days in Corfu.

"Times were different in those days," she says. "We had no electricity, so I applied for permission to erect a wind turbine. Even though there is always breeze here beside the sea, it was turned down."

She confirms what Edward Lear said in 1855: 'This wind is what makes the island so healthy, & I never could understand why there are no fevers when there are marshes of such extent'.

"You are an eco-friend?" I counter.

"Of course I am. 20 years ago in New Zealand we were warned about what man could do to our climate. The arrival of the hole in the ozone layer was an early warning about global warming. My mother was an active member of Greenpeace. Do you remember the sinking of the *Rainbow Warrior*?"

"By the French?"

"The boat had just returned from the South Sea Islands with 300 islanders on board. They had been contaminated by nuclear fall-out from US H-bomb tests. The French intelligence services, who wanted to stop the *Rainbow Warrior* returning to obstruct their own nuclear tests, mined it, killing a photographer."

"That's terrible," I comment.

"Well, at about the same time, we in New Zealand were alarmed at the depletion of the ozone-layer, particularly over the Antarctic. A hole had appeared in the stratosphere and the reduction in our protection from radiation threatened us with an increase in skin cancer."

"But the CFCs have been banned, haven't they?"

"They have and now the ozone layer has started to recover. I am sure it's the same with global warming: it's man made and we must all do something about it."

I am completely in agreement with her. "Hence your wish for a wind-turbine?"

"And Air New Zealand's use of bio-fuels in their jumbo jets."

"Could we have turbines along the shore here?" I ask cautiously.

"Definitely out to sea, why not?"

I decide that *Kafesas* is the perfect end of a walker's second day. The food is wonderful and our hosts are enchanting.

"If walkers stop off here in the winter, when the bus service to the resort has stopped, how do they get back to town?" I ask.

Miriam points to the road beside the taverna. "They walk to Argirades, less than two kilometres inland, where buses pass from Lefkimmi every hour."

What a delightful way to get home.

Day 3: from St. George to Ano Pavliana
A British day

Flowers 8, Scenery 6, Underdeveloped 5, Challenge 4, Hrs 6
See map on page 35.

Again the team will follow the Trail today. As expected we will see more development as we move north. The scenery will improve as we get into our first mountains, which adds to the challenge at the end of a long day. However, we are to enjoy our first major surprise of the journey: the beauty and the abundance of the flowers will be truly staggering.

Jannie picks up our morning guests, Denise and Mitch, at Alonaki Bay Taverna, just north of Lake Korission, where we will stop for lunch. Afterwards they will return home, which is only a couple of kilometres away. Bill and Barbara will then take us to the end of our day's walk. Barbara will walk the first half of the afternoon and her husband will walk the second, finishing high above their lovely new house.

As one expects from a Dane, Jannie is exactly on time at our rendezvous. Once Denise and Mitch have been squashed into the Discovery, we trundle down the main road to Lefkimmi. After the long straight at Linia, we turn down the narrow two-kilometre track, now asphalted, to Issos beach. We have loved this so-called 'Sandy Beach' since the early 1970s. With its shallow water, it is a perfect place for children to learn to swim, and for adults to learn to windsurf.

We look south-east to the resort of St. George, a 3.5-kilometre strip of small two- and three-storey hotels, shops, restaurants and bars, with the large all-inclusive Aquis Sandy Beach Hotel at the nearest end, about a half-a-kilometre along the shore. Purists follow the Corfu Trail along the length of the resort, which is served by a bus in the summer, and finish at Paramonas Bridge, where they walk inland to pick up the bus from village of Agios Mattheos. Walkers following Aperghi Travel's schedule also stop overnight at Paramonas.

Turning north-west, I begin to question my 'plan'. The mountain above Agios Mattheos and that of Agii Deka in the far, far distance remind me of the view of the Twelve Pins from Connemara Golf Course beside its almost Caribbean beach on the Atlantic coast. No way would I contemplate such a long walk in the West of Ireland, but today we will be treading the sands that were host to the Bond film 'For Your Eyes Only'.

Mitch, in his late forties, checks his watch. "We'll be at lunch in under 2½ hours." It is one of those watches that is used by divers.

"Altitude, please, Mitch?"

"Whoops, minus 44 metres." He smiles.

He strides off with Charles and Denise, who stops and picks up something from the beach. She is a real beachcomber. Today may not be too rewarding as the local litter-pickers have collected the winter's flotsam and jetsam. She catches up and overtakes the leaders. I am impressed; she is an athlete as well.

Larger logs have been left on the beach and assembled into immense sculptures. This used to be the hippy beach of nature's children, usually in nature's dress as well.

In the rear, I can bore Sydney with my memories. As the hard sand on the sea's edge grows nothing but seaweed – thankfully absent today – he has little else to do but listen.

"Soon we'll turn inland over the dunes. Your time will come," I tell him.

"Those are not real dunes, but hard hills of sandstone. Little can grow on them," he complains.

"Not like the dunes of my golf links in Deal ..."

"Linking marsh and sea!"

"... with the nesting skylarks and the migrating birds."

I tell him about the enormous dunes of the Jutland coast and my courting days. Sydney is glum. This is not going too well.

"Look out to sea, Sydney – the island of Lagoudia. We used to windsurf out to it."

"But there is no wind."

"Every afternoon at three, the wind would come up and reach Force 4 and we would race all the way there and back." I exaggerate slightly. "Lagoudia is where the fishermen go; they find loads of fish in the reefs around it."

I think we are now finally on common ground.

After exactly 30 minutes we go round a point on the shoreline and just before some small cliffs turn inland, past a pink plastic chair. With a high dune to our left, Mitch and Denise lead us towards the lake, still out of sight. Hilary's *Guide* tells us that if we can see the lake, we must go further left. There are tracks of quad-bikes in the sand, less damaging to the roots of shrubs than the dreaded cross-country bikes which have destroyed much of the dunes to the south.

Suddenly we are in a paradise within juniper woods; the glades are carpeted by a million flowers. Sydney is incredibly happy. I trot behind him, kneeling down before everything he points out, my camera clicking crazily to capture these enchanting moments. This area is a long way from the tourist invaders, who keep to the seashore. It is on one of Mitch and Denise's secret walks. Perhaps for two months of the year, nature's beauty blooms and then dies away as the summer sun scorches the dunes.

Sydney and I are now following a rural track, with occasional glimpses of the mountains to the north, far behind our leaders. Suddenly we come to a mud beach beside the lake where billions of mosquitoes have just hatched. When mankind has wiped itself out, these insects will take over the world. I am truly scared. The swarms are everywhere, surrounding us in a fearful frenzy. We run like madmen, keeping as close to the shrubs as we can, so avoiding most of the black clouds on the lake's edge. Though I have bare arms, I feel no bites; perhaps the new-born mosquitoes have not as yet tasted blood.

Ahead there is a high bank of dried seaweed, pulled out of the lake to allow the water to flow into and out of the sea. A wooden bridge crosses the canal to the coast. Yellow paint has been dabbed on it; I can wake up from my nightmare. Our leaders are waiting patiently on the marked Corfu Trail for Sydney and his side-kick, both of us grinning at our frantic escape.

Before we can continue, I want to inspect the sluices that trap the fish in the lake. Mitch tells me that there have been fish traps here since Venetian times and that sea bream and grey mullet are still bred in the lake. I watch fascinated as two fish farmers, pictured on page 43, work above the traps which catch the fish as they make towards the sea. In a shed beside the water, the roe is smoked and then sealed in molten wax to preserve the unique flavour. Though *avgotaraho* is more expensive than the processed smoked cods' roe used for *taramasalata*, its taste is unique.

"One hour to go," announces Mitch; "you have a choice: along the beach or along the track?"

Sydney and I insist on the inland route; he is still chasing flowers and I find walking on sand tiring on the old legs. We now enter camper van country. During the tourist season nature lovers, mainly from Germany, will holiday beside Halikounas beach. A south-sea island style wooden cabin, playing gentle music, will open for drink and food. Now we are at peace with nature. A huge grey heron resting beside the lake flies off, lands and watches us pass.

It is time for Mitch and me to talk about his life on the island.

In the UK he had been a self-employed electrical engineer working on under-floor heating. I tend to like engineers as they

85

usually voted for me in the past. I always used to claim that when canvassing in Richmond one would meet lawyers, whilst just over the river in Twickenham, engineers would come to the door. They often worked at Heathrow. Mitch's hunting ground was in fact near Stansted airport. Each summer, he and Denise would come to Corfu, where they saw something rarely seen in England – the sun!

So in 2005 they sold up in UK, came to Corfu and set up a solar heating business. They bought a three-storey concrete shell, constructed illegally as it was too high and its back-staircase was too close to the boundary of the property. Undaunted, Mitch knocked off the top floor and staircase and then built an extension to look out over the lake and the sea in the distance. His advice to ex-pats who think of working in Corfu is to be 100% legal.

He has now made what will one day be a zero-energy house. Thermometers are fitted outside and inside the house. In the winter, if the temperature outside is greater than inside, he leaves the doors open. As the temperature drops he closes the thick patio doors fitted with 20mm German thermal double glazing.

Inside there are six thermostat-controlled temperature zones set at 24C in living areas, 21C in bedrooms. Glycol from two solar panels passes through a heat exchanger in a dual cylinder, with the upper half at 70C for hot water, and the lower 50C for under floor water heating. The whole system including controls and piping cost £2,500, which will be paid back in less than six years. For seven months of the year he has 100% hot water and heating for free. For the rest of the year, two electric boilers top up the heat at a cost of 4.1€ per day against the 9€ average in Greece, because he has installed both wall and ceiling thermal insulation and extra LED light bulbs: the old 25 and 40 watt ones have been replaced by ones using 2 and 3 watts respectively.

"What's next?" I ask. "How about some wind turbines?"

"I've seriously thought of putting some small ones on the roof of the house, but the wind is a bit erratic inland. Off shore, though, there is plenty. I watch the kite-surfers most days of the year. I'm more interested in solar PV panels. I have even applied to the EU's Centre for Renewable Energy for a PV grant, but they are only available for houses over 40 years old."

"As ours will be in two years time," I exclaim excitedly. "And when we are not in Corfu, we will be able to sell back the electricity we generate. From England, I will be able to use Google software and check the energy being used or sold."

"And see if you turned off the immersion heater when you left!" he grinned. "Talking of Google, have you heard that Inland Revenue in the UK are now searching for independent villa owners who rent out their property abroad, but fail to declare the income for tax purposes?"

"As you say, being 100% legal these days is the only way to avoid being caught."

"Getting a good accountant and listening to advice are also a must if you are thinking of setting up in Greece."

Now Mitch is building a pool. "Are you going to heat that with solar power as well?"

"Yes in time, I will need four more solar panels; meanwhile I will invest in a cover."

We are now north of the lake and on the edge of the coast, which has been badly eroded. Looking back south we see Paxos in the far distance; in the north we can just make out the Diapontian islands. Except for the occasional house, the west coast is completely undeveloped. Moments later, as if out of the desert, we arrive at an oasis. It is our lunch stop at the Alonaki Bay Taverna, where Jannie and Rachel are waiting.

"Exactly two hours twenty minutes," says Mitch.

A mynah bird, leaping around in a cage, welcomes us: "Hello."

It's warm enough to sit out under a canopy, with trees and flowers all round. A large meal should not be a priority in the middle of a long walk, but I have ordered a few vegetable dishes: *tsigarelli*; broad beans, artichokes, peas and potatoes from the oven; baked courgettes and potatoes in garlic sauce; french beans (the first of three crops for the year) and fried courgettes. Everything is grown in the fields nearby. This is one of the most fertile areas on the island. On the road here in the morning I noted four garden centres growing roses.

Then the speciality of the house is served: fried baby shrimps from the lake. They are slightly crunchy with a delicate and delicious taste.

My mobile rings. "The road has disappeared," says Barbara, our companion walker for the first part of the afternoon. "Thank goodness Bill stopped in time. We'll have to drive round the long way, so we'll be late getting to you."

Over lunch, thanks to excellent food and the delightful company of Denise and Mitch, I change from a time-driven maniac to a laid-back lounger. Who cares about being late?

In due course, Bill and Barbara arrive and we say our goodbyes to Mitch and Denise. Our new guests have recently retired to Corfu, and the hustle of life back in the UK is becoming a distant memory. Both teachers in their previous life, Bill is bearded and could become my mentor in my new attitude to life. Barbara is blonde and bubbly. She has volunteered to take the baton on the next leg of the adventure, according to Hilary's *Guide* a two-hour stroll, through olive groves on the sea side of the conical shaped mountain above Agios Mattheos to Paramonas Bridge. Bill will then lead us up the path to Ano Pavliana, a pleasant climb of an hour and a half, which I had achieved without difficulty during my planning and training period.

We are ready to leave, so Jannie can take Rachel home.

"When do I pick you up, John?" she inquires.

"My map shows a distance similar to this morning. Hilary suggests it'll take half-an-hour more, but she always over-estimates times to be on the safe side. Let's make it in three hours; that's at five o'clock," I add hopefully.

Charles and Barbara set off. There's lots of laughter ahead. I doubt if we will see much of them. Sydney and his gofer follow in equally good spirits. There are lots of flowers to admire and photograph.

"There's an even better clump of the blue one over there," I suggest, when we have spotted yet another species.

"But you have to climb through the nettles and the brambles."

Sydney balks at such adventures as his knees are too precious. Clad in my Teflon golf trousers, I have no fear of stings. A few minutes later, I return in triumph. We admire my efforts on the camera's little screen. And so we go on.

After heading inland towards the mountain, we turn back towards the sea, the first of a couple of zigzags. Ahead we see Charles and Barbara waiting for us. In fact they are discussing a hole in the road.

"Bill was right," exclaims Charles. "The road has literally disappeared."

Now I'm the expert at such matters, having suffered a 60-metre pot-hole in the road below our house, so I insist on inspecting the damage. "The road, the pipes, everything has disappeared into the sea," I exclaim.

"Get back, John. We don't want you to follow the road," Charles jokes.

The expedition photographer insists that there is no danger. I am lucky as well as foolhardy. The picture, shown on page 48, is worth the effort.

We set off back inland, through an area of smallholdings with little houses in large gardens filled with vegetables growing profusely in the fertile soil. This is not tourist territory, but a land cultivated by local villagers. There is no need to put up fences; people all know each other around here. The flowers bloom crazily in the open verges. Sydney is ecstatic and I am enthusiastic.

"Look at the wild fennel, John. You wouldn't see that in mainland Greece; the goats would have eaten it."

"Sensible animals: wonderful flavour for a salad when young," I suggest. Few goats are to be found in the south. There are more in the northern mountains.

"Marvellous with oily fish," adds Sydney.

We come to a junction with a wider road; to the right about a kilometre away is the 13th-century fort of Gardiki, now restored. Those with more time, particularly those in the parties organised by Aperghi Travel that end their day's walk at Paramonas, could take a short deviation and look at the fort. We must turn left to Paramonas, where Bill will take over as our guide, and then quickly press on, as we have the long climb to Ano Pavliana at the end of our day.

In 1862 Edward Lear climbed Mt. Pantokrator, the conical mountain above us, named after the monastery on top. 'We reached Ag. Matthaios, a finely placed village. [Then] to Mt. Pantokratora, a very pretty & hot pull! – the view of Lefkimi, Albania, & other 'islands' very beautiful, & opposite Fano & St. Angelo etc. We set out again [from Ag. Matthaios], the scenery very beautiful – broken rox & superb olives & so round the Ag. Matthaios mountain to Gardiki, or Palaiokastro – a castle like [?] Bodeino or any 12th century gray ivied walls, but with immense olives about it. The long plain & sea foamy, a beautiful scene, but the vast olives are for studies not sketches'.

The next 3.5 kilometres are along one of my favourite roads on the island: a dark spooky journey under ancient olive trees so high that they block out the light. Tracks off to the left lead down to secluded and little known beaches. In some summers these are covered in glorious golden sand; in other years little is left as the strong sea scours the coast.

The olive harvest is over and the black nets that catch the fruit are being folded up, to be put down again at the end of October. Wild flowers appear in patches where the trees have produced fewer olives, which happens in alternate years. Sadly, the use of chemicals against the fruit fly has poisoned some of the groves, which makes the land looks barren.

Half-way along the road, we see an old gun emplacement which is now a ruin. I wonder if it was built during the Second World War by the Italians or the Germans.

On our left, we begin to get glimpses of the sea. An occasional new house is under construction. Linked fencing is already in place, which indicates the owner is foreign.

Unbeknown to us, we have been steadily climbing. Suddenly ahead, a vista opens and we can see the magnificent expanse of the west coast with its mountains falling into the sea. This is great, as we have now left the rolling southern hills of the island and we are entering my country – the mid-island west coast.

In 1968, Jannie and I moved to New York. We took with us two little children and a map of Corfu – the Greek Army map used in the war. Excited by my work which kept me away from my little family for 6½ days each week but unimpressed with the 'city which never sleeps', I dreamt of a place beside the Mediterranean, on the island we had fallen in love with. Each night I would bring out the map and study the contours. In front of me now, I can see my chosen paradise: the joint bay of Skala and Paramonas, hemmed in by mountains well over 400 metres high. In my first book, *Greek Walls*, I tell of how our dear friend George found a perfect site for a small house in Paramonas just back from the coast, and how we returned to London to collect the money before rushing back to Corfu – only to find the owner had suddenly doubled the price. Forty years later, the plot still lies empty and we have moved further up the coast to our present paradise, Agios Gordis.

Just out to sea, rocks break the surface, indicating reefs which in the old days were teeming with fish, including the shy and ugly Mediterranean grouper, smaller than its Caribbean cousin but just as tasty.

It is here that the guests of Aperghi Travel will spend their night, and also where Hilary ends her third day on the Corfu Trail, with a walk of two kilometres along a conifer-lined river valley into Agios Mattheos, where a bus can be caught back to Corfu Town.

Bill is waiting on the bridge over the Paramonas River to take us on the last section of what is becoming a very long day. He, with his fresh legs, and Charles, with his long ones, rush off on the main road rising up from the valley. Sydney, with the metronomic rhythm of a marathon runner, is keeping pace. I struggle; we are going uphill. Seeing problems behind, he slows down.

"Have you noticed the white irises beside the road?" I haven't as I'm concentrating on putting one foot in front of the other. "I've seen them before in Morocco." Silence. "Have you been to Morocco?"

"No, Sydney."

"They are planted to keep the goats away."

"But there aren't any goats here; we've discussed this."

Another silence. He's in deep thought. "They could have been planted to mark the boundaries of the plots of land."

"In Corfu, people use olive trees to mark their property." I'm not sure he believes me.

Bill and Charles are waiting for us beside a concrete ramp up to the right. I am spurred on by the sight of a yellow mark. We are soon climbing what one could barely call a path. Further on, we see a man working in the fields. He reminds me of the ewes on our first day: his eyes follow us as we pass.

"*Ochi.*"

We look at Bill, who has walked this way only two weeks before.

"Are we trespassing?" asks Charles, who knows that '*ochi*' means 'no'.

"I don't think so," replies Bill as he comes to a halt. Our farmer stands up and smiles. Then he points in the opposite direction. We retrace our steps and continue up the mountain.

"He's met the likes of us before," I venture. I check on Hilary's *Guide* later, and she does warn the walker: 'Ten minutes on, after circling a cultivated plot, it becomes increasingly overgrown', which is exactly what it does. Photography ceases as we steadily climb; it seems that flowers like light, and we are now squashed in by myrtle and oak, the latter scratching Sydney's bare legs. I reckon that a donkey, even without its panniers, would find this a difficult path, which is small compensation. Of course, a goat would have no difficulty but I have already decided there are no goats in these parts and, anyway, I'm not a goat.

After twenty minutes, we stop where the path widens and where I had previously taken a group photo of the Sunday walkers (see bottom of page 40). I have no urge to repeat the exercise with the depleted team, though Bill points out his house way below. He phones Barbara, who appears at the front door; we all wave. We continue climbing and stop again where rocks overhang a steep drop down to the coastal road.

"If this view is a taste of what is to come, the Corfu Trail will be more like the other walks I have done," claims Charles, our well-travelled expert. "I normally walk in the mountains, where the views are open all the time."

"So you don't like the Corfu Trail, then?" I ask crossly.

"Of course I do; it's just different from what I'm used to. This has been flatter, though the views are beautiful and the flowers have been great."

"What you mean is we don't spend all day climbing up and

down mountains. It's just as well as I would be dead by now," I add.

The view of the coast stretching away to the islands to the north is indeed spectacular, but I am expecting the splendour of our trip to be more in the intimate nature of walking through olive groves than in the great vistas Charles is used to in the Alps and the Apennines.

"Bill, how long before we finish?" I ask.

"Twenty minutes."

"I'll phone Jannie to say we're nearly there. Great, we are exactly on time." My mobile has been turned off. "Oh no, I hope she hasn't been phoning me."

Jannie is already waiting for us at Ano Pavliana. When I tell her the good news that we won't be long, she seems rather angry. She must be the most tolerant person in the world – to put up with me – so I'm alarmed. I am not surprised she is already waiting for us, because she is incredibly punctual. I always tell people who might be in Copenhagen on a Saturday evening with nothing better to do, that they should drive along a suburban road a couple of minutes before the hour; if they see parked cars with people waiting inside, they have found where a party is being held.

"Jannie's a bit peeved," I announce.

"That's not the Jannie we know. What time did you say we would finish?"

"Five o'clock. I told her we would take three hours. It's twenty to, isn't it?"

"John, it's twenty to six, not five!"

I have never walked so fast: over the brow of the ridge and down into the village.

"I phoned you, at least twice," Jannie exclaims. "You never answered. I thought you had had a terrible accident."

Profuse apologies and a glass of old fashioned lemonade calm her.

As we take Bill home he invites us round to hear their story.

Their first visit to Corfu was in 1993 when their girls were eight and six. They sat in an apartment at Kalami, with a lovely sea view, and watched the ferries go by.

"Over a G&T, we decided that we could live like this!" says Barbara. "The day we got home, we enquired about buying a holiday home from the UK office of Corfu Property Agency but they were beyond our means."

With their children at school, and their work as teachers taking up so much time, they decided to visit lots of other Greek islands and also Spain. Sometimes during a summer holiday they managed to get to Corfu and also to some other place.

"And you chose Corfu, the best of the lot?" I ask.

"We learnt a lesson while holidaying in a villa in Spain. We stayed for a month but began to feel increasingly vulnerable when strange people constantly called trying to sell miscellaneous things. Our hire car was broken into and one of the girls was frightened by someone knocking on her window in the middle of the night."

"And is Simon Jenkins' article right?" Everyone in Corfu knew what he'd said. "He compares Corfu to Spain with its 'towns reduced to such ugliness'."

"He's totally wrong. Corfu does not allow high-rise buildings, whilst Spain does. We really like Corfu Town, as it is vibrant all year round, and we are not far from the mainland, with magical places to explore. The island is so green with fantastic scenery around every corner. But above all, the people are so friendly."

"You were working in England; but gave everything up to live permanently here?"

"We had always wanted to live abroad; to get away from the miserable weather." Barbara pauses. "The UK is brilliant when the sun *is* out, but in Corfu it is out even in December. We had missed a gap year when we were young, so we wanted our break later in life – a bit of adventure."

Bill takes up the tale. "We arrived on May 1, 2006. We worked several summers with a holiday company, not for the money but for something to do. We made some good contacts and got some cheap tickets to the UK. Barbara taught English to a young Greek boy, who also had numerous other out-of-school activities, including tennis lessons and German lessons, all funded privately. Sadly, Greek education seems to favour learning by rote. We heard about one girl who could read Shakespeare but failed her exams because she had not memorized the answers to the standard questions. Of course, they have problems later if they go to University in UK as they haven't been taught how to take notes or voice reasoned argument."

"We really liked Agios Gordis," continues Barbara. "From May to October we only mixed with Greeks; then we joined Hilary's Saturday walks in October and met ex-pats for the first time. The owner of the resort's car hire company found us a flat to rent in nearby Kato Garouna and we started looking for a house to buy. We found half finished property, some not large enough or too near the boundary or some even more illegal. In the end, we decided to find some land and build. We were introduced by CPA to an engineer, who they said was the only 'honest' one on island."

"There are others who are," I suggest, in defence of Nikos, though I know that the few bad apples have unfairly given the profession a bad name.

"My first question was whether we needed an architect. Andreas's answer was that we didn't as he was an engineer and we could design the building between us. The daughter of our Greek family had heard of some land for sale near Pentati and she suggested we should 'Go and see it *now*, not tomorrow', even though it was getting dark."

I laugh. "That's one of the delights of this country;

everything happens now or sometimes in the vague future."

"We asked Andreas what he thought and he said it 'had got prospects'. He then agreed to manage the project. Neither of us speak Greek, but Andreas spoke good English. He had received an MSc at Exeter. He asked us what we wanted, and we told him something not too big, perhaps a two-storey house with a basement."

"Which will raise the ground floor slightly and which Greeks like as they can convert it later on," I suggest.

"Yes. They enlarge the windows and make it into a gym. We use the space as a games room with a pool table, dartboard and a fruit machine, which we brought from England," explains Bill. "We also have a juke-box but it's a bit temperamental. As it is a terraced site, we have a view, from the top floor, over the olive trees to Paleokastritsa. We wanted the house in traditional style, which would soon look as if it had been finished a long time."

"And that's exactly what you have got," I comment. "What was the secret of your success?"

"We went into great detail during the design phase so when planning permission was granted – which took some time – the builders could get on and follow the plan. Of course, it is possible to apply with a single square on the plan, but we didn't want trouble later on," explains Barbara. "Andreas got various quotes and we chose a builder who started work shortly afterwards."

"16th November 2007," chips in Bill. "It was a wonderful, fairly dry winter, so the building was finished within a year."

"It seems you had very few hassles. Why was that?" I ask.

"Firstly, because the engineer managed the project; secondly, the foreman could speak English and would always answer our questions; and finally, and probably most importantly, we lived only fifteen minutes away and could respond instantly. If we had been in the UK, the result could have been very different."

"We were also always prepared to listen to advice. The Albanian workmen who did the stone-work and paving made several suggestions for changes to the exterior layout. We trusted their judgement, and the final result proved them right."

"You must have had some problems," I propose, remembering the many we had overcome.

"We have had one which we have yet to fully solve," Bill admits Bill. "We have found out about the waterfalls that come down the mountain. At the start, the builders bulldozed two terraces into one. It exposed the raw earth which last winter swept seawards through the pool." I remember that this was the problem we had in 1971, when the rain carried our retaining wall down the mountain.

"In conclusion, are you happy with your decision to live in Corfu?" I ask.

"Yes," confirms Barbara. "Corfu is a very safe place. Our neighbours know if we are away, and they blow their horn if they are passing and see us in the garden. We allow plenty of time to get to town, as we expect to meet goats and hens on the road or an old lady leading a donkey! I think, if we lived in such a remote area in the UK, we would be worried about safety, and perhaps of burglars."

In 1855 during his first winter on Corfu, Edward Lear commented in the same vein: 'It is a great comfort that one may walk anywhere in safety'.

Day 4: from Ano Pavliana to Pelekas Homeward bound

Flowers 3, Scenery 6, Underdeveloped 7, Challenge 6, Hrs 5
See map on page 36.

Yesterday we climbed up away from the coast for the first hour and a half of the official Trail's Day 4. Today we will miss out the rest of that day's walk and two thirds of Day 5's by descending to Pentati and Agios Gordis, walking the length of the beach and then climbing up to Aerostato, from where we will follow the final third of Day 5 to Pelekas. In the autumn I hope to complete the two-day loop around Agii Deka, the highest mountain south of the great Mt. Pantokrator range, in two reduced length hikes, each of three to four hours.

I chose Ano Pavliana as our overnight stop because it is not only on the year round bus route into town but it also overlooks the picturesque bowl between west and east coast mountain ranges, through which we have driven to the south of the island each day. It also has a busy café-bar to rest in whilst waiting for a bus.

A less exhausting option to climbing up from the coast and then dropping down again to Pentati would have been to continue along the lovely and little used road from Paramonas to Pentati and then down to Agios Gordis past the Aquis Agios Gordios Hotel to pick up the summer bus back into town. It takes the same time as yesterday's walk, is easy to follow and would be ideal for hotel guests walking from the Aquis Sandy Beach Hotel in St. George.

Sydney will be disappointed today as it is raining, not unusual for late April, and most of the flowers will be closed. Charles will be delighted because we have the hardest climb of our journey so far. They will both, I hope, be surprised by the lack of development, even though we pass through a major resort.

I have been looking forward to this section because it is across my back yard and we will walk with my friend Fotis, whom I first met in 1966 when he was a toddler in his father's taverna on Agios Gordis beach. I say 'walk', but that is too tame a word; he prefers something more strenuous. He has just returned from running the whole way round Mount Olympus which, at over 2,900 metres, is Greece's highest mountain. Though he was some way down the field, he was more annoyed that a woman had beaten him.

"I followed her all the way, but couldn't overtake her," he explained when we were planning our day together. I was not sure he really wanted to overtake her!

Fotis spends his winters contemplating the continuous roar of the sea at his empty taverna on the beach of Agios Gordis, or walking through the mountains around the bay.

Last Easter, he caused consternation in the village of Pentati. "I was on my way up to the top of Mount Pantaleimon, the mountain which you can see from your house," he explains. (It is from there that paragliders leap whenever the wind is from the north-west, landing ages later on Agios Gordis beach.) "I met the priest in Pentati – he must be 80 years old. He offered to come with me, and in just four hours we had reached the summit and returned. Next morning at the church service the priest was missing. He was still in bed!"

At the end of the season he will walk the 1,000-metre-deep Vikos Gorge and then run a 10-kilometre race in Athens. Finally, he will go off to Mount Athos, made famous in the UK by Prince Charles' visit. No females, human or beast, have been allowed there since 1060, and only those men with religious or cultural interests may enter.

"For two months before I will be mentally preparing for it," explains Fotis.

"Are you near God?" I ask in my innocence.

"No, he's everywhere."

"Then what is so special about Mount Athos?"

"It is impossible to explain. I know every path and every monastery. When the boat arrives, it is the most magical moment. At 6pm it is dark; so I go to bed. I sleep until two in the morning then spend four hours in church, which is optional. I then walk all day for ten days, staying in a different monastery each day. Sometimes I walk to the top of the Holy Mountain itself, which is over 2,000 metres high."

"How much do the monasteries charge?" I ask in my mercenary way.

"Just €25 a day, at all the monasteries, and that includes the food."

I have always been impressed with the excellent behaviour of the Greeks. "Does the existence of a flourishing church make your youngsters so much more polite than ours?"

"No, not really. It is just that we respect our elders."

Jannie picks up Fotis at the junction (and bus stop) of the resort. We drive up the south side of the valley to Kato Garouna, then turn right through Kato (Lower) Pavliana to the rather lovely village of Ano (Upper) Pavliana.

"John, we are not in a hurry, are we?"

"Of course not," I reply.

"Can I show me something special?"

"Fotis, whenever have I said 'No' to such a suggestion?"

"Then we won't stop in the village."

We continue up the Pentati road to the four-way junction on the top of the ridge, along which we now drive for 2.5 kilometres through the rushing clouds. We catch glimpses of the sea 425 metres below and then the central valley. At the end of what was once just a fire-break but now is a recently made up but unasphalted road we come to a little church.

"The villagers of Ano Pavliana fought a mobile phone

company who wanted to erect a mast here. They won; so they built a church to give thanks for their victory. The large sign outside said 'PROFITI ILIA ESTAVROMENOU'. I believe this refers to the prophet Isaiah foretelling of the arrival of Jesus and his crucifixion.

I stand in wonder at the view. Four mountains, each about five hundred metres high, rise up above the central valley. As the wind almost blows me off my feet, I have a wicked idea. What would happen if wind turbines were erected, straddling the fire-breaks to their summits? Would the villagers of Ano Pavliana fight against them as they did against the mobile phone aerial? Would the villagers of Agii Deka fight them as they did against the 'golf-ball', which helps pilots land at the airport? Would the villagers of Agios Mattheos fight them even though in the war there were guns placed on top of their mountain? Would I and the other residents of Agios Gordis fight them if they were on top of Pantaleimon? Or would they be accepted, if everyone were to receive free electricity to compensate for the damage to the visual environment?

We go back to the junction and, leaving Jannie to return home, the team led by Fotis, sets off down the newly asphalted road to Pentati. In the hour we take to descend, not a single car passes us. A cynic might question why so much money has been spent on re-surfacing the road for the twice daily bus service from Town. I, however, can remember the first time we drove on it in 1971: it had been almost impassable, with great rocks blocking our way.

Walking four abreast, we learn a lot. Fotis, our hunter-gatherer, stops and picks a blue flower.

"*Aquilegia alpina*," says Sydney.

Fotis sucks it. "Nectar, delicious!" he announces.

"Fotis, careful! Eating the seeds or the roots can be fatal," warns Sydney.

We start discussing the far-flung Greek empire.

"Charles, have you ever been to Alexandria?" asks Fotis. "It has a beautiful sea front."

"The Greeks burnt it down," Sydney comments.

"No, it was the Romans," Fotis disagrees.

I think it was due to a Greek-Jewish civil war, but prefer to mention the British involvement. "Nasser kicked us out."

"And that was the end of the British Empire," says Fotis with a big grin.

"Careful, now, Fotis. Sydney is a Commander of the British Empire."

Fotis later points out the 'X' painted on the olive trees. "It marks who owns it." This rather disproves Sydney's theory of the irises.

After the rain, there is a rather unpleasant smell. "That's from the chemicals sprayed on the olive trees to eradicate the dakos flies," explains Fotis. "As a result, in June, there will be no fireflies either."

We arrive in Pentati and I notice a new road has been built. Fotis says it's because there have been landslides. I am alarmed at the damage done by the rain above the west coast. We walk through the narrow main street of this very pretty village and then, after three minutes, bear left at the sign 'Footpath to Agios Gordis'. After 200 metres, where the road goes left to the harbour, the beach of Fieroula and Ortholithi, we keep straight on along a muddy track. I point to a pile of rubbish on a corner.

"Why can't they use wheelie-bins in the village?" says Fotis angrily. "Last year a man threw stones at me when I suggested he should not use it as dump."

The mountainside is now towering right above us. We carefully make our way round a narrow path with a high cliff falling into the sea. At water level, but out of sight, is a secret cave. Just offshore, a double rock juts up inches above the surface; it also has its secret, a narrow passage a metre high through which brave (or idiotic) people can swim. I take tremendous care here, using my stick as a third leg; a few summers ago a lady fell and broke her leg. The ambulance couldn't get to the end of the beach, so a four-wheel drive pick-up had to be used to rescue her.

'It's better to be late in this life, than early in the next,' was my father in-law's favourite saying, so I take extra care. Though this is a popular route in summer, I hope those who take it will be very careful, particularly after rain.

Until now, there has been total peace – not a sound. As we turn the last corner before the almost vertical clamber to the rocks below, I am shocked by music coming from the all-inclusive Hotel Agios Gordios. The workmen, who have their radios on full blast, are completing the renovation of the hotel ready for the coming summer season. My first reactions have been mixed. The new owners have upgraded the facilities, which must be good for their clients. But they have also added a Sushi Bar, which is unGreek to say the least. My Greek friends, however, tell me they would like to try the restaurant. Finally, they are building a beach bar, four feet above the little cove at the near end of the beach. Assuming it doesn't get washed away in the winter, it will definitely be a success, though it competes with Fotis' taverna, *Theodoros*, a hundred metres along the beach. In the autumn, I will find out how this all-inclusive has affected the resort.

I look across the resort to the Pink Palace complex, the other 'all-inclusive' in the resort. This stands out near the bottom of the road down from Sinarades, perhaps 500 metres further down from our house.

In 1965, Spiros Grammenos, now in his 70s, built the original café-bar half-way along the beach. In 1972, he added 20 rooms on the beach and then built the Pink Palace disco nightclub at the present site, on our road but 400 metres from the beach. By then we were on speaking terms since, in the previous year, he had worked for his father, Stamatis, in erecting our little summer-house.

"*Kalimera, Spiro*," was then the most I could manage.

"Good morning, Capitalist," he would reply.

In 1999, the night-club became what it is now – a pleasant hotel with 160 air-conditioned rooms, open all year round, with full and half-board at a very reasonable price. In the end perhaps Spiros was the capitalist; but he had worked very hard for his success.

Back in 1967 his brother Yerasimos had constructed the International Hotel, 100 metres north along the beach from the original Pink Palace café-bar. Its name did not adequately describe its lack of luxury, but it did indicate a potentially new market – the back-packers of the world. In due course it was the Pink Palace where they made their base in Corfu.

I look for our own home, on the mountainside up the road from the Pink Palace. It is hidden in the olive groves which stretch along the length of our lovely two-kilometre beach on which my children and grandchildren have had such wonderful holidays. Behind the house what looks like a monstrous, multi-storey carpark stands derelict. Ten years ago Yerasimos built a four-floor extension to his father's house, but the planning authorities stopped further work on it as only a two-storey extension had been approved. Perhaps Nikos and Mitch can get together and convert it into a solar power station!

Fotis, who has walked on ahead, welcomes us with coffee and soft drinks. We sit gazing out to sea. The murmur of the waves is unbelievably soothing. One day, if I ever slow down, I will idle my days away in this heavenly spot.

The mountains surround the bay like an amphitheatre; we are the stage. Inland is Agii Deka, the highest mountain south of Mt. Pantokrator. Perched on its side is Ano Garouna, which Edward Lear visited in 1862. He said: 'To Garouna. Wonderfully lovely place & beyond, to the bay'. The bay was of course Agios Gordis.

It is time to move on. The southern end of the beach is pure golden sand. We jump across the river that flows through the resort in the winter, and walk north along the shore. The prevailing wind is from the north-west, so the current washes the fine sand southwards, uncovering pebbles then stones at the north end.

We pass the original Pink Palace, and then Yerasimos's place, and soon the stones become rocks – ideal for Nikos' 'Summer Storage Heater'. Not many years ago, it was the 'nudist' beach, with its bar in the bushes. As it didn't have electricity, the authorities turned a blind eye to it.

On the west coast, where there is no proper harbour south of Paleokastritsa, villagers construct little refuges for their fishing boats. We pass one called *Mavrespetras*, built from the black stone which gives it its name. It has been slightly dredged, so it has a sandy bottom. At the far end of the beach, a pair of six-metre-high rocks stands guard. Between them there is a natural deep and secluded pool with a mottled green and blue bottom, accessed only from the sea.

Perhaps 300 metres above the beach is the famous view point of Aerostato, the 'station in the sky', which is our next destination. 50 metres after the last house and 50 metres from the end of the beach we climb up a narrow path and pass three houses one behind the other. The path becomes a rough concrete road which passes on the right a little church, one of the three Fotis' uncle built in the area. At its end, we meet the track which has run parallel to the sea from the hairpin bend where we live on the road from Sinarades to Agios Gordis. We turn left and at the end of the concrete wall of the house on the junction there is a sign up to the right to Aerostato, which we follow.

Fotis is in the lead. Suddenly he stops, stoops and picks up a piece of dried grass, with which he opens a minute round woven door covering a hole in the bank. Inside, a spider is hiding. I remember Gerald Durrell describing such a find in *My Family and Other Animals*. Fotis pokes the grass into the hole and sure enough the spider grabs it in self-defence. He slowly eases out the little creature. Now I know how Gerald Durrell must have felt; this is a wonder of nature. Fotis smiles knowingly to his audience – I wonder how many other magical mysteries he has uncovered – and returns the spider to its home.

With our Natural History lesson over, we set off for a twenty-five minute-climb up the steep path. Every five minutes, I hear Fotis call back. Our Olympian athlete is worried about his old friend. I am tempted not to reply so he can come down and rescue me. At the top, we meet the road which goes left to the viewpoint, past an excellent taverna, in which our builder Nikos Merianos once treated us to the Corfiot speciality, *Kouneli stifado*, a stew made from rabbit, red wine and heaps of little onions.

Today, we turn right to meet the Corfu Trail, which has just passed through Sinarades, my local village in which many of the workers on Agios Gordis spend their winters. The way turns left up a steep incline to a little church, where the villagers meet on Easter Sunday and then slowly follow their brass band, the Sinarades Philharmonic, back to the village. On the Sunday after Easter, the Philharmonic leads a procession from the main entrance of the village, along the main road into town for half a mile, and then through our neighboring village of Kouramades and back to the village cemetery. (See page 44.) These are the emotional experiences that make Jannie and me feel so blessed that we have found Greece.

It's good to be back on the Corfu Trail. The short cut has saved a day, and thanks to Fotis we have not got lost. We continue north on the coastal ridge with splendid views to the west. After a kilometre, we turn inland and start descending towards the valley road which will eventually reach

Paleokastritsa. Ahead, on the hills opposite, are three magical villages, Kouramades, Kalafationes and Varipatades, which together with the large village of Sinarades provide glorious opportunities for gentle walking. They are easily accessible by bus from Corfu Town, which is only twenty minutes away. All four have retained their traditional centres, and each is a thriving community in its own right.

In 1864, just before he left the island – to return for just a few days in 1877 – Edward Lear described the scenery: 'We walked to the plane tree fountain below Kalafationes: most lovely. Those immense olives, light-trunked, dark-stemmed against the background, & the gleamingness & sparkle of the lemon & orange beyond & through. A wonderful world is this Corfu'.

Edward Lear tells of his trip in March 1856: 'We walked to Kalafationes – a village some miles off – & by chance we arrived to see the dance with which all country weddings conclude; it is a very pretty sight. On a sort of rising ground, where the churches are usually built, this ceremony takes place: a long string of couples hand in hand, & close together, moving in a circle to music, & proceeded by the *choregos* – a man who capers & dances before them, backwards. The first couple are the bride & her mother, & all the jewels & finery they possess. The 2 we saw were literally covered with plates of gold, & coins threaded like necklaces about their heads & necks. Each of the dancers holds a handkerchief in one hand, which the next in order holds also; they advance 3 steps, & go back 2, & so by degrees get round the circle. The bride & her mother keep their eyes fixed on the ground. There were perhaps 40 couples'.

As we descend, it feels as if we are turning south. We stop at the next junction in the path and ignore the yellow waymark.

"Hilary's wrong," says Fotis with a smirk. They have been friends for a long time. "We turn left along this path."

It looks familiar as I have walked the area with my daughter in the past. After fifty metres, I begin to worry. Sure enough, we come to a dead-end.

"No, Hilary's right," confesses out guide sheepishly.

As we retrace our steps, I remember the October when Louise and I had made the same mistake. We had been rewarded for our deviation by finding a pomegranate tree ripe with fruit ready to pick. We gorged ourselves as we savoured the exquisite flavour of our discovery. It is one of the pleasures of the Saturday expeditions with Hilary that the walkers, in particular the Greeks, help themselves to wayside fodder.

We soon turn north again and, after walking parallel to the valley road, we take the tarmac road towards Yaliskari Bay and its hotel, perched high above a little sandy cove. Before the brow of the hill from where a narrow goat's track leads down to the beautiful Kontoyialos beach, we turn right for our sprint for home – well, my companions did the sprinting – finishing at the wide hairpin bend before Pelekas, where Jannie and Rachel are waiting.

I eventually stagger in to be met by my best friend, who is worried.

"Fotis says he was thinking of getting a helicopter to rescue you," Jannie says.

This hairpin bend brings back happy memories of our first holidays on Corfu. In 1967, we parked our little Fiat here and took the path beside the red mansion all the way down to Kontoyialos. There my Corfiot friend George and I, with our wives watching, played cricket on its soft sand with Michael from St. Lucia and Rosa from Spain. Not another person was on the beach. Later we would return and hunt for grouper on the reef offshore.

The path has been replaced by a road, but it is still possible to get to the sea by following little paths from Pelekas village through the olive groves which tumble down the mountain to the beach. There, modern tourism has taken over: the recently upgraded Aquis Pelekas Beach Hotel sprawls across the bay.

Hilary and I would like to advise the guests at the hotel: "Leave your all-inclusive luxury and discover the other Corfu, Sinarades and the villages across the valley, and perhaps take a walk back along the Trail to Agios Gordis. Then why not walk down the coast to St. George of the South and stay at the Aquis Sandy Beach Hotel? Finally you could continue on to their Capo di Corfu all-inclusive at Lefkimmi."

We challenge the Aquis UK and Greek management: "Why not become the catalyst that brings new tourists to our lovely island, not just to your resorts but also to the Corfu Trail which connects up your hotels? Why not provide multi-centre walking holidays and offer luggage transfers between your hotels? Perhaps encourage your guests to meet the locals – they are incredibly friendly."

This reminds me of a story told to me by one of the senior coaches at Chelsea Football Club, where my grandson Sean from the Bahamas trains. The coach went to Jamaica for a holiday. (Sean's mother is Jamaican, so I can vouch for the story's authenticity.) He stayed in an all-inclusive, whose management discouraged the guests from meeting real Jamaicans. One evening, he escaped from security and joined some local lads for a kick-about, an apt description of the game they play. His first contact with the ball was seconds before his first near contact with a player's foot, which he dodged; Jamaicans, like Sean, play with bare feet. After a couple of Ronaldos and a Cryff, the coach shot and scored. From then on his team-mates shouted at each other: "give it to Whitey!" Locals are indeed friendly.

The four walkers join Jannie and Rachel in the Land Rover and drive up right through Pelekas to have a drink beside the Kaiser's Throne, a huge rock on top of a cliff over the valley below. It was named after the Kaiser who, before the First World War, would be chauffered over from his Achilleon Palace above the east coast at Gastouri to watch the sun go down over the sea, way below to the west.

This viewpoint offers the best panorama of the centre of the island: to the south, the whole of our fourth day's walk from Pentati; to the south-east Agii Deka with its golf-ball radar installation on top, and Gastouri with the Kaiser's Achilleon Palace; to the east, Corfu Town and the mainland in the distance; to the north-west, tomorrow's walk to Myrtiotissa, Lawrence Durrell's 'best beach in the world', and on across the Ropa Valley and the Marmaro Hills to Paleokastritsa; and to the north and our last three days across the Mt. Pantokrator ridge to the developed north-east corner of the island.

For anyone who has not been to Corfu before, I recommend visiting the Kaiser's Throne for its fantastic view. Walkers should take out the Freytag & Berndt map and follow the route before setting out on the Corfu Trail. Hilary's *Guide* suggests it should take ten days to cover the 220 kilometres, that is, twenty-two kilometres or fourteen miles per day. In 1857, Edward Lear, at the age of forty-five, would find this an easy challenge, as he averaged four miles per hour: 'We set off to the other side of the island, & got to Myrtiotissa – having started at 12.30 – exactly at 3 – 10 miles. At 4 we set off, returning by a bit of coast & the village of Pelekas, & arriving in town at 6.30'.

Pelekas has an interesting history. Seen from afar it reminds one of a Tuscan town, perched high on a hill. In its centre it still has pretty archways and a lovely square and church, but the village lacks the old tiled roofs of its neighbours across the valley. It looks less Corfiot, and that is because, in the 1980s, concrete box extensions with flat roofs were added by the villagers to capture the tourist market of the moment: Inter-Rail travellers from Scandinavia. 1,800 beds were provided for these independent visitors, none of them on package deals. In the evening perhaps a thousand of them would congregate outside the five bars in the village square, blocking the road through the village. Perhaps uniquely, there was not a single tour operator's office; seven local travel agents issued the tickets for onward travel to the mainland and Athens and for the return ferries to Brindisi. This was no sudden invasion: from the early 1970s hippies had been coming to Kontoyialos, the beach below the village, which could only be accessed by foot.

On one occasion, the police received a complaint from the villagers that some naked revellers had been seen on the beach. Rather than walk down, three local constables drove to Glyfada, the next beach up the coast, to hire a boat. None was available so they hired three pedaloes to make their short journey, without difficulty as the sea was as calm as glass. The hippies ran into the sea to welcome their visitors, pulled their vessels ashore and invited them to Yiannis Taverna for refreshment. An hour or two later three inebriated policemen pedalled home; the owner of the pedaloes doubled the rental rate for late delivery.

After resting up at home, we go down to our beach again for dinner at O Theodoros. In summer I order fried fish as the sun sets, and then swim until I am called back to the table. Tonight it is dark and cold, so we eat in the family room inside: an honour.

In the season, when asked what is on the menu, Fotis will answer 'everything'. This means all the usual Corfu favourites, plus Olga's meat balls with home-made tomato sauce. Olga is Theodoros' widow; they opened in 1960, the first building on the beach. I quote from my first book *Greek Walls* of our first visit in 1966.

'(Theodoros) then introduced us to his small attractive wife Olga. Their daughter Maria, a pretty smiling four-year-old with blond hair and green eyes, and their son Fotis, a shy one-year-old, watched as gazozas were brought to this young couple sitting at a concrete table beside a mile of silver sand. We wondered if they realised that this was heaven on earth. How could they? They didn't know of cold, wet northern Europe with its smog and pollution.'

In hindsight I think now the sand is gold rather than silver. Olga's meatballs are the same. I quote again.

Our friend 'has told Olga that her meatballs taste the best in all Greece. He then asked her what she puts in them – because it certainly isn't meat.'

Of course it is meat and mighty good they taste. Nowadays, the food is cooked by Hannah, the very beautiful Czech wife of Tassos, Fotis' younger brother. She has learnt many of her skills from Olga, who still pops in to help.

We order two portions of meatballs, two fresh red mullet and *kalamari* for Jannie. *Tarama* and Greek salad start us on our way with a few carafes of the excellent house wine. Our wine-taster Sydney approves of the red. I like the white with my pan-fried fish.

By now you know Fotis rather well; he is cautious and thoughtful, quite a philosopher: he can sit for hours watching the sea beat on the shore. Tassos is more boisterous; he lived for the first six years of his life on the beach and then moved to Sinarades with his parents in 1981. Throughout the winter he also returns to the beach every day.

In summer 2001, when he was the coach of the juniors at Corfu Tennis Club, I suggested, over a glass or two of his excellent wine, he couldn't beat my son Peter, who was arriving soon from the Bahamas.

"How much do you want to bet?" he asked.

"You decide."

"Your Land Rover," he proposed.

"And if you lose what do I get? Your car! No way. Will you wager your taverna?"

"Of course! I will win!" he said confidently.

Well, I am now the owner of a wonderful restaurant on the most beautiful beach on Corfu. Tassos, of course, says he was only joking! Fotis just raises his eyebrows.

Over the years, the brothers have built up a large number of regular clients. Many use the taverna as a base for the day: the parents sip their drinks whilst the children make sand castles. Others, like us, prefer to eat and swim at the end of the day. Some just have a beer. Many of his guests were from the Agios Gordis Hotel, their neighbours on the beach. I am interested to find out if this is still so now that it is under new management, as part of the Aquis chain.

From my random sample in the autumn, it is obvious that the upgrading of the hotel has been a success. Everyone has praised its location and its value for money. Indeed, one couple were particularly delighted when they were upgraded from full board to 'all-inclusive'. Their only regret was that, in consequence, they then stayed their whole week in the hotel. Such tourists are the ones that used to pop in to Theodoros. The brothers were philosophical: it's what happens, they say. I am more concerned that the mini-markets have lost business, as the guests of the old hotel no longer buy a bottle of wine for the evening; they now get them as part of their holiday package. I decided to visit three friends who provide accommodation locally.

The first is Sea Breeze, located right on the beach. It is open throughout the season and also at weekends during the winter. I do not apologise for comparing it to the Bahamas, with its beautifully tiled new dining area overlooking the sea and covered to let the breeze blow through. It is run now by two brothers. Yiannis is married to Helena, the daughter of local councillor and my good friend, Spiros Mazis. They have two sons aged 13 and 8; the former is named, as is the usual practice in Greece, after his grandfather Spiros. The other brother, Vassilis, also has two sons aged 13 and 8, the elder called Stamatis after his paternal grandfather.

Their clients are mostly English. They have 60% returns

and pride themselves on knowing their guests personally.

"As the coach from the airport comes round the bend, they look down on the resort and say 'it's home'," claims Yiannis.

In 1975 their father and mother opened a few rooms in their house, which was set back off the beach and has recently been replaced by an annexe. In 1981 they built a snack bar on the beach and then, two years later, added rooms above it. When Yiannis returned from the army in 1990, they added a top floor. In 2001, they built two pools, one for adults and one for kids. They now have 20 rooms with a total of 50 beds.

On one night each week they have a barbecue and on another they organise Greek dancing. Their tour operator runs excursions, and most people take the bus into Corfu Town at least once.

Theirs is a story that is heard all over Greece, and is the reason why, even in a tough economic climate and with competition from the upgraded Agios Gordis Hotel, they are still such a success.

Their view of the sea-bound rock of Ortholithi, the mountains behind and the Diapontian islands to the north, on a clear day make their location rather special. Last year a Greek Cypriot diplomat who had travelled the world sat down on their terrace and said: "This is one of the most beautiful places in the world, and Corfiots do not realise it because they live here."

I join two elderly couples from Scotland. Their beer arrives.

"Here is your tall glass," says Yiannis who, knowing each client's preference, provides the personal service of which Greeks are rightly proud. They actually stay nearby at the lovely Villa Sophia but come every day to eat and drink beside the sea. It is their fourth visit to Corfu, once to Paleokastritsa, once to Arillas in the north-west and now twice to Agios Gordis. "It's such a peaceful resort," they say. "This time, we have already been twice to Town by bus and once to Paxos by boat."

A couple from Bradford explain that it is their third time in Agios Gordis, the first in a small place then twice at Sea Breeze because "we can see the sun set". They like the Greek people, having been to twenty Greek islands but only back to Crete, Kephalonia, Lesbos and Corfu. They have also been to Spain.

"Is Corfu going the way of Spain?" I asked.

"Certainly *not*," says Mrs Broadbent. "Corfu is the last island we visited, because we had read that it was over-developed. We have been pleasantly surprised, as all the buildings on the island are low-rise. We particularly like it here as there is no road in front of the hotel; it's more family oriented."

I then met a large family from Warwick, consisting of grandparents, parents and six-year-old Sophie; it was the week before half-term. In fact there were four generations on the island; the great-grandmother, in her 80s, was staying in Kassiopi. In the 1980s the grandparents had visited Paleokastritsa at the end of the season, but were transferred to Sidari; "as it was in the old days," they added. The parents had been to St. Stephanos in the north-west twice, Arillas once and Agios Gordis three times.

"The island draws us back," explained the father. "We've been to Crete and Zante, but Corfu is the prettiest. The people are friendly, the food is excellent and the resort is not-overcrowded. It's quiet but there are things to do."

"And Sophie?"

With the enthusiasm of all six-year-olds, she chips in. "I really love the sea. I can swim in it. Well, that's when it is calm. I also like making sandcastles."

"We love Corfu Town, its old buildings, its little stone-paved streets, the washing hanging out," said her mother, with equal enthusiasm. "I close my eyes and I can imagine I am in Venice."

Finally I interviewed a younger couple from the Isle of

Wight. It was their sixth visit to Corfu and their fifth to Agios Gordis.

"The first time we stayed in St. Stephano in the north-east. We didn't take a boat out as I work with boats in England. Our first week here was in the Agios Gordis Hotel. We read our books, the Durrell ones and your own; we had nice walks and we made friends with Fotis. He didn't know about the Isle of Wight, but he was very proud of having been to England, to Liverpool of all places."

"To watch the football," I suggest.

"We stayed at a couple of villas: one was disappointing, the other was very nice. Now we stay at Sea Breeze for its tranquillity. It's not very Greek though," he jokes. "It is very clean. The Greek people are much friendlier than in Minorca; the Corfu people are particularly friendly. As an island person I understand the problems: the children leave and there are extra costs because of the ferries. Now when I visit Corfu, I feel as if I am coming home."

I ask Yiannis if he had thought of offering his guest a guide to local walks. He hasn't, but I note that Aquis are doing so at the big hotel.

"It's a good idea, as we open immediately after Greek Easter, when the flowers are at their best," he says thoughtfully. "They could also walk to Sinarades to see the Folk Museum, to see how they lived in the 19th-century. It's strange for the visitors, and even for some of us Greeks."

I move north along the beach to the Romantic Palace, which is owned by Michael and Anna Pangalis, whose Romantic View was destroyed when the main road below our house collapsed. From Kato Pavliana, he is handsome and dark; she is blonde, blue-eyed and beautiful from Thrace. Her home was Orestiada, half an hour from Turkey and half-an-hour from Bulgaria, the last town before the border on the road to Edirne. I told her how, in 1962, I hitch-hiked through the town on the way to India. My last lift was with a lorry-load of Greek Army conscripts, who whistled at the local blonde, blue-eyed belles. In contrast, the Turkish conscripts on the other side of the border hadn't a whistle between them.

In 1987, Anna was working for a travel agent in Stuttgart. She popped into Michael's champagne bar for her lunch-hour snack and they have been together ever since. They returned to Corfu and opened up their little hotel in 1990. Half their guests are English; the others are German, Dutch and Scandinavian. Everyone has been before. After staying at the Romantic Palace for fifteen years, one English couple has bought a house in Sinarades.

Michael is a football fanatic, and has coached on the island and on the mainland. Alexis, their eldest, having played for the Greek youth team and Panathinaikos, now plays in Cyprus; Akis, their second son, plays in Corfu. Sixteen-year-old Stella, however, wants to go to university.

Theirs is a fun place to stay: on Thursdays they have live music with a two- or three-piece band. Every evening, Michael shows off his Greek dancing skills, which include lifting a table in his mouth. Then Anna joins in for just one dance. Their family entertainment was one of the reasons why we fell for them.

Anna's food is better than ever, if that is possible. She cooks special dishes from Thrace, and Michael grills fresh snapper and sea bass on the charcoal grill.

"Has the new hotel affected you?" I ask her.

"It has made no difference at all," she replies, agreeing with Yiannis at Sea Breeze.

My final call is to Steven on the Hill. This establishment opens from May to October and is full from June to September.

"We only miss the few extra people from the Hotel at the beginning and the end of season, as the more people we have, the better the atmosphere," explains boss Steven. "Because of the recession, the resort has generally not had a good year, though the Dutch come out of season to walk; Holland is so flat that they like it here with the mountains all around. In July and August, Greeks and young Romanians arrive by car. We have been fine, as 70% of our guests, mainly British, have come in previous years. One Englishman has been here 55 times."

That's not a bad record, as they only opened the restaurant in 1986 and their rooms in 1987. I can recommend their food; we attend the Volanté String concerts held around the island in October, which Steven and his younger brother Vlassis cater for.

My resort of Agios Gordis and our village of Sinarades are rather special. Many of the young have never left because the area is so lovely and there are work opportunities for them in tourism. So everyone knows everyone and it is a very close, safe community. I think Steven should have the last word.

"I was in the same class at the village school as Fotis and Magda," he explains. (Magda is Pink Palace's Spiros Grammenos' daughter.) "We all love the beach. When I was just three, I was given a little tricycle. One day, I set off alone from the village without anyone knowing. I cycled the four kilometres all the way down to Agios Gordis to see my parents working in the olive groves." It is the local families, not the international chains, that make Greece unique.

Day 5: from Pelekas to Paleokastritsa
The west coast villages

Flowers 6, Scenery 5, Underdeveloped 7, Challenge 5, Hrs 6
See map on page 37.

Today we will follow the Corfu Trail from Pelekas to the centre of the Ropa Valley and then head west to Giannades where we picnic for lunch. The Freytag map we are using shows the Trail continuing along the topographically boring Ropa Valley and cutting west to Kanakades. It was from this pretty village with an exquisite church in its square that our friends Roger and Pat led Jannie and me, on a trial walk, to beautiful Liapades. Hilary today will fill in the link from Giannades to the Trail above Kanakades. Later in the summer, when the road over the Ropa Valley is tarmacked, she will recommend a parallel route along tracks and paths and will update her Guide on the web. We hope the Freytag map will also be amended. (It has been.)

On our trial walk, the sun was out and the flowers were fantastic, so I am marking my floral experience high. Jannie also walked the trial day but found the climb up from the Ropa Valley difficult. That was when she decided to take on the job of transport manager.

Our first target today is Myrtiotissa, the beach that Lawrence Durrell described as the 'loveliest beach in the world'. Edward Lear in February 1857 was also enchanted: 'In a little sheltered harbour – not unlike Amalfi – under great rocks, lies the little convent of Myrtiotissa – so called from the myrtle covered cliffs all round. After my great Athos monasteries, this is a wee little one, with 3 monks only; however it is clean & decent, & they gave us a cup of coffee each, which was not unwelcome'.

Today, we revert to Charles' transport plan. He drives us

to the end of Pelekas, where he leaves his Suzuki. Jannie and Rachel will meet us for lunch and then pick us up at the end of the day, returning to collect the little jeep. The three of us set off from Pelekas through the olive groves parallel to the road to the Ropa Valley. After a few minutes, I check in my pocket for some notes – and find the Land Rover keys. Charles is not amused as he has to return home to give them to Jannie and then drive back to meet Sydney and me when we get to Myrtiotissa.

At the junction with the steep road down to the sensational beach of Glyfada – our favourite in 1966 but sadly now very developed – Sydney and I continue along the waymarked path into the olive groves. Those short of time could continue along the main road which Charles will take after his diversion, and meet the Corfu Trail again after 500 metres; but we have a major adventure ahead. I had considered saving the two hours and the long descent to the sea followed by a hard ascent, but I wanted to return to one of the paradises of my youth, which I had been told by a Greek friend had undergone a dramatic change.

First though, I must tell of one Findlay Gordon, a golfer of some repute. In the 1970s, soon after the golf course on the Ropa Valley opened, he played there in an international golf competition. After the game he invited his caddy into the clubhouse for a beer. The Australian caddy suggested he knew where the drink was cheaper, so off they went. Three days later Findlay returned without his money and without his shirt. He recalls he might have gone to Myrtiotissa, which became infamous as the island's nudist beach.

Over the years the clientele's orientation might have changed, but their lack of clothing hasn't. Now here is the story a Greek friend told me. The local villagers noted the goings-on of the foreigners, but as Greeks their 'liberal' attitude accepted such matters. However, it was hinted that the monk in the monastery might be 'slightly gay'; he seemed to be very friendly with the youngsters on the beach. One day, however, a naked man was found dead on the beach, under the Monastery. The villagers were now extremely spooked: what punishment might befall them? Next spring, not only had the young men disappeared, but the beach had also. It had been completely washed away! Rumour has it that a dredger was seen working off-shore during the winter. It would be dramatic to suggest that some heinous plot had been carried out, but dredgers off the west coast have been seen before; where else do the beaches on the east coast, such as Ipsos, get their sand? After a violent storm all the sand can be swept off a beach to form a sand-bank offshore, ready to be sucked up for the highest bidder.

Sydney and I sit waiting for Charles beside the rough track down to the sea. Eventually he arrives, complaining about the state of the road. I point out that until a road has been asphalted it can become seriously eroded over the winter. It was not many years ago that Myrtiotissa was only accessible by foot or on donkey.

We descend the last hundred metres and I stand on the narrow track beside the now departed 'loveliest beach in the world' and mourn its loss. Does the water trickling out of the springs in the cliff which almost overhangs the beach still taste as fresh as on our first visit? Today it is raining, so I cannot tell. We walk along the track, which rises up past the Monastery, still open and in use. From our second day onwards, I have spotted this bleached white building standing guard over the west coast.

Soon we leave the narrow path to inspect an old olive press. A huge millstone remains, a reminder of literally hundreds of presses which once existed over the island; some are still to be found in derelict ruins, others have become features in renovated houses, many lie in the open in olive groves, and an unknown number have become part of the foundations of modern buildings. The horse-drawn rotary mills crushed the olives into pulp, which was then layered between fibre mats in the press. The top wooden plate was screwed down by long wooden levers, squeezing the oil from the pulp into a shallow basin in the stone bed of the press and out of a groove, to be collected and stored in stone vats, for local use or for transportation in goatskin bags to Corfu Town, and eventually to Venice to burn in the lamps of the city. Here was an early example of a bio-fuel.

After a hairpin bend in the track, we turn back towards Pelekas and start climbing a concrete road up the seaward side of the mountain of St. George. The views south get better with every stride: Aerostato, Pentati and the mountain above Agios Mattheos appear under scudding clouds racing in from the open Mediterranean. Perhaps one of the disadvantages of a walk like this is that we have not left time to linger and take in the majestic scenery.

Another downside is that Sydney cannot stop and inspect the rare plants he sees. He told me that in Crete he would cut off a flower and some leaves and then analyse them in the evening. This approach enabled him to discover new varieties of both tulip and daphne. Sadly, on this expedition, we are always rushing: travelling to and from each day's walk and then going out for a meal in the evening.

These west-coast cliffs offer a completely different terrain to others we have met. The variety of its flora was the reason it was designated a *Natura 2000* site. Poor Sydney has just his side-kick to discourse with. My low level of expertise and slight deafness lead to odd conversations such as this: "Sydney, what's that plant: the tall one with yellow flowers with white edges shaped like monk's hats?"

"*Phlomis*," he replies, "Jerusalem Sage."

"*Filonius*. I'll call it *Thelonious*: Thelonius Monk, the great jazz pianist?"

"Who?"

"The inventor of bepop." I don't think Sydney and I are on the same wavelength. "Jannie and I go to the Copenhagen Jazz Festival every July; it's wonderful for us oldies."

After half an hour's steady climb up from the sea with the Ropa Valley now appearing before us, we stop for a well-earned water break. Further up the hill are some telecom aerials. Though hideous, they are accepted for the sake of our mobile phones. Perhaps one day wind turbines will also be accepted. There are already fifteen wind turbines on Kefalonia. But I am sure Hilary will fight them; she loves her island as it is. I got her to agree that a possible and more acceptable form of alternative energy could be derived from a solar power station on the broad Ropa Valley.

On Easter Monday, villagers from Pelekas walk to the church at the top of the 390-metre-high mountain of St. George for a picnic. It brings home how ancient beliefs still flourish so strongly in this materialistic modern world.

Today we drop down to the Ropa Valley and walk through the golf course, where as a golfer I should play more often; but I don't because Corfu is far too precious to spend one's time walking after a little white ball. The island will never compete with Spain and Portugal as a golfing destination; there they have hundreds of courses to tempt the golfers and closed communities of luxury housing surrounding each course. Nevertheless, it is an asset to the island and indeed constitutes a good test for the average player. Swedes and other northern Europeans turn up in great numbers in October for the weeks of open competitions.

The golf club's neighbour is the large gypsy encampment. I have a soft spot for Gypsies: they recycle waste material. In the early days of the golf course, the youngsters honed their skills at recycling by doing a good trade in lost balls, although they sometimes didn't realise a ball on the fairway was to be left in place and not picked up and sold. My soft spot for the

Romanies dates from 1970 when I canvassed in Orpington for Eric Lubbock, now Lord Avebury, whose Caravan Sites Act 1968 provided for 400 caravan sites in the UK. Sadly though, the car-loads of travellers I took to vote did not save him from losing his seat.

We now walk along the centre of the Ropa Valley. After four and a half days it is the first part of the Trail to disappoint me; it is flat and open, much of it swampy. In spring sheep graze on the lush grass, and put on weight ready for the barbecues to be lit on Easter Sunday.

In summer, out in the open, it must be unbelievably hot. I thought how lucky we were that the English architect who designed our house in 1970 provided slats at the top of all doors. In the summer, as the cool air moves up through the olive grove, under the veranda and through the house, we stay cool. In winter, some air movement is also good as it keeps the house dry.

Our main worry in the summer is from fire. Rising above the whole length of the west coast is one huge olive grove. God help us if, with a strong *maestro* (NW wind) blowing, it caught fire. We would be wiped out. A few years ago an area to the west of the town was badly burnt: the umbrella pine wood of Kombitsi was all but destroyed, and the inferno driven by a northerly wind reached Kalafationes, where a Venetian mansion with a priceless library was gutted.

Across the Ropa Valley, near the gypsy encampment, we see a derelict three-storey building. In the summer, it is used by the fire-fighters, who sit there playing cards. They are permanently on guard. On most mountains, firebreaks have been constructed, enabling the Fire Brigade to get quickly to the source of the fire. Planes fly over the island throughout the day watching for the first sign of danger.

Hilary plans to change the route across the Ropa Valley taking it straight on at the entrance to the golf club, then swinging left to skirt the Theotoki estate and along the picturesque valley south of Giannades. Over the years, as roads are tarmacked and development takes place, the Trail will evolve. The *Companion Guide* website will always show the definitive, current route, waymarked by yellow paint.

Where the track meets the road crossing the Ropa Valley, Jannie and Rachel are parked. I think Charles would rather like to walk the two and a half kilometres to Giannades where we are stopping for lunch, but he is out-voted. We climb into the Land Rover and set off to meet Hilary. She is waiting on the road to Marmaro and insists we come in to see a new pet; she already has two dogs. In her garden is Spiridoula, her neighbour's three-month-old tame lamb, who we all fall in love with. How long will it be before she is returned to the flock, and then finished in the pot? Everyone wants to stroke her long soft curly hair, which reminds me of my grandson's, also the object of too much attention. We are ready for our picnic; it's been a long morning.

"Let's have it in the village square," suggests Hilary.

"We can get six in the car," I propose.

"With the dogs? No, let's walk." Noone volunteers. "Come on, John."

This is the first time I've walked with Hilary alone; normally I'm just one of the Saturday walkers. We race out of her garden, along the path next to the field through which the updated Corfu Trail may go, and up through the back alleys which lead up the hill on which Giannades is perched. I decide that she is now more Greek than English; she walks like a Greek – very fast.

"One of the pleasures of walking the Trail is that we enter a village along paths trodden over centuries by the villagers returning home from their olive groves," she observes. I feel like an unwilling donkey.

"Except for Spartera on the first day, when we actually left by the main road, it seems we've missed out on this pleasure," I tell her.

"Then you haven't been following my instructions." Which was true, but I am not going to blame Charles and, anyway, the road we had taken through Pentati had been my idea. "All the time I am trying to keep the Trail off tarmacked roads," continues Hilary. "Now the Ropa Valley path is being asphalted, I am planning another way. I'm nearly there; I just have to get agreement from the owners of a couple of olive groves we will have to cross."

The rest of the team is waiting at the square. The view across the Ropa Valley to the hills on which live Roger and Pat, our next guests, is not to be missed. It has been said that a Corfu village is not a village unless it has a square with a large tree to give shelter and a cafenion to give nourishment. With its unparalleled vista, Giannades meets the criteria almost completely though, as it is already siesta time, its minimarket and cafenion are closed.

Hilary, whose knowledge of the villages on the island is unequalled, explains that many of the locals are pensioners, having worked in Germany. This gives the village a feeling of prosperity.

"Giannades originally was higher than this, overlooking the sea; but pirates attacked it; so the inhabitants moved inland. You can still see village fortifications with gun holes in the walls of the houses. Most of the chimneys are Venetian: built of bricks with half-bricks missing to provide air vents."

After an excellent lunch prepared by the transport manager, Hilary strides off through the village with high houses on either side.

"That arch over there, John, is the one in your book of Theresa Nicholas' sketches." One day I will stop writing and visit every village mentioned in *Corfu Sketches*, to check on how the buildings, alleys and gateways have survived the so-called progress that has come to Corfu. Hilary points to the stone corbels jutting out from the wall of a fine old building. These trusses or brackets which are about 50 centimetres long are to be seen on many old houses in the villages. A cross pole used to be inserted in the holes you see to connect adjacent corbels. Then an awning was hung from the pole to create a primitive form of air-conditioning. This doubly pleases me as, on the one hand, the roof of our veranda acts as an awning and, on the other hand, Bill and Barbara's pergola is held up by corbels. They have kept traditional design alive.

Outside the village we start a slow climb into the Marmaro Hills, an area of the island that is new to me. The higher we go, the glimpses of the Ropa Valley become more majestic. Perhaps my idea of a solar power station on the plain may not be so visually acceptable.

"Do you know why verges are being strimmed at this time of year?" asks Hilary. Of course we don't, but we do agree that the loss of flowers is regrettable. "It's because the Greeks don't like snakes. They hide in the long grass." Country folk have obviously heard of people being bitten. We townies believe if you make enough noise, the snakes will run away.

I ask Sydney the name of a tall plant with bunches of little yellow flowers on the end of stems which become hollow as it gets old.

"Alexanders," butts in Hilary.

"*Smyrnium Perfoliatum*," adds our botanist.

"*Smyrnium Olusatrum*," Hilary contradicts.

Sydney, ever the gentleman, replies: "Hilary knows more about local flowers than me."

I think I'm more interested in Smyrna than Smyrnium.

In 1922, Kemal Ataturk drove the Greeks back to Smyrna, after they tried to take back Constantinopolis and their original empire in Asia Minor. The Greeks had been encouraged by the British, who then refused to come to their rescue when the

Armenians and Greeks were being massacred on the portside. Ethnic cleansing and a mass transfer of populations followed. I mention Smyrna to Hilary and how my journey to India had drawn me to the *rembetika*, the tragic music of the refugees.

"I have more *rembetika* tunes on my I-pod than of any other music," she tells me proudly.

"I had a lousy musical childhood," I said. "I can only remember one record; I think it was the only one my father had. It was by a contemporary of his, the great Irish tenor, John McCormack:

'If you ever go across the sea to Ireland,

Then maybe at the closing of your day,

You will sit and watch the moon rise over Claddagh,

And see the sun go down on Galway Bay'."

"So when you stop writing, John," says Hilary, "you'll stay in Corfu and watch the sun go down over Agios Gordis Bay."

"And watch the moon rise over Agii Deka. The Irish are like the Greeks: their Diaspora dreams of its homeland. That trip gave me my love for the *ipirotika clarina* and the *bouzouki*. In the autumn, Hilary, we will go to Platopigatho Taverna near Sinarades, the most magical place in Corfu, hear the *bouzouki* and ask our friends to play the *rembetika*."

After 40 minutes we meet a concrete road coming up from Kanakades on the floor of the Ropa Valley.

"This is where I leave you. John knows the way from here." We say goodbye to our excellent guest – or are we the guests on Hilary's Corfu Trail?

Charles turns to me and announces in his best Sandhurst voice (though I don't think he was in the army): "Carry on, John."

"The last time I was here," I recollect, "my friend Roger was climbing up the hill, hand in hand with Jannie. She was on strike; she had already told me my 'gentle ascent' was a lie. We were 250 metres above the village and had been going straight up for over half-an-hour; and that was more than she was prepared for." I pause. "Sydney, we'll soon come to a whole olive grove covered in honesty, so unbelievable in the dappled sunlight."

"*Lunaria*," he insists.

"After that long climb, I remember that Jannie suggested I didn't know what honesty is."

"I'm not sure if I believe you either; you said the weather would be fine," Sydney quips. "It's been overcast all day, with intermittent rain. How far have we to go?"

"Less than an hour. Don't worry, Sydney; it's downhill all the way to Liapades, a most beautiful village containing many old mansions and an exquisite square with a great plane tree in its centre. Then we'll sit opposite the church and have a well-earned beer."

I point out the field of honesty, but they are also on strike today; flowers are the same as people, they like the sun. At this point we are overtaken by a very old lady on a very old donkey. It is almost in a gallop, which is very odd.

At the edge of the village we have a choice: straight on along a very narrow waymarked path, or right and left along the main track from the olive groves. At that moment the heavens open and we run for the shelter of the bar. It is closed. From the top two corners and two sides of the square, and even from the church, rivers are pouring down towards us. The old lady on the donkey and the local bar owners obviously know more about the weather than me.

We take shelter under the veranda of another bar on the lower side of the square. "Charles, how much further does Hilary say to the Paleokastritsa road, where Jannie will be waiting?"

"Only twenty minutes." He reads on. "But listen to this: 'The path climbs very steeply and at one point you have to climb a small cliff (there are footholds and a rope!)'."

"That's not for me. I'll phone Jannie." Twenty minutes later the Land Rover appears, slowly ploughing into the raging river just as we had been taught at the Solihull off-road centre. Wet but happy, we return home; transport arrangements are working well.

I do recommend a drink at the bar overlooking the church. There is a little grill room, open all year round and well used by locals, in an alley just above the square. For those exhausted by the day's trek, the Cricketers Taverna on the road down to the beach offers excellent food, a friendly welcome and rooms to stay in the season. They offer walking and cycling holidays in spring and autumn.

For those that finish the official Trail walk on the main road from town to Paleokastritsa, I recommend a visit to Doukades, 1.5 km towards town. Looking east, a high cliff rises up. On a pinnacle sits the little chapel of Agios Simeon. The stiff climb up from Doukades to the chapel is rewarded by a panorama of the whole of the island south of the great Mt. Pantokrator Massif to Agii Deka, with the Ropa Valley in the near distance and the bays of Paleokastritsa to the west. On returning to the picturesque village of Doukades, you can enjoy a traditional meal at Elisabeta's taverna on the square. Since 1949 her wine, more purple than red, has fascinated her clients, but it should not be drunk before making the ascent to the top of the rock.

The main road, which Dimitris Charitos referred to scathingly on Day 2, was built in 1823 by soldiers of the British garrison. John Forte, previously the British consul on the island, wrote how Sergeant Wheeler at the time complained of his Sunday routine: 'At an early hour troops march to Church ... after Service the garrison march into the country and have a sham fight. The troops return home in the afternoon, swears all the time they are cleaning their things, in the evening gets drunk and goes to bed. You will say this is a fine way to keep the Sabbath. It cannot be helped the men are employed through

131

the week making the new road.'

Pat and Roger, who I had hoped would have been with us for the section of our journey, are in England. The British community on Corfu comprises those settled on the island and itinerants like ourselves. Roger has recently retired from his own successful business, which organised individually-tailored travel holidays for those rewarded by their companies. This has taken him all over the world, from China to South America.

On our trial walk earlier in the year I had a chance to discuss Australia.

"Jannie and I visited Australia just before I retired. We drove down to Margaret River in November and saw the fantastic wild flowers. I reckon those on Corfu are just as good."

"I agree," said Roger, "but the wine over there is better."

"We flew to the Red Centre and walked King's Canyon. I think the Vikos gorge is more impressive."

"That's true. And the villages of Zagoria are incredibly beautiful."

"We then walked round sacred Ayers Rock. It is not as moving and spectacular as Meteora."

"OK, John. Where's this leading?"

"We finished in Sydney. I prefer the view from Anemomilos across Garitsa Bay to the view across Sydney Harbour."

"Maybe, but you didn't watch cricket at the MCG," insists Roger.

"We watched the warm-up match against England at Lilac Hill and ate the local meat pie, which is aptly called a 'rat's coffin'. It wasn't as good as eating *tiropita* and watching the cricket on the Esplanade."

"You have a point, but you are biased," claims Roger accurately.

"You know why?" I explain. "I can travel by train from England to Venice, chill out for a day beside the Grand Canal and then take a ferry to Corfu. Or I could fly, say, to Hong Kong then chill out beside the harbour and then fly on to Australia. How much carbon will I save by coming here? That's why I am biased."

Roger is more interested in Corfu than carbon emissions. "People don't realise that we are the centre point of south-eastern Europe. You could add lots of other locations to your trip in Greece, like the remarkable Prespa Lakes on the border with Albania and Macedonia, with their magnificent bird life; and Kastoria on the lake with its history of the fur trade and its beautiful old mansions. Then there's Ioannina with its old Turkish quarter and beautiful lake with the island where Ali Pasha was killed."

Ali Pasha was the man who gave 'despot' a bad name. In Byzantine times, a despot was a sub-sultan or governor of a 'despotate'. Unfortunately Ali Pasha had become rather like an Afghan warlord. He had too much power and did terrible things, such as killing his cook if his favourite meal, a *kleftiko*, was not up to standard. (Sometimes I think, after an awful meal, that this is not such a crime. My recipe for *kleftiko* is in the chapter on food.)

The story goes that Ali Pasha desired a young Greek girl; he then took seventeen but they all said no so he threw them in the river to drown, but in the end a thirteen-year-old liked him and they lived happily ever after, which is not quite true as in 1821 the Sultan sent agents to assassinate him. An oracle had already told him that when his beard turned red, he would be dead. On the island in the lake Ali Pasha was killed and his head cut off, which made his beard red.

"In retirement, we will spend much more time here in Corfu. We'll harvest our olives, travel around Greece and relax at home in the sun," explained Roger.

This is their story. In the 1980s, Roger and Pat bought a 400-year-old Corfiot farmhouse after an English couple had split up. They inherited a 'maid', who walked a kilometre up from the valley twice a day, plus a donkey, which grazed on their land, eating the grass and the lemon trees. One summer they went out with a doctor friend who, on the first evening, smoked his pre-dinner cigar at the top of the property by the pool. He soon returned.

"Roger, does your donkey often lie down?"

"Not usually," Roger replied.

They went back up to the pool and saw four terraces below the donkey looking asleep, but bloated. The tell-tale sign of flies confirmed the worst – the donkey was dead. Roger refused his friend's offer to do a post-mortem and got on the phone to Apostolis, interpreter, local expert and now friend.

"Stoli, help. The donkey's dead at the bottom of the cliff. We must bury it."

"I'll get a couple of the Albanians to dig a grave," Stoli suggested.

Next day, they arrived carrying their picks and shovels. "They say the ground is too rocky," reported Apostolis. "Don't worry, my friend has a bulldozer."

"Please get him here soon, Stoli," said Roger. "The donkey is beginning to stink."

Two days later, Mr. Digger and his fifteen-year-old son arrived, the former driving the bulldozer, the latter sitting on top of the monster with his moped in the shovel. Apostolis turned up to take control and translate.

Mr. Digger got to work carving a road down the four terraces and finally digging a grave for the now seriously decomposed donkey. By now it was dark and dinner time. Roger, the good host that he is, offered Apostolis some food.

Mr. Digger suggested a drink, so Roger poured him a glass of wine which he refused.

"Whisky?"

Roger searched out an unopened bottle of his best duty-free Black Label. They sat down to celebrate the funeral of the donkey; Roger and his friend drinking wine and the three Greeks the whisky.

Flies and wasps can be a nuisance in the country, but hornets, though rare, are a real problem. One appeared and landed on the old stone wall. Smack! It was killed by an expert blow from Apostolis' bare hand. Another appeared. Smack! It was also squashed. A third appeared and entered the gas lamp which was illuminating the drunken celebrations.

"Have you a blow-torch?" asked Apostolis.

Roger returned with one and Apostolis got to work. Roger could see his lovely old farmhouse going up in flames, but Apostolis was an expert. Hornet number three was no more.

Conversation turned to ghosts, which Apostolis assured his audience really do exist. In English and Greek, he told his story.

"I remember, walking with my girl, through the olive groves one night. It must have been about Easter-time. In the distance, we saw a ghostly-white apparition. I took her hand and promised to protect her, so we carried on. It was getting closer and closer."

Roger, doctor, Digger and son were spellbound. Apostolis paused theatrically.

"And?" asked Roger.

"It was a blossoming lemon tree in the moonlight!"

With the bottle now empty, they got up to leave. The son staggered to his moped as a safer option to riding the bulldozer home. The others listened in trepidation as the sound of the machine slowly disappeared and as somehow he got down to the valley. Digger mounted his steed and with shovel waving frantically, he also departed.

This left Apostolis, the hero of the evening, to brave the walk through the olive groves to his car at the gate of the property.

Roger and Pat have many such stories about our island and its people. They usually tell them across a long rustic table in their 'baronial dining room'. In one corner there is a large stove, slowly burning olive wood from their own trees. Another, brought overland from Ludlow near where they live, warms the sitting room. The thick walls of the farm house maintain the heat in winter and keep the house cool in summer.

In previous Octobers, this great room has been the venue for concerts by the Volante String Strings, with 'Steven on the Hill' from Agios Gordis providing the food. Fine houses all over the island now host similar events, thereby contributing to the musical tradition of the island.

After our 'trial walk', a few weeks before we set out to complete the Trail, Jannie and I joined them for dinner. Our future guides, Dierk and Christine, were the other guests. Pat and Roger justifiably pride themselves in their cooking. In Corfu, we are particularly blessed with fresh vegetables and other produce. Roger produced a rabbit *stifado* unequalled in the tavernas on the island. His recipe is included in the food chapter.

Conversation started on the issue of tourism on which Roger has strong views. He has, of course, been involved in the business most of his life.

"All-inclusives could kill the island," he began. "In the 1970s, the Club Med was the first on island; in fact it set up the first Club Med outside France. It has now left Corfu and the site is derelict, but it did offer sport, classical music and culture. So what about the present crop? On Roda beach they offer full board for €41. The food is recycled. The 800-bed complex at St. Stephanos costs just €39. They put nothing back into the economy. If all it offers is a beach then we cannot compete on price with Turkey which lies outside the Euro zone. Corfu should be selling itself better. I picked up some brochures from the World Tourist Organisation three years ago. They looked good and contained excellent material but they were hidden under the counter. There was almost no publicity on the island. The success story of Corfu tourism ilies in the repeats: visitors love Greek hospitality and the family-run hotels which offer personal service, and they come back again and again. We must encourage the visitors to spend their main holiday on the island and then take short breaks to Corfu Town.

"Have you read *Riddles of Venice*? It contains six treasure hunts. That's what we should be offering on the short breaks to our World Heritage Site. The cruise operators should also be suggesting walks through the Old Town.

"Short holidays depend on the airlines. I campaigned to get easyJet to fly to Corfu. This year they are flying from Gatwick five times a week starting on April 1st, from Manchester on Monday and Friday from May 1st and from Bristol twice a week from May 24th. Now that Marfin Bank has bought Olympic we should get a better service from Gatwick, and Aegean are flying twice a day from Stansted via Athens."

By now it was late. Roger suggested we should carry on the discussion on one of Hilary's Saturday walks. I preferred to get on to my favourite topic: energy. Dierk and Christine have built a house on the west coast cliffs above Giannades; it is famous for not being connected to the mains electricity supply. Our hosts began to yawn. It was indeed time to drive through the dark olive groves down to the valley and defer the energy debate until another day.

Day 6: from Paleokastritsa to Agros
The best view in Europe!

Flowers 6, Scenery 8, Underdeveloped 5, Challenge 7, Hrs 6
See map on page 38.

This morning we have a pleasant two-hour ascent past what many claim to be the 'best view in Europe', from Lakones on the great ridge which crosses the north of the island. We then pass through the 'rock cleft' shown on the front cover of the book and enjoy a 1½-hour amble down the 'Roman Road' with its equally spectacular vistas, to finish on the Bay of St. George. After lunch (without alcohol!), I will stagger up a knee-softening 25-minute climb. We finish with a 1¾-hour jaunt through the rural idyll of the still unspoilt north-west.

For me, this is the most challenging day of the trip. For my partners, it is the standard fare of walking holidays; for our two brilliant guests, Dierk and Christine, it is a stroll in the park with their dog Valentino, a pure-bred collie. For flower-lovers, we pass a few excellent areas to which tour operators take their clients. The name Paleokastritsa is synonymous with tourists, but as usual the Trail leads us away from roads and development.

In April 1855 Edward Lear wrote of Paleokastritsa: 'we went to a quiet little bay . . . such a pretty little place! It is surrounded by great rocks, on one of which is a convent, & on another an old castle; & if this place were anywhere else it would be a watering place. The beauty & the quiet of the place is delightful. [Next day] we employed in going up to the old castle, a beautiful excursion half way, the rest barren. The fireflies: they are here by millions now from 8 to 10 every night, & are certainly better animals than frogs. The whole land is like a fairy scene lit up with myriads of tiny lamps.'

Seven years later he visited again and noted: 'Wonderful bay & rox. We lunched at the monastery – & afterwards saw the bones of an old whale.'

According to John Forte, "experts reckon it could have weighed 50 tons. The local legend amongst the monks is that it is a cetacean which spewed forth Jonah."

Lear continues: 'Very beautiful place. The beauty of colour & reflection in the convent rocks & bay at early morn is summut wonderful . . . And now: *how* still! *how* silent! – even the bubble surf so far below is scarcely heard! Palaiokastritsa memories, if I live, will live with me. For at this beautiful place there is just now perfect quiet, excepting only a dim mum of myriad ripples 500 feet below me, all round the giant rocks which rise perpendicularly unbroken to the sky, cloudless that, save for a streak of lilac cloud on the horizon. On my left is the convent of Palaiokastritsa, & to my left is one of the many peacocktail-hued bays here, reflecting the vast red cliffs & their crowning *prinari* [holm oak], myrtle & sage. Far above them, higher & higher, the immense rock of St. Angelo rising into the air, on whose summit the old castle is seen a ruin, just 1,400 feet above the water. . . Few views can be more fine than that looking to the Doukades & Lakones rox at dawn.'

Five days later he summed up his visit: 'Accursed picnic parties with miserable scores of asses male & female are coming tomorrow, & peace flies – as I shall too. Palaiokastritsa is becoming unbearable from the number of visitors & picnics.' 150 years later, the same sentiment can be heard.

Our walk today starts just after where the road to Lakones bears right from the main Corfu Town to Paleokastritsa Road.

Our guests today represent the European Union. Dierk is German, Christine is French and their dog Valentino, whose name could be Italian, is Greek.

Dierk is an engineer and worked at the European Space

Agency sending up satellites; Christine worked in client relations for Airbus in Toulouse. These two successes have shown that European countries working together can compete on a world stage, which individual nations would find more difficult to do.

Working in Toulouse they used to sail their boat from Port Vendres to the Balearic Islands for holidays. When they finally became free from the constraints of employment they first sailed to Tunisia, where they stayed for a year before continuing east till they landed on Corfu – their boat is berthed in the Old Fort Harbour. Like Odysseus they fell in love with the west coast. They bought Hilary's walking book, and walked by themselves for two years before meeting the author. On Saturdays, they are regulars on Hilary's expeditions. I am confident that today we can put away the *Companion Guide* and just follow in their footsteps. Others walking the Trail should follow Hilary's detailed instructions with great care.

The road up the mountain to Lakones is popular with tourists in their hire cars and their buses. I am therefore delighted that the Corfu Trail follows ways far from the traffic. These are the original footpaths that villagers took through their olive groves to the valley and then on into Town. Over the years, houses have been built along the route, so the Trail can appear to be blocked in places. Hilary has managed to keep the way open and marked. We pass a piggery; its animals appear very wild. Dierk points out a spring which used to have drinkable water; now it doesn't. Eventually we are forced onto the road as we enter the village of Lakones. In season, it is a bottleneck, with cars queuing at traffic lights so that they can creep in single file between beautiful old houses.

Out of season it returns to its traditional roots, with the local philharmonic band parading through its narrow main street on October 28th , which is known in Greece as *Ochi Day* to celebrate the day in 1940 that Greece's dictator General

Metaxas rejected the ultimatum from Italian dictator Mussolini to surrender by saying 'No!'. Within hours Italian forces had crossed the Albanian border. Heroically, the Greeks pushed the Italians back. Hitler had to come to the rescue of his wayward ally, and in April 1941 he launched his assault through the Balkans into Greece. The resulting delay to Operation Barbarossa, the planned attack on the Soviet Union, was critical to the eventual outcome of the war. Greece must be the only country in the world that celebrates the start of a war rather than the end – perhaps understandably as in 1945, the nation after a horrific occupation by the Axis powers and widespread famine, entered into the tragedy of the Greek Civil War. The partisans, mainly Communist though not supported by Russia following Churchill's agreement with Stalin that Greece would 'belong' to the West, fought the Royalists who were backed by Britain, who also received an *Ochi* from Metaxas, and then by America.

Once through the village, we enter tourist territory. The first and original taverna on the left is appropriately called Bella Vista. The view is indeed one of the 'best views in Europe'. Lear wrote: 'The view from [hill above Lakones] is vastly grand & lovely at sunset'.

To the right are two bays separated by the promontory of Vigla, on which sits the Monastery of The Assumption of The Virgin of The Old Castle (Paleokastritsa). In the centre is the promontory of Agios Nikolaos on which, in ancient times, was situated the town Paleohora and under which, in the early 1970s, the Greek Colonels constructed what was rumoured to be a base for American nuclear submarines. Now, on its left side is the harbour, the only refuge for large boats on the west coast, which lies within two sheltered bays on which the Hotel Paleokastritsa stands. Across the final great bay is the village of Liapades and a little cove where the novelist Emma Tennant lived before a Russian millionaire bought the house. He thought he had bought the beach as well, but the day trippers in their boats from Paleokastritsa thought otherwise. The people won!

Stretching into the distance to the south are the cliffs of the west coast. On a clear day, one can make out the mountain above Agios Mattheos, which we passed on Day 3. This extraordinary panorama appears to be composed of just three colours: the pale blue of the sky, the dark green of the continuous forest of olive trees, and the deep blue of the open sea.

The Monastery above Paleokastritsa claims to have been founded in 1228. The original building was burnt down by the pirate Boucicault in 1404; the Turks razed its successor to the ground again in 1537 during their first siege of the island; but the rebuilt building survived a second siege in 1715, though the inhabitants abandoned the Monastery and took refuge with the local population in the fortress of Angelokastro, a kilometre past Bella Vista. Though Paleokastritsa was the original resort on the island and has been crowded ever since, its Monastery offers a tranquillity which defies the modern world.

The Trail continues along the main road – a section which, at 2.3 kilometres, is the longest stretch of asphalted road on its whole length – before cutting down through olive groves to Krini and crossing the road which goes to Angelokastro. This impressively situated fortification stands on top of cliffs which rise 400 metres out of the sea. From the top one can look right across the island to Corfu Town, suggesting that it was important as a look-out against marauding pirates.

In the delightful diamond-shaped village square of Krini is a traditional coffee bar, but we do not stop as we have just had our break at Bella Vista. North of the village is a peaceful valley where the old cobbled track has been concreted over. This indicates that some development will soon take place. In the gulley beside the road are the tell-tale signs of black contaminated water from the effluent of the olive presses, which Dimitris Charitos had complained about in our interview at the end of Day 2.

In 2007, the Durrell School of Corfu held a two-day seminar entitled 'Cleaning up the Mediterranean'. One of the best speakers was a German who had lived for fifteen years in the north-west of the island. He was 'practically involved in ecological and lifestyle issues, agro-tourism, marine conservation, the protection of species and nature, waste management and recycling'. He mentioned his battle against the black waters which pollute the local rivers. I hope this will not lead to full-scale war between him and the locals.

Sadly, environmentalists can be very aggressive. At one time, as Chair of the General Purposes Committee of Richmond Council, I was faced with a battle between fishermen on the Thames and the Friends of the Earth who were campaigning against the use of lead weights. I invited both sides to meet, for the first time, over a glass (or three) of wine. By the end of the evening they had all become friends, as they realised that they had a common passion: the love of the river, its peace and its wildlife, and in particular the swans. Local tackle shops agreed to stock alternative weights, and we set up a Swan Sanctuary on Corporation Island opposite Richmond riverfront, with appropriately planted vegetation and a large notice publicising the new use of the island. Sadly swans can't read, but happily the anglers can. Swans are back in their hundreds all along the river.

Soon after Makrades the Trail narrows and we pass through the cleft in the high rocks, that features on the front cover of this book. In front of it is one of the most spectacular views on the island. Far below us is the beautiful bay of St. George, finishing at the Cape of Arillas, with the double coves of Porto Timoni either side of the promontory. In my early wind-surfing days, the nearer one was our destination. The further one, I was told, hid scantily-clad damsels; but they were never at home when I visited. In the distance are the Diapontian Islands: Mathraki to the left; Othoni in the centre and most distant; and Erikoussa to the right.

Mathraki, the smallest island in the group, with an area of three square kilometres, lies six kilometres off Cape Arillas and contains a few small hotels and tavernas. Its beaches are of powdery sand and are surrounded by reefs, rocky shelves and islets that attract all the fishing boats in the area. If the fish stock of the Mediterranean is ever to be regenerated, Marine Reserves must be set up. At the Save the Mediterranean Symposium, the area between the Diapontian Islands was considered a suitable site for such a reserve. Having just walked the length of the island, I believe the reserve should be extended to the whole west coast. An area off the east coast of Corfu, where the seaweed Posidonio is abundant and where small fish breed, has already been made a *Natura 2000* site. Small scale Marine Reserves are set up after consultation with local organisations. Since 2006, a ban on trawling has been enforced in the area from Corfu to the heel of Italy. Such conservation would be a long-term benefit to tourism on the island, as scuba-divers and snorkelers would see more marine life. Obviously, the livelihood of local fisherman must be respected as well.

Erikousa, whose landscape resembles that of the opposite shore of Sidari, is just two kilometre in diameter. Its name is derived from the heather bush (*reiki* in Greek, *erica* in Latin) that grows there profusely. In June 1972, we visited its wide sandy south-coast beach and camped overnight in the yet to be opened generator building. The sea was fluorescent with minute fish. Today it is a popular day-trip from north-coast resorts.

Othoni marks the westernmost point of Greece and is 11 square kilometres in size, rising to almost 400 metres high. In the war the Italians, who occupied Corfu, exiled young Corfiot males to the island – a pleasure to be cut short when they were moved to concentration camps in Italy.

After the war, the depleted population of the island emigrated to America. They sent their hard-earned dollars back to Corfu, where they bought flats overlooking Garitsa Bay. In 1960, Socrates Katehis, then aged 12, went with his grandfather, father and brothers to New York. After selling hot dogs for two years, the family set up a Greek Restaurant on Broadway. Socrates met Agatha, who was from Erikousa and whose family had bought a flat from my dear friend and engineer Petros Kardakis. They have now returned to Corfu and own *Nautilus*, our beloved taverna by Anemomilos on the south side of Garitsa Bay in Corfu Town. Their son also works there as a waiter. For lovers of seafood, I do not apologize for itemising the taverna's Greek style fruit de mer: fried large prawns, steamed mussels, fried mussels in batter, marinated octopus, fried squid, fried whitebait, fried hornbeam (small sardine) and fried hound (firm white fish).

We are now past the 'rock cleft', north of Makrades, where rocks squeeze the Corfu Trail from both sides, and start descending down the 'Roman Road' to the broad bay of St. George. Thankfully, this ancient cobbled way, which was possibly the link between the fortress of Angelokastro and the castle at Kassiopi, is too narrow for cars, so I hope it will never be concreted over. We make a great traverse across the north-facing escarpment. Looking up from the bay, I have often been reminded of the raw Highlands of Scotland; it is a bleaker mountainside than the olive-and-cypress clad centre of the island.

Within a few metres of our descent, we pass a coach-load of Scandinavians, who are inspecting the the bank beside the track. We overcome our initial animosity towards trespassers on *our* Corfu Trail, when my few words of Danish come in useful and we find they are floral enthusiasts. They are being bussed around the island to see the sights and the flowers. The party has had coffee at Bella Vista and they tell me they will have lunch in St. George. There are calls of '*se her*' and they rush over to 'see' what the caller has found 'here'. They have certainly found a fantastic bank of yellow flowers, which makes me feel proud I'm almost a Corfiot. For them it seems a perfect introduction to the Trail. Sydney in his professional way suggests I take a photo and then says something in Latin followed by "we've seen all these before". Such superior behaviour! I ask Christine what the flowers are. "Mustard". Trust the French member of the team to know a culinary plant.

We zigzag down the mountain, looking out for the yellow waymarks that indicate a short-cut which leads us off the path through the olive groves. Suddenly we are met by a thicket of bamboo.

Eventually we arrive at the bay's edge. As the photo on page 48 shows, the road has been destroyed over the winter and we have to navigate across the huge concrete slabs which lie jutting at angles. A hundred metres on, the road becomes impassable as a great landslide has come down the mountain. We climb down to the beach and clamber round the obstruction where it has reached the water. To those that complain about pot-holes on the island, I say the power of nature in the winter in creating pot-holes is greater than the power of man in summer to fix them. Once the rain has finished in May, workmen travel round the island trying to fill up the holes before the tourists and their cars arrive.

I have promised my companions lunch at one of the tavernas on the beach. We walk round the bay and find every single one is closed. Heaven knows where the Danish busload was heading. We return to where the Trail leaves the beach and make inland.

"Where's the lobster you said we would have?" asks Christine.

"Don't worry, I'll find something." I accost sundry locals whose English is worse than my Greek. Eventually we are directed to a mini-market. I buy ten baps, a packet of sliced cheese and sliced ham – 20 slices in all, plus a plastic knife and some napkins.

"Each of us can have either two English sandwiches or four Danish open sandwiches."

"Is that all?" queries Sydney, whose stomach is almost audibly complaining.

I return and buy five Mars bars,

"Christine, this is British cuisine!" I lament.

She is not amused. "Yes, English cuisine!"

"But we love French food," I add to placate her. Glancing at Dierk, I continue: "And German würst."

"And Danish herrings?" he replies with a smile. "But you are a European, John."

"I'm not," says Sydney, almost choking on his sandwich. "At the Department of Energy, I was responsible for relations with Brussels."

"Though I was pro-Common Market," adds Charles, who had been Sydney's boss, "I am opposed to the socialistic tendencies of those that would build a super-state."

"Well, so am I," I respond.

"I reckon we could be going that way," he argues.

"That's rubbish, Charles," I respond in anger. "Europe is a Union of sovereign states. It's the likes of you that scaremonger about straight cucumbers and the loss of national identity. Dierk and Christine haven't lost theirs."

I was born and raised in East Kent. As a Dunkirk baby, I was aware of the terrible war being fought just across the water. Oddly enough in those early days, I didn't hate the Germans; we'd beaten them. My brothers waged war against our neighbour, an Italian, by flying a kite over his house and then releasing a 'bomb' of rubbish on his house; later I became good friends with an Italian prisoner-of-war, who fascinated me by chewing tobacco. For some weird reason, at the suggestion that a bridge might be built across the Channel, the boys at Harvey Grammar wanted to machine-gun the French but I insisted we let in the French girls. Indeed, my first tender experience was at the Grand Hotel in Folkestone with a French girl in the lift I operated – a life of ups and downs! Perhaps all this explains why I became very pro-Europe and eventually married a Dane.

The Europe I was born into was at war; the Europe today is at peace. For all its failings, the European Union should be credited for this achievement. Dictatorship was defeated and democratic roots were planted in Spain, Portugal and, particularly, Greece – encouraged by the Union. The collapsing communist Eastern Europe has been replaced by democratic institutions, nurtured by the Union. Yes, I am a European.

I have over the years developed a deep affection for the nation my father fought twice. Our journeys to Corfu, in the spring and in the autumn, go through Germany to Venice and then on by ferry. We stay at an inn in the centre of one of Europe's most magical medieval towns, Rothenburg-ob-der-Tauber. The Zum Greifen has become our third home and Frau Klingler now welcomes us as part of the family.

Charles rises; he is the diplomat and wants to avoid an international incident.

"I have been studying Hilary's *Companion Guide*. Three and a half hours gone; two and half hours to go! Hilary says the first half-hour is a very steep climb."

I know Hilary well enough. She grades her Saturday walks from 1* to 5*. I can just manage a 3* which she defines as 'moderate, some steep climbs'. 'Very steep' must mean a 4* – difficult/rough terrain – or 5* – only for the fit! I am starting to fear our coming walk. Perhaps I should have studied the *Companion Guide* before we left this morning.

Hoping in vain that he has made a mistake, I insist. "Let

me read that, Charles." Hilary does indeed say 'there is a very steep ascent'. She also says 'we must always keep to the most uphill track and the climb is about 40 minutes in total, 20 minutes very steep'. I don't like this.

It takes me two minutes to walk up the almost sheer 40-metre drive to our house; this path is even steeper. With flower-covered banks and cypress and olives above, it is a beautiful though rough track. I keep on telling myself this. I conclude that it must be a 5* and I am *not* fit. I time the steep ascent at 25 minutes – I'm slow as well.

We enter Prinilas and stop. Charles is reading Hilary's instructions. "'Reaching the village road at the top, turn left and continue 3–4 minutes to the village cemetery.' It must be wrong."

"No, we turn right and there's an alleyway up to the right," says Dierk, who knows this part of the Trail well.

"Sorry, I must be in the wrong village," says Charles.

Five minutes later we get to the cemetery.

Still confused, Charles looks at the *Guide* again. "Oh, I missed out a line!"

Sydney grins but doesn't say anything. I mutter something about looking at the map at the back of the *Companion Guide*. A ringed number 9 in the text tells us where we are and refers to a ringed number 9 on the map; this trail finding is easy if one looks at the map.

A hire car drives up and the passenger asks if we know where the Corfu Trail is. This is not such a stupid question, when one knows that the aim of the Trail is to avoid roads as much as possible. The English couple park their car and join us as we take a narrow track next to the cemetery and descend through orchards of almonds and oranges, to arrive twenty-five minutes later at Pagi, the next village. In the 1970s it was here that we used to stop, on our way to St. George for a picnic, to buy fresh bread out of the oven on Sunday mornings. The little shop is still there.

I ask our new companions if they would like to walk back, but they insist on continuing with us. They have come all the way up from Agios Gordis, where they are staying at the Aquis Hotel. It proves my point that, once tourists leave their hotels and explore the island, they fall in love with the scenery and are ready for the Corfu Trail. They add that the à la carte restaurant was not included in the cost of their holiday, and anyway why would they want to eat sushi when they could do so back in London. They have been with us for an hour as we reach the marshy valley bottom. Faced with fording the river, they sensibly return to their car. I decide that nice people walk the Trail!

If it is less than ankle deep, it is not in full flood. After heavy winter rain, it is probably impassable, but today we wade across the river which, after some rain, is flowing gently. Jannie and Rachel are waiting for us at the other end of Agros, and they drive along the main road to meet the fearsome five. Sydney insists we stop at the bar/store and have a beer. What an excellent fellow!

With the ladies in the front, the men in the back and our guests plus Valentino in the boot, we chug off home, over the Troumpetta Pass, through Doukades, where Elisabeta waves to us, to the Paleokastritsa road. The school run has gone perfectly. We drop off Dierk and Christine, who have been excellent guides and company, and agree to go to lunch with them in the autumn.

* * * * * *

In October Dierk picks us up in Giannades, telling us that the little Toyota Aygo we use when we have no books to take to Corfu will 'bottom out' on the way to their house. He takes us on what he calls the 'scenic route'; later in the afternoon, we return by an alternative route, which, after a few glasses of wine, seems to me just as scenic. His Suzuki jeep climbs carefully over each rock in the road and falls back into the following hollow. Part of the track has recently been concreted. Dierk and Christine chose their spectacular site from eight extremely remote plots on the west coast. It is in the Marmaro hills at the point where they rise up 200 metres above the sea. Our walk along the Trail suggests that there will always be such places for people who want seclusion.

In the winter, their house is accessible only by jeeps which ride high off the ground. In May a bulldozer levels what has not been washed away from the surface of the track over winter. We drive over the brow of the hill and look north to Paleokastritsa, Bella Vista and to the Diapontian Islands, and south right down to Paxos in the far distance. Nearby, down the coast, is a secluded cove which is only accessible from above with the help of a rope. In the summer, tourist boats arrive from the resorts further afield to enjoy its remote location. Our hosts prefer to swim in their infinity pool which has fantastic views out to sea. Fresh water is pumped up from three deep wells.

We stop at the entrance to their property, a great expanse of olive trees; their gate is closed. I get out and remove the unlocked chain.

"It's to keep the animals in," says Dierk. I would have expected to be told it was to keep the animals out. Two donkeys, which they have fostered from the donkey refuge, lie in the shade of the olive grove watching the new visitors. We drive down past their stables, to which the she donkey will often go, we are told; the male only follows when the weather is bad. It is truly luxury accommodation with plenty of hay.

Valentino, the other animal, appears at the front door with Christine, to whom he is devoted. He was also adopted – the Greeks are not great animal-lovers – and is jealous of the new 'babies', which is Dierk's name for the donkeys.

We are led into the house, which, with its autumn colours,

feels very French. It's a homely home: open-plan with comfortable leather sofas and a large kitchen area, perhaps an indication of a great meal to come. The full-width floor-to-ceiling sliding doors bring the olive grove into the house, making it a soothing home as well. We pass through to a patio which is raised above the property and has slippery tiles to stop the donkeys getting into the house. The flower beds are surrounded by lengths of two-inch-wide white tape, which surprisingly stops the donkeys from eating the flowers.

"Wonderful animals," says Dierk, "much more efficient than a motor lawn mower and excellent producers of fertiliser." Theirs is a low energy house. They are not connected to the electricity grid and generate their energy from the sun and the wind. If necessary, a small 5KW diesel generator can charge up the large storage battery in less than one hour to cover their daily consumption. Behind the wood burner is what Dierk calls the 'system collector', a box taking heat from the wood burner and two solar panels, which passes it through a heat exchange to two circuits: one for under-floor heating and the other for domestic hot water.

On the patio table is a large carafe of excellent home-made wine and a vast plate of nibbles: nuts, special Corfiot crystalline strawberries, figs and bagel-shaped biscuits. The husbands sit at one end debating energy issues, the wives are at the other end discussing important topics: houses, the island and food. I tell Dierk about my friend Nikos and his solar panels.

"The feed-in-tariff sounds good, but a seven to eight year pay-back for the investment on solar PV is slightly too optimistic," he replies. "We've just been to Athens for the International Exposition for Renewable Energies and Environment. The business of photovoltaic systems seems to have increased enormously due to subsidising by the governments. A new law in Greece ensures that DEH, the state electricity company, buys the excess energy from individuals at such a high price that the investment is recovered after less than ten years. A lot of companies offer kits, with a typical 5kW installation costing about five euro per watt, all included."

"Athens is such a pleasure to stay in now that the infrastructure has been improved," comments Christine, more interested in cultural than energy issues. "I visited the museums and exhibitions and also the shops. The new Parthenon Museum is really remarkably well designed and the statues are so well arranged."

"Of course 40% of the originals are in England!" Dierk points out.

"I don't know if your percentage is correct, Dierk, but surely they should be moved from the claustrophic basement in the British Museum back to Greece. But tell me more about the exposition, Dierk," I ask.

"The photovoltaic part of the exposition was very large with mostly German, Italian and Chinese firms being represented. England was not present, but a Scottish firm offered wind generators. Their 6kW model costs about 25,000 euros."

"If I wanted to build a solar park on the Ropa Valley, how much would it cost?"

"A Mega watt container from China will cost you about one million euro. DEH will pay you 300,000 euro per year, meaning you break even after three years – and then you have a comfortable income!"

"What's the catch?"

"The cost for the site, the mechanical support, the interconnections, and the power conversion and control systems will double to treble the cost. Still it is an interesting investment. The business for supporting elements is very much booming; the big firms providing aluminium window frames have all developed supporting systems for photovoltaic panels. However, I was most impressed by the large sun trackers for solar parks."

"So what is your personal interest, Dierk?"

"We have a 500 watt generator at present, but with the pool we need more power in the summer, and in winter we have to run the diesel for about an hour per day. I had planned to cover the garage with a 5kW photovoltaic generator. I also want to increase the wind generator power. Sadly, off-grid systems do not play an important role in today's market and they are not financially supported by the government."

"What are your conclusions?"

"The prices for photovoltaic panels have become interestingly low, so now the key element is the cost of the support systems. Somebody stated years ago that even if we can make solar panels as cheap as street signs, we will still pay a lot more for solar energy than we do now."

"Don't depress me, Dierk. Then what is the solution?"

"In the far future, we will reduce our personal energy consumption by being more conscious of the issues, due to the increase in energy costs and even more by energy shortages. Concerning our consciousness, the main problem is that we do not have a feeling for energy, only our bodily endurance. Let me give you an example. There is a 1000 kilogram vehicle on a frictionless rail of 1% inclination and 10 kilometres in length. It will take only 100 Newton to push the vehicle up the track, just like a supermarket shopping cart. A couple of hours later you will be 100 metres higher and you will be rewarded for your effort to create energy."

"Dierk, I forgot about Newtons the day I left university. Please give it me in one sentence," I plea.

"John, if we had more respect for energy, we would presumably be more careful with its use."

"Then what about us installing Nikos' 'summer storage' heating in a super-insulated room in our basement in England?" I ask.

He laughs. "With English summers?"

"I would buy a lorry load of shingle – it's easily obtainable from nearby gravel pits along the Thames valley."

Dierk, the typical engineer, takes my notebook and draws a circle representing a boulder and a formula: $V/F=R$. As a Cambridge Maths graduate with the all-time worst degree, I take him to be saying that very big rocks are much better at storing heat than many pebbles. I face defeat again.

He's a believer in nuclear energy and green transport. He draws me a pie chart of forecasts for future German energy production, with solar just a sliver of the cake. "It's political in Germany. Ever since the Greens came into power-sharing, we have stopped all building of nuclear plants."

Christine, the perfect French hostess, smiles at me knowingly. The perfect English guests decide that it would be most impolite to mention the nuclear plants next to Calais, which I worry could be the target of a lunatic wanting to wipe out my beloved East Kent; I had already tricked Charles, the top nuclear civil servant, to admit that an expert insider might just be able do a 'Chernobyl' if he was so 'minded'. I also don't point out to Dierk that in 2008, England had installed 6MW of solar PV power against Germany's 1,500MW; he would again mention 'grey England' or 'German engineering'.

Returning to the pie-chart, he points out the energy produced in Germany from 'waste'. I think that if the Lefkimmi waste disposal site is ever built – which I doubt – it could generate energy.

I move on to energy conservation and Nikos' polystyrene walls.

"In England, I bought loft and under-floor insulation equal to the total floor area of our house. As it's a two-storey house, I had, in fact, bought double the quantity I needed." This probably confirmed how bad a mathematician I was, but then I had trained as an engineer. "Wayne, our daughter-in-law's brother, used the surplus insulation when renovating our stables into a two-bedroom house. It uses almost no energy at all. He is now unemployed; there are no jobs in construction in Nottingham where he lives.

"During an earlier recession my brother, whose company was the largest installers of cavity-wall insulation in south-east England, used to argue that unemployed construction workers should be taken on by local authorities to install all forms of insulation in areas of most poverty for *free*. It would save paying benefits and would target energy saving, and hence saving heating costs, to those that need it most and are least likely to claim for grants. I think he had a point."

We agree at last and get up to eat. But first Christine gives the uneaten bagel-shaped biscuits to the donkeys to their obvious delight. Five-star donkey hotel this!

Then we receive real French hospitality. For starter we have home-made paté and lettuce salad plus stuffed tomatoes Provençal. For the main course we are offered two types of fish, picked up from the market in Town by Dierk at seven o'clock, baked on thin slices of potatoes to stop them sticking to the pan; hot aïoli made of garlic, egg yolks, olive oil and lemon juice; gratin dauphinois and mixed vegetable stew. The cheeses are Danish blue for Jannie and peppered Greek for me. We continue with apple compôt on a biscuit cake with a strawberry on top. Finally we are served coffee with Tortuga Caribbean Rum Cake from Grand Cayman.

Euro-sceptics should recognise that the culture of the European nations will never be desecrated by the Union. Burgers and KFC may come, but French cuisine will always rule.

Dierk and Christine's house is unique.

"Was it built by a Greek?" I ask.

"We started with a local engineer, but he agreed to leave. We then took over the project," explained Dierk.

I am impressed and ask him: "How is your Greek?"

He replies: "Very good. The only people who do not understand us are the Greeks." So much for the British stereotype of the humourless German!

"So what's the secret?"

"Buy locally. We had great support from Moskou in Agios Ioannis."

"From Sasha?" I enquire as we had bought our tiles from her.

"Of course. You get personal service in Corfu," adds Christine. It is something we rarely get from shops in the UK now.

"But how can you deal with everyone, when you are out of range of mobile phone reception?"

"It was difficult as Greeks can't survive without their mobiles, but we managed."

I hope they will visit us one day and try authentic English cuisine: a Pakistani meal at Gifto's in Southall.

Day 7: from Agros to Spartilas
Corfu, overdeveloped? Not true!

Flowers 6, Scenery 7, Underdeveloped 9, Challenge 4, Hrs 6
See map on page 38.

*This is the Corfu that tourists pass through but never see.
We start on the main road to Sidari, bypass the village of
Horoepiskopi, cross the main road to Roda and Acharavi at
Rekini and finish on the road to Mt. Pantokrator. Except for
passing through two villages, Valanio, not far from Nimfes, and
picturesque Sokraki, where we drink ginger beer, we walk along
many tracks unmarked on the Freytag map. We would have
scored 'underdeveloped' 10 but for a recent visit by a bulldozer
between Sokraki and Spartilas intent on converting a path to a
track.*

*The olive groves along our route are old and well tended.
This is because nearby there are villages, little changed over
time, in which families still harvest the fruit over winter. In the
spring, black nets lie under the majestic trees. The flora are
therefore restricted to the verges.*

For a description of the scenery I must defer to Edward Lear,
who visited the area in June 1855 and who wrote in a letter
back to England:

'I think it highly probable that you will not be able
(all at once at least) to pronounce the address of the place
[Horoepiskopi] from which I write this: so you had better call
it Hokus Pokus at once, as all the English do here. Hokus
Pokus is a village 14 miles from Corfu over the north side of
the Pantaleone pass. It is on a double rocky hill in the midst of
a valley entirely full of splendid oranges & cypresses, just as
if it were in a basin; on the other side of the basin are several

other villages, & to the north all the hills slope away to the sea, beyond which the Khimatiote [Albanian] hills are seen. This Hokus Pokus is the centre of the villages in the north of the island. Although the scenery is exquisitely beautiful, yet it has too little variety to engage me much, nor are the lines of the hills so fine as on the south or city side. Pagus seems pretty, but there is a monastery at Nimfes which is really placed most picturesquely: immense cypresses stand up against the evening sky, & the great rocks & far, still landscape & lilac channel are very noteworthy.

'The whole 2 hours walk [from Horoepiskopi] to Sokraki was under wide olives, by the side of a stream where blue dragon-flies, green frogs, & lizards, & yellow butterflies abound. The village itself stands high at the end of the valley, & just above it is a rock, from which you see looking south, all the Corfu world.'

I am delighted to note that Edward Lear took two hours for his walk, the same time as we do, under the leadership of today's guest, Hilary Whitton Paipeti. Her name has come up many times before in this book, which is dedicated to her. For those that have not met her, the following incident illustrates someone who has done more to retain the character of our beloved island than anyone else. In doing so she might have made a few enemies, but Hilary's heart is in the right place.

A few years ago I was on one of her Saturday walks. It was in a beautiful area in the south-east of the island, which the Trail does not pass through. We had climbed up from Boukari, where the best fish restaurants on the island are found, and we were walking through olive groves with the east coast far below and the mountains of the mainland in the distance. In the lead was Hilary. Suddenly I heard her screaming. The rest of us, including her dog, Lulu, backed off in a cowardly manner. She was confronting four burly men, carrying chain saws. The evidence of their guilty act lay on the ground. I understood little of her vitriol – my Greek vocabulary is devoid of the words she was using. The men, probably Albanian, might not have followed her tirade either, but they knew the gist of what she was shouting: "Stop cutting down our olive trees." They stood their ground for a few moments; then, in submission, they laid down their chain saws, retired and took a drink of water.

Dog owners are meant to be like their dogs. Hilary does not look like Lulu, the pepper-and-salt haired mother. She may have long curly blond hair like the son Bruni but she is more bullterrier than wimpy Corfiot mongrel: Lancashire bullterrier, but bullterrier all the same. Hilary's original dog, Ira, looked much more like her– they once won a 'dog-owner lookalike' competition, which Hilary regards as a very great compliment to her. Ira knew every inch of the Corfu Trail, and would stay in the lead at all times. Often, when they met walkers, it was Ira, not Hilary that was recognised.

Hilary successfully battled in her magazine *The Corfiot* against those that have cut down Corfu's olive trees for the pizza ovens of Italy. The *Daily Telegraph* then took up the story. MP Nikos Georgiades, brandishing the article from the paper in the office of the Minister of Agriculture, succeeded in bringing in a law stopping all cutting below three metres; olive trees of that height recover after only a couple of years.

I now mention a subject where I am in danger of being severely bitten: global warming. Hilary supports David Bellamy, who does not believe that 'climate change' has a human cause. But when it comes to Bellamy's campaign to stop the destruction of the rain forests, we are on the same side, though my argument is more about our grandchildren and their grandchildren than his orang-utans.

Personally, I am convinced that the burning of the forests and the loss of carbon sinks will be a major contributor to the increase in carbon dioxide in the atmosphere.

Hilary is a person of many talents. Firstly, she is a writer, with many books to her name; including her latest *Corfu4Kids* (see www.corfu4kids.com). Many of these are on the subject for which she is known – her walks all over Corfu.

Secondly, she was the founder and still is the editor and publisher of the *Corfiot*, Corfu's English-language monthly magazine. Its monthly editions – so far 220: the length of the Corfu Trail in kilometres – have been the source of invaluable information on living on Corfu, such as the location of her Saturday treks. All would agree that the *Corfiot* is a campaigning paper; it has fought over-development and environmental damage to the island, such as the felling of olive trees and the relocation of the island's in-fill site to the south of the island. She has also fought the use of toxic fruit-fly sprays and the cruelty to animals which can often be found in Greece, particularly against donkeys and dogs.

Finally, she has been involved in the property market. Her knowledge of the villages of the island is unique. On having her as our guest, I agreed to her request that property would not be a subject of conversation. But at the end of the chapter I bend the rules by passing on her views on the villages on the island, the rise and fall of Corfu's mansions, and residential tourism.

Our day starts on the Ropa Valley, where we pick up Hilary, waiting by the go-cart track. With Sydney in the back seat with the rucksacks, she climbs into the boot of the Suzuki with Lulu and Bruni. We drive up the 'Colonels' Road' as I call the wonderful link between the south and north of the island, through Doukades of Elisabeta's fame, and over the Troumpetta Pass to Agros.

As we extricate ourselves from the car, Sydney breaks the ice by asking Hilary: "Your dogs smell?"

"No they don't" she replies indignantly.

"Well they smell like mine when they have picked up the scent of foxes."

Charles immediately changes the subject.

Soon after setting off on foot from the centre of the village, I notice a Corfu Trail sign has been changed.

"Probably by the owner of a local taverna," suggests Hilary. I realise, not for the first time, that if we had not been escorted by our guests, it would have been difficult to walk the Trail without the *Companion Guide*.

We leave the main Sidari road at the sign to Agios Athanasios Monastery, which turns out to be for nuns rather than monks. Appropriately there is a sign outside: 'Please do not enter unless properly dressed.'

Soon we leave the minor roads and take the main tracks into virgin countryside. Hilary starts to forage, picking wild asparagus from the verges to eat. On one Saturday walk, I noticed that her fellow accomplices behaved like a swarm of locusts, stripping this delicious wild vegetable from the side of the road. Under Hilary's instructions – her recipes in the *Corfiot* are an essential for healthy living – we all had asparagus omelette for supper that evening.

Hilary sees a couple working in a field and calls over "*kalimera*". She explains to Charles that Corfiot locals are extremely friendly and one must always say "good day" to them. She reminds me of the local politician, constantly in touch with her constituents. A couple of years ago, she was asked to stand in the Corfu elections on an environmental platform, under the PASOK banner. She declined. "I'm not really a Socialist," she explains. In fact she is an Independent, so independent that for the sake of international relations it is perhaps just as well that she chose not to stand.

By now, we have left the hills at the start of our walk and pass through low-lying verdant land, with lilies and other flowers growing beside the tracks. After an hour and a half, we cross the bridge over the river Typhlopotomas, which enters the sea at Sidari, and arrive at Rekini on the main Corfu-to-

Roda road, where we stop for a coffee. Behind the café-bar archaeological excavations are being carried out; all over the north of the island ancient settlements are being discovered.

My map suggests the next part of our walk will follow a minor road to the quaint village of Valanio, deep in the middle of nowhere, though not so far from Lear's village of Hokey Pokey on the right and later Klimatia on the left. It was here, as he pointed at the lovely old Venetian mansion which Theresa Nicholas had sketched, that a local wanted to buy my mock-up of *Corfu Sketches*. Was the village named after *klimataria*, I asked, the pergola which had been erected in front of the house and on which vines are still grown? I must return to the village one day and give him a printed copy of the book! Beyond Klimatia is Nimfes, named after 'Water Nymphs', with its ancient mini-monastery. The name comes from the fact that all the streams that drain from Mt. Pantokrator flow through this area, which is aptly known as the 'Paradise Plateau'. All the villages around are linked by footpaths, with Klimatia as the centre.

Following Hilary's Corfu Trail, we stay on the minor road for just 100 metres. On the right is a wooden sign: 'Municipality of Esperion, Footpaths Network for Tourists – Map of Footpaths Network' with an arrow pointing to 'Entrance and Exit'. This is just what I like: a tourist trail, though few know about it, as the publicity is non-existent. For this to change, an enterprising person must follow the example of more mature holiday destinations and place in every hotel a rack for fliers that describe all the tourist attractions in the locality.

Within a few minutes we are descending through the dense undergrowth down a slippery, steep bank to the river, which is in full flow.

"So this is what the Greeks expect from their tourists?" Charles asks Hilary.

"They built a bridge over the river but it was washed away in the November storms," she replies with a shrug. I sense she has little faith in local initiatives: they start with good intentions but they are not maintained.

By now, boots and socks have been removed, and we follow Hilary safely across the river. Socks and boots are put back on and my three companions climb up the other bank.

"Wait," I shout, "I have lost a sock – yet another bloody sock." Losing one sock on Day 1 was an accident, but losing a second on Day 7 is more than carelessness: the sock-gods are against me.

Eventually I give up the search and we continue along the south bank of the river. The walk meanders through a fabulous shaded glade, a perfect place for a summer stroll. Trees overhang the route as in a tropical rain forest. A visitor dumped here with a blindfold on would have no idea, once vision was restored, that it is Greece. Orchids poke their noses up from the undergrowth as we pass through a dense thicket.

"The holly is like the one we have at home," I suggest to Hilary. "But the berries are redder than these and they cover the tree in December before the birds eat them."

"John, it is not holly," she corrects me. "It's a holm oak and the berries are not berries! They are parasites."

I am humbled by the expert. "You mean like mistletoe?"

"Exactly," she replies with a smile. She knows I'm a bit thick when it comes to flora.

We are now zigzagging up from the lush dense valley through which the river flows; it never dries up even in summer. Half-an-hour after coffee we arrive at the village of Valanio with its picturesque square and mini-market, the key to the survival of a village. Hilary points out buildings with stone surrounds on doors and windows, through which goods were once sold when they were shops. KKE posters indicate that the village offers strong support for the Communist Party which, in the 1980s, was described as Euro-Communist rather than Soviet Communist. The Chinese Communists (Maoists) were over in Albania.

Working villages in Corfu always have a surprise in store. In Valanio, the surprise is the overpowering smell of jasmine from climbers in full bloom. A few magnificent buildings suggest better times in the past.

Soon after Valanio, we are 'off-map' and on ancient tracks which are still very much in use by the locals.

"Sokraki is still an hour away but first we have a fast yomp," Hilary announces happily. I had heard Paddy Ashdown, my ex-leader, use the word, and I wasn't sure I liked it.

In fact I find this part of the Trail a joy to walk. It leads us slowly up and then slowly down through a vast forest of olive trees. The black nets which cover the ground still contain the olives which have fallen and which will be collected every day or so and taken to the press. In the centre of the island on Day 5, we had passed through other olive groves. Some were wild and not harvested; others had their nets already gathered in. In the Marmaro Hills the wild flowers coloured the countryside a brilliant blue. Here the olive groves are more mystical, majestic yet gaunt and grey. Photos of these two groves are on page 46.

We meet an old man picking olives out of the fold in the netting into which the fruit rolls. Hilary repeats her canvassing.

"He's 72," she announces. I look at Sydney but refrain from asking him whether he could still pick olives at the same age. I note that five-litre feta tins which used to be used to collect the olives have been replaced by plastic ones.

On top of the ridge half-way along the 'yomp' there is another wooden sign for the 'Footpaths Network for Tourists'. It indicates the 'Historic Place 'Queen's Leap', Return from (sic) the same road.' I congratulate the Municipality of Esperion on their choice of terrain. Way below us is the spectacular uninhabited valley of Melisouthi, the 'ditch of bees'.

"A few yeas ago they wanted to turn the valley into a great reservoir," Hilary explains, "but it didn't go ahead. Here we are not much more than five kilometres south of Acharavi as the crow flies, in some of the most unspoilt countryside on the island."

Nearing the end of our yomp, we descend into the valley and meet a bridge on the asphalted road from Klimatia to Zigos, the village where the owner of the Rouvas, the wonderful restaurant near the market in Corfu Town, lives and grows the fresh vegetables which make his lunches so tasty. I have an outstanding invitation to inspect the crop, but sadly no time until the autumn.

It is now time for lunch – a picnic of cheese, bread, tomatoes, olives and onions. Bruni joins in, rejecting the onions but eating the olives, stones and all. Funny animals, dogs!

My map indicates that, by road, we are 2.5 kilometres from Zigos, which is the same distance from the village of Sokraki.

"Edward Lear wrote that he took two hours to walk from Hokey Pokey to Sokraki. We took 30 minutes to get to Valanio plus an hour on your 'yomp', Hilary. How can we do the last five kilometres in half an hour?" I ask innocently.

"Because we are walking directly up the side of the valley! It is the worst climb on the Trail," she adds with a wicked grin.

However, today's is not as bad as yesterday's hellish ascent from the Bay of St. George up to Prinilas.

Hilary picks up a few cartridges as we climb. "There should be a law which forces hunters to return the same number of used ones before they can buy new ones." I think this eminently sensible idea would lose her a lot of votes in a country where any bird, however small, can be shot.

Just before the top we come to the tell-tale signs of habitation ahead: a rubbish dump. This reminds me of the south of Iran, where visitors coming to an oasis from the desert knew their journey was at an end when they met the ring of human excrement encircling their destination.

We enter Sokraki through a narrow alleyway and immediately come to the picturesque triangular shaped square. Its southern side consists of a small but lovely house which Hilary would like to buy for herself. On each of the other two sides there is a little café-bar. Emily's Restaurant, on our right is a favourite for walkers in need of refreshment as the village is at the top of the steep climb from the north or reached by the hair-raising hairpins up the Pantokrator ridge from the south. Emily is inside preparing snacks, whilst her husband Stathis serves the customers. The house speciality is ginger beer – the genuine drink, made in Kalafationes, of lemons, ginger, sugar and water– just as it was brewed during the British occupation 150 years ago.

The only downside of the square is its location on the car-borne tourist trail. After nearly seven days on foot, I suddenly take an aversion to the motorised fraternity. There is barely a handful of parking spots in the centre of the village, so thankfully most of the cars do not stop. Sokraki is typical of the villages in the area with its collection of beautiful old but small houses, each using olive wood for their lintels. Hard and strong, they have lasted hundreds of years.

The last leg of the day's trek is four kilometres long through a shallow valley to finish at Spartilas, which sits precariously half-way up the 900-metre high face of Mt. Pantokrator. Thankfully, there are no more climbs – the last one up to Sokraki was enough for one day.

After Sokraki, the terrain changes from olive groves to pine and deciduous forests in which ancient fields lie fallow within stone walls. In years gone by vegetables would have been grown by the villagers for the market in Corfu Town as well as well as barley for their own use. The vegetables would have competed with produce from Lefkimmi, brought by boat from the quayside we lunched beside on our first day.

Just before we get to Spartilas, what look like allotments are still being cultivated in an area called 'Campos Spartilas'. (Does 'campus' come from this word?). The families of the village split up the plots, so that all share the land best for growing vines or vegetables. Instead of the little wooden sheds used in northern countries, old appliances such as refrigerators and even cars are used for storage. Such a sound recycling idea!

After passing through Sokraki's ancient fields, the Corfu Trail narrows to a footpath between low trees. A holly oak stands high beside its neighbours. Hilary explains that this unusual specimen has grown unimpeded, having reached a height too tall for goats to keep it as a bush. The path is well marked by the yellow spots on the trees, so I do not fear getting lost.

"However did you find this path?" I ask our guide in amazement. After the open vistas through the olive groves earlier in the day, we are now passing through almost impenetrable forest!

"Theresa showed me," Hilary explained.

Theresa Nicholas, who sketched the town and the villages, moved even further up in my estimation. "And who showed Theresa the path?"

"She learnt it from Ann Nash," referring to Corfu's famous painter of flowers. "Ann probably was told by the villagers of Sokraki, who would have used it in the old days as the route to Spartilas."

At this point, the path is crossed by a wide mud road, recently cut by a bulldozer. "Oh my God, the vandals! How dare they destroy this virgin forest?" Hilary is suddenly on the point of tears.

The path continues, but no longer dark and mysterious, as the future road runs parallel a few metres away. Ancient stone terrace walls and an ancient well have been flattened. What is the reason for this destruction? Hilary is already planning another campaign, but I fear it is too late.

"I cannot believe the local council is constructing another road!" she mutters furiously. This is a dilemma for an island with such fantastic potential for walking: does one utilise the wild Corfu Trail loved by serious hikers or manufacture roads for car tourists?

Jannie is waiting at Spartilas, where we settle down for a beer or coffee. A local English couple see Hilary and come over to discuss the new road. They have been responsible for keeping the Trail open through the forest, a task for which they deserve our total thanks.

Hilary can at last relax, and she tells us about her vision for the future of walking on the island.

"Walking in Corfu is like a three-layered pyramid. At the top we have a single Corfu Trail. This links with the middle layer of thirteen regional networks," she explains enthusiastically. "Some of these are currently sketched out in my *Complete Book of Walks*."

"And the bottom layer?" I enquire as I have ideas for this.

"I have selected 30 villages with a café-bar. Each will be the starting and end point for a round trip, which passes through the alleyways that lead to the surrounding fields or olive groves, then following the original paths which make up the historic network found all over the island."

I am sold on her plan as it will bring an income into the villages. "Perhaps we could also have resort-based local networks?"

"With local hotels becoming involved. This is what Fried Aumann will tell you about on your last leg of the Trail. He has waymarked – in blue – paths through the Paradise Plateau which lies just south of his Country Club in Acharavi. Local councils are already getting involved. They see it as a way to get grants: €74,000 for your Parelion Council, John, just for notice boards and useless maps; €100,000 for the new Tourist Trail down from Old Perithia; goodness knows how much for the Queen's Leap path we went along today."

"My friend Spiros Mazis, who is a member of the Parelion council, tells me the notice board in Agios Gordis has disappeared already," I comment.

"The other trouble is that the Trails set up by the communes are not maintained," she adds. "Let's start by getting the Corfu Trail more widely used. Already Aperghi Travel (00302661048713) offers individual and group walks with the British-based organisations, Walk Worldwide and Explore World-Wide. Ramblers World Wide (01707331133) Holidays use parts of the Corfu Trail in its programme. Our problems are also maintaining, waymarking and re-routing the Trail to bypass new road construction."

Jannie drives us through the narrow roads of the north of the island, back to collect Charles' car in Agros, and then we drop Hilary home in the Ropa Valley. We promise Hilary a meal at *Platopigatho* in the autumn. Tonight Charles, Rachel and Sydney are taking us, their hosts, to another one of our favourite restaurants, *Klimataria* in Benitses. Nikos Bellos, the owner, left the port from 1974 to 1983, when the village was almost destroyed by a vast influx of tourists. Many of these moved on to Kavos, leaving Benitses to be born again. Now with the old village hidden behind its landscaped square and its excellent fish restaurants, it is a pleasure to visit. Its new marina should be open in 2010 but first it must complete the work agreed in its planning application before getting electricity.

Klimataria, which specialises in fresh fish from the harbour, was opened in 1997 by Nikos and his wife Lilly from Dun Laoghaire in Ireland. As it is a small place it is essential to phone first (26610-71201) and book one of their few tables. It is well worth coming as every dish is a winner.

For starters, we have white *taramasalata*, aubergine salad

(*melitsanosalata*), courgette croquettes and marinated fresh anchovies. These have had their backbone removed, and are marinated in lemon for two hours; then finely chopped garlic and oil are added and they are left overnight. Nikos also produces a plate of spicy-hot sardines, cooked in a casserole with red pepper, onions and oil, which we devour.

Nikos then appears carrying a 1.7 kilogram grouper. I immediately recognise its mournful mouth.

"Niko, it's rather small, isn't it?" I ask. "In the Bahamas, where my son lives, they are far larger."

"The Mediterranean grouper is a smaller cousin," he explains. Perhaps in defence, he points to a picture of him holding a 3.5 kilogram fish.

I didn't mention that I found the cost of the Bahamian grouper was so high that I cooked a curried Jack instead. An onlooker in Nassau fish market had warned me that the Yellow Jack can be poisonous if not cooked enough. This curry didn't come undercooked!

For the main course we choose best beef meatballs, red mullet, huge prawns, and octopus well beaten then slowly cooked. Chips are forbidden as Greeks eat slabs of bread without butter.

To finish us completely we have start of season *fraolies* on meringue – they are sweeter than the baby strawberries we have at our Twickenham home in Strawberry Vale – followed by profiteroles and oranges in liqueur.

* * * * *

In October, we keep our promise to take Hilary to *Platopigatho* which, surprisingly she has never been to before, as it is very much for Greeks only. She loves the food and the music and is delighted that Alexis plays *rembetika*.

After our spring adventure she had sent me some old articles from the *Corfiot* dealing with the subject of property, which she forbade me to discuss on our walk. They deal with the villages and Venetian mansions of the island and also with what she calls 'Residential Tourism'.

The first article appeared in November 2003 and was titled "What's in a Village?"

'A stone-cobbled footpath climbs from close to the entrance of the Magic Life Club Hotel at Nissaki, winding between the olive trees. In autumn Sea Squill spikes the ground, and you may find a rare, retiring Narcissus. Glimpses of the sea come in an ever higher perspective. A half-hour walk and you suddenly emerge from the trees. Houses are ahead, stone-built like the path. You reach them at a yard laid with old paving stones and shaded by a massive holm-oak tree, perhaps the oldest on the island, and certainly the most venerable. A low wall invites a rest to recover your breath.

'You would like a drink too, after the ascent, but if you have not brought your own, you are out of luck. A little stone house tucked into the corner of the patio was once a kafenion; now, with only half a dozen houses occupied in the vicinity, it stands empty, derelict. The village square, whether an extensive space or no more than a widening in the street, is the focus of a settlement. Without one, a village has no heart. Katavolos lost its heart when the kafenion closed, and folk no longer gathered in the tiny square for coffee and gossip.

'Down on the coast, Nissaki straggles along the main road, a necklace of expensive villas, with the exquisite little harbour with its tavernas and fishermen's cottages as the main jewel. But Nissaki's heart is in its square, where the church, the kafenion and a paved courtyard are the magnet for every type of social event.

'These features are repeated in different combinations all over the Greek world. The square, the church and the kafenion. And in the square, planted close to the kafenion, the Tree of Idleness for shade while you sip your coffee or ouzo. Back in the 1950s, a resident of Cyprus warned Lawrence Durrell: 'if you intend to work, do not to sit under the Tree of Idleness.' Most readers assume that this tree, subject of a full chapter in Bitter Lemons, *is* the Tree of Idleness, the one and only tree with the ability to induce torpor. But it is a metapohor; Durrell was identifying a state of mind rather than a specific location.

'The combination of square, kafenion, tree and church is found all over the Greek world, characterizing and defining the lifestyle of the eastern Mediterranean. Where they are absent, this lifestyle perishes. A village is no longer a village.

'There are said to be over 100 villages in Corfu. But are they all villages? If they have no square, no kafenion and no church, the essential features of such a settlement, then they are not. One model is Kinopiastes, the central Corfu village which is home to the famous Tripa Taverna. In the main square, the huge Church of the Virgin, with its finely carved marble door surround, abuts a coffee bar. There's no Tree, but people sit out under the awning, on the honey-paved alleyway. Just off the square on the other side, the street widens where several alleys branch off. No fewer than three kafenions huddle at this spot, known locally (but not on any map) as Kokkoros after the oldest one.

'The Mayor of Achillion, Stefanos Poulimenos, is often to be spotted here, faking inactivity but in reality keeping his finger on the pulse of village life. He was born just around the corner, in an old, now derelict, house. Village President before he became Mayor, Poulimenos has worked for nearly 20 years to turn Kinopiastes into a showpiece. The settlement has an advantage in its proximity to Corfu Town, and the nearby passage of an hourly bus service, but careful civic planning has made it into a most desirable location to live. Where there once were ruined eyesore buildings, little squares now extend, an arena for the social life of the people who live in the immediate neighbourhood. It's a real village, and its growing population reflects the fact that people want to live there.

'Where are the other squares, the ones which distinguish a real village from a settlement which is no more than a hamlet? Doukades with its large church, two tavernas and three kafepantopoleia (coffee bar and grocery store combined), with lots of room to sit and watch vehicles getting stuck on the sharp corner. Sokraki with its plane tree shading a diamond-shaped square where you feel the peace of the mountain seep into your veins. Strinilas with its famous elm tree and, at Stamatis' little restaurant the best egg and chips in the world. Benitses with its tree-planted harbour square and top-class restaurants and bars. Agios Mattheos with its linear 'square' lined with pavement cafes. All villages with a heart. Then the other villages, marked on the map as such. The ones that are not villages. Alepohori. A big square but no church, and only a water spring to drink at. Komianata. A sweet, well-tended square, but apart from some attractive buildings, nothing else. Poulades. Just a kafenion at a road junction, and a few scattered houses. And there are never any people around, in these villages that are not villages. I found another one the other day – Tzetzeratika. It's one that's not on any map. A lovely peaceful settlement. The folk tell me that they sit in summer in a shady lane which runs beside a ruined house, because it's coolest in that spot. Maybe I'll open a kafenion there. Then it will be a real village.'

The second article, 'The Rise and Fall of Corfu's Mansions', was in the July 2005 edition of the *Corfiot*.

'We climbed one hairpin bend after another on our way up the mountain. Through the olive groves, the sea appeared in a more vertiginous perspective at every turn. Then, at a little hamlet, we set off on foot along a stone-cobbled path winding through olive trees. Nets were laid out on the ground to catch the fallen fruit – but it was June now, long after the harvest was over, and their presence was evidence that the proprietors no longer took care of their groves. Through the encroaching brambles, we glimpsed a strawberry-tinted wall while, high above, a green shutter rattled in the breeze. Here, in the slopes above Nissaki, we had come across one of Corfu's abandoned mansions. In a region where property on the coast is snapped up, hidden houses in the hills are left to moulder towards decay, for the landed families can no longer maintain the lifestyle of past generations.

'Mansions like this one were a product of the Venetian era, remnant of a medieval feudal system that had its origins with the Angevin lords, who ruled the island in the 13th-century. When Corfu was added to the great dominions of Charles of Anjou in 1267, the island was divided into four bailiwicks (which are still evident in the traditional regional divisions of Oros, Girou, Messis and Lefkimmi) and twenty-four fiefs, held either as royal demesne or by barons on behalf of the crown. This was the pattern upon which the Venetian nobility's estates developed. With the Ottoman Empire slashing its way across the Balkans, people sought safer havens. Corfu, never taken by the Turks, offered security. So families came from many locations, and those with wealth and initiative became the nobles of Corfu. Of the great clans, 'the Marmoras, Theotokis and Prosalendis were of Byzantine extraction, the Capodistrias and Giallinas from Dalmatia, the Voulgaris from Epirus, the Sordinas from the Veneto, while the Pieri were French... the Kourkoumelis and the Flamburiaris (moved) from Cephalonia to Corfu.' (*Britain's Greek Empire* – Michael Pratt).

'It was this period which saw the construction of the great country houses, 'residences intended originally and principally as a base from which to oversee the gathering of agricultural produce and to supervise the labourers which toiled in the service of the great landowners. These buildings, manor houses in essence, were used as temporary residences at harvest time and are characterized by their extensive storage capacity and generous provision of various outhouses.' (*Noble Houses of Corfu* – Despina Paisidou) At the same time, the great families mainly resided in a grand house in Corfu Town. Some, like the Voulgaris house next to Saint Spiridon Church, still are in the hands of the original families, though the features that set them apart from the average urban Venetian apartment building are often only evident when you cross the threshold. In later years, many families were unable to maintain this town base, and many migrated to the countryside on a permanent basis. After union with Greece in 1864, the landed gentry gradually lost their riches and status. In 1912, the Corfu Land Act forced them to surrender much of their estates to the peasants who worked it, though some retained enough land to make agricultural life viable. Until the 1960s when developing tourism swept away the labour base, the Manessis family's San Stefano estate still ran to 240 acres, as did the Kourkoumelis estate at Afra; but here the land had once stretched to five thousand acres. Land rich and cash poor. In her delightful book about Corfu (in Greek), Ninetta Laskari of Agios Markos remembers the 'poverty food' they would eat in times of need: 'When we had nothing to eat, we would take a couple of handfuls of olives in brine, five or six onions, thyme, oil and garlic. We soaked the olives all night, then cooked them to form a bitter paste. We drained this and put it in a frying pan with oil, seasonings, onions, garlic and water to cover. We stirred it while it cooked so it didn't burn, until all the water evaporated.'

'The last century saw many of the landed families living in genteel poverty. Many estates were broken up, mansions decayed and were abandoned. Some, like the Manessis, saw where the future lay and moved into tourism, and a huge hotel stands close to their famous mansion, still in the family. At Fundana, Spiros Spathas, descendant of the Giallinas family, converted storage areas into lovely studios for visitors, enabling him to maintain his mansion as a family home. For other mansions, standing derelict in the countryside, this could be the only solution.'

Hilary's third article from the *Corfiot* deals with 'Residential Tourism – A New Future for Corfu?' It was in the October 2002 edition.

'In villages all over Corfu's countryside, lovely old houses stand abandoned and derelict. While many of these buildings, just a short drive from the beach, are ideal as holiday homes or more permanent residences, the local property business has so far disregarded them in favour of modern developments. Unlike in France and Italy, where the demand for old properties has been apparent for years, local estate agents have shown little interest in offering buyers the chance to purchase a character house in need of renovation.

'Now, a team of people in Corfu and overseas is in the process of creating a new market out of these so far neglected dwellings, by promoting residential tourism. Residential tourism makes an enormous contribution to the local economy, a contribution that has not to date been recognized. In addition to the money brought into Corfu for the initial purchase of the property, many other sectors benefit. For example, funds are required for renovation work, which usually employs small building firms rather than large contractors. Once the house is ready, it requires furnishing. And since it makes sense to buy heavy items in Corfu, local stores benefit.

'And it does not stop there. New owners invite families and friends to stay, people who might otherwise not visit Corfu. Once settled, residential tourists' spending is spread out, not focused on a four-month season or on a particular resort area, and the little shops which serve villages in the neighbourhood of the newly inhabited homes gain enough business to stay open. While many of the new buyers intend to use their home for holidays, some aim to become permanent residents.

'A few have not only moved to Corfu full time, but have

also set up successful businesses. Ben and Claudia have established The Invisible Kitchen, a catering operation which fills a neglected place in the local market. 'We've found our niche and it seems to be working well,' said Ben. 'We love what we're doing and it's nice to do it in such a fantastic place.' The couple bought an old stone house in a village off the beaten track near Acharavi. 'It's so quiet,' continued Claudia. 'yet you still have people to chat to and give support. There's no traffic passing through, and essentially that's very important to us.'

Now as we sit in *Platopigatho*, thinking back on our walk, I was able to tie these three subjects together in the context of the north of the island: the area across the great ridge of mountains, away from town. The Corfu Trail ends at the most northerly point on the island, east of the town of Acharavi. My last interview will be with the co-founder of the Corfu Trail, Fried Aumann, who owns a gorgeous country club on the coast just outside the town. He keeps his spa open throughout the year and also liaises with the Invisible Kitchen, which offers excellent food at reasonable prices. I have always been surprised that these could be a success out of season, as the resorts elsewhere on the island are closed from the end of October to the end of April. The reason is that there is a large ex-pat community based on Acharavi. This 'residential tourism' has helped keep this part of the island ticking over in the winter.

For those that love rural Corfu and fancy becoming the squire of their own demesne, then the northern slopes of the Mt. Pantokrator ridge could be the place to find their Venetian mansion, as there are many to be found even if they are now derelict. Converting the house and outbuildings to provide bed and breakfast accommodation would generate an income in the summer. In the winter, the harvesting of the owners' own olives would add to the pleasures and the pocket. Guests would be entranced by the peace of the countryside, and for sure would be willing purchasers of the vintage extra-virgin for sale. Hilary tells me of an English couple living in Klimatia called Julie and Eddie, who provide Greek hospitality with en-suite accommodation. The income supplements their pensions. Eddie, however, is also a master carpenter, which is useful if there's conversion work to be done.

Some of these mansions are in or near the multitude of villages that Hilary sees as ripe for encouragement. For me, the part of the island she led us through was an eye-opener. Whenever I have returned to the resorts of Roda and Sidari I feel depressed; I no longer recognise the undeveloped Corfu we fell in love with. But a day's walk through the hinterland brings back memories of the old days, the unspoilt countryside and the quaint villages.

"Can I raise the forbidden subject, Hilary?" I enquire after a litre of excellent local wine has been consumed and the music is in full swing.

"What's that, John?"

"Property. In particular, village property. Even you fancied that little house on the square in Sokraki."

"It's not easy living in a village," Hilary has to admit. "Most village houses are very small and there is usually no parking outside. In the recent past, a family would live in just 60 square metres; sometimes three generations with eight children would squeeze in; village houses are often sub-divided, with perhaps a room owned by a cousin in Athens. The young now move out and build on a plot outside the village, which is owned by the family. You therefore must get agreement from a number of relatives before you can buy."

"You say that 60 square metres is small. Before we renovated our house we had only 72 square metres into which we fitted an open-plan living area, three very small bedrooms and a bathroom."

"But you have a terrace and olive trees round the house. Most foreigners want similar outside space and a view, so they usually buy on the edge of a village. One can, however, convert a centrally-located house into a one-bedroom holiday home with a sofa-bed in the living room to be used just in the summer. If wooden windows and doors are used, the character of the house still fits in with the neighbours. I call this re-antiquation," adds Hilary with a chuckle.

"But if you want double-glazed windows, uPVC is the only option," I suggest.

"Not true," she replies. "There are still many craftsmen that make traditional wooden windows with double glazing. You can renovate authentically and still have mod cons!"

Probably a hundred houses on the island have been converted for foreigners on the island. Many have beautiful views.

As we finish our discussions, I hope that the many who fall in love with Corfu might share our dream, find a little village house, convert it and become part of the community.

Day 8: from Spartilas to Agni
Over the top to the end of our journey

Flowers 8, Scenery 9, Underdeveloped 5, Challenge 9, Hrs 6
See map on page 39.

Can this really be our last day? And what a day it promises to be. It consists of three parts: a sheer 45-minute climb up a gulley on the face of the Mt. Pantokrator massif, an hour and a half crossing the karst plateau to the road to the Mt. Pantokrator peak and finally two and a half hours on the gradual descent to Kentroma, above Agni on the main road from town to Kassiopi.

The first two sections follow the Corfu Trail. After a further half an hour on the Trail descending gently to the High Col, we cheat. The official route, taking three and a half hours, finishes at Kaminaki, half an hour south down the coast from Agni. From the High Col, it drops down to the right to the deserted village of Old Sinies, climbing again out of a wide valley to drop finally down to the sea. It follows rough tracks and cobbled mule paths and has a spectacular view of the coast near its end.

From the High Col, we will instead walk straight on along the first half of the final day of the official Corfu Trail, but in a reverse direction, leaving the other half of the final day to the autumn. This cunning plan saves us time and means we will make Agni for a late lunch. We will also be able to enjoy the company of our last guest, Patricia Cookson, founder of CV Travel, on the descent from Mt. Pantokrator to journey's end, hopefully without complete exhaustion.

This final leg offers fantastic vistas during the first and last sections, the ascent and descent of Mt. Pantokrator and a thrilling walk through the 'lost world' of the karst plateau.

181

As the lover of mountains, Charles will be in his element; Sydney will be excited by the orchids and other flowers on the plateau; and I will be knackered and thankful if we three old men manage to complete our journey.

Today we make an early start, as it is the best part of an hour's drive to Spartilas, and then, two and a half hours' climb and walk before we meet up with Patricia.

"Good morning, John," announces Charles breezily. "How is Noah?"

My most important job on the holiday has been to check out the weather, which has been typical for spring in Corfu: sun and showers. I use the website of the National Observatory of Athens (www.noa.gr).

"The overnight storm is expected to pass Mt. Pantokrator by ten and we should have a lovely afternoon."

Charles delivers us safely to Spartilas by nine o'clock. It is still raining in the village and the face of the mountain is completely obscured by clouds.

Over a cup of coffee we debate our options.

"If Noah is right, the clouds will have cleared once we get to the top," suggests Charles, the optimist. "And then Sydney can see all these rare orchids you have been promising us."

"I could miss out the climb as long as we can somehow get to see the orchids. What do you think, John? You are the local." Sydney may have a one-track mind but he is very practical.

"I remember Hilary telling me how she and a friend had started out from Spartilas in sunny weather, but had been quickly overwhelmed by a storm that crept up on them from behind; they were battered from the south by sleet, which, hitting the cliff, was wind-driven upwards. She said it was impossible to turn into it and descend, so they continued to climb and took shelter in the chapel at the top until the storm abated."

"But, John, you are not Hilary!" suggests Charles with a wicked snigger. Sydney joins in the laughter. "All Sydney asked was what you thought, not what Hilary thought." Are my partners mutinying and daring to suggest I am becoming too dependent on Hilary's opinion?

I wonder if Charles treated his Minister in the same derisory way. So I come clean with a worry that has been nagging me for a few days. "I came down the cliff a couple of weeks ago. Though the gulley was dry, I found it extremely dangerous. After the overnight rain, it will probably be a river. I'm for driving round the mountain to Strinilas and then taking the road to the summit."

"And miss the orchids?" asks Sydney, raising his voice. He is far too nice a guy to suggest I am a wimp, but I don't want to climb straight up for nearly an hour in zero visibility and storm driven rain.

"Then we will leave the main road half way between Petalia and the summit and take the fire track which circles round the mountain. I've never been on it but it will extremely rough."

"I am all for bad weather alternatives," concludes our leader. "Then that is settled."

We drive up to Strinilas, where our epic trek was debated on Easter Saturday over egg and chips. I point out to Sydney the great elm tree in the village square. "The Elm Tree Taverna over there used to be owned by a Dutch lady. I think she left after tourists kept on asking her why the tree didn't have Dutch Elm disease."

Taking me seriously, Sydney replies "It's because the disease was only in the UK. It has been endemic there since Anglo-Saxon times. Every two to three hundred years the population of the beetle grows to such a point that the disease returns and kills off the beetles, and then the cycle starts again." Sydney is the most knowledgeable of companions.

We carry on along the main road until we see a Mountain

Refuge board on the right. It displays a map which indicates we are at the junction with the fire track. We are still in the clouds. This is just as well, as I am sure Charles would never have risked his hire car if he had known how huge the boulders are and how deep the pot holes can become after the winter rain.

"The track is fine where the Corfu Trail crosses it," I reassure him.

"And when is that?"

"I don't know," I confess. At that moment a huge wireless aerial appears right above us. "Good heavens, I think we are lost. The only aerial I've seen up here is right on the summit of the mountain."

"We are doing this for you, Sydney. Breaking the car, getting lost; all because of some orchids."

Two minutes later we come to a little valley. "I recognise it," I yell quickly. "The Trail crosses somewhere near here."

We park the Suzuki and walk back along the fire track for fifty metres. Sure enough there is a yellow waymark painted on a rock opposite a narrow path dropping down from the road. Another yellow mark confirms that we are on the Corfu Trail.

After seven days of olive groves Sydney is excited: he has trekked in the mountains of Crete and once found the fifth tulip on the island. Cyclamen are his speciality but they come in the autumn in Corfu. In the little valley below the road, we find a paradise of flowers – yellow, white, pink and blue – striving to rise above the lush green grass between the limestone boulders. At that moment the clouds part, allowing blue sky and a glimpse of sunshine through; this is truly heaven!

Guided by the waymarks, we follow a gully through a tunnel of holm oak, with the mottled sunlight shining on the wet leaves, into a green moss glade covered in white *siniotiki* stone boulders.

As we leave the glade, we see on the left a threshing floor

and now roofless little stone hut, where the farmers would have sheltered whilst storms raged. It was here that I photographed Dierk, Hilary, Fried and Christine with their three dogs on our way down to Spartilas three weeks before.

We return onto the Trail and after a hundred metres take a little diversion to the left.

"Orchis italica," shouts Sydney. "Come and look at the Italian man orchids." Sure enough, there is a beautiful flower containing a cluster of purple little men with their distinctive five limbs. As I capture this moment on camera, Sydney calls out again. "And here's a bee orchid," followed seconds later with another whoop of delight. "Whatever is this?"

I inspect the little pale yellow orchid. "That's Hilary's secret. She says it is only found up here on the plateau."

Even Charles joins in. The three of us are inspecting every plant in this extraordinary fifty-metre-square of untouched Eden.

I break off and lead my partners the short distance to the edge of the plateau. Far below is Spartilas, with the great bay to Corfu Town beyond coloured a steel grey as it reflects the scudding clouds which overhang the whole island, indicating the storm is over. Could we have climbed up the face of the mountain? Perhaps we could have, but it is better to be safe than sorry, and as the clouds have only just left the mountain, it would have been a race against time. Instead we have been able to linger with the orchids and can now inspect the derelict chapel of Taxiarchis.

Hilary tells us a little about the extraordinary history of this place in her *Corfiot* article, appropriately titled 'Chapel in the Clouds': 'But even off this almost forgotten path, and hidden by a thicket of trees, is a place that's not on any map – the Chapel of Taxiarchis. The Taxiarchae are the Archangels Michael and Gabriel, to whom the chapel is dedicated. Its name-day falls on 8 November, and it's certain that no-one visits the location to celebrate, even to light a candle. Who's bothered nowadays to climb that path from Spartilas?

'When I first visited the chapel many years ago, it served as a place of refuge. From that time, I've watched the chapel fall into ruin. Today, the roof has collapsed, and the mountain's sometimes severe weather is eating into the beautiful ancient frescoes which cover the internal walls.

'A friend made an attempt to pin down the owner (like many out-of-settlement chapels, it's a private establishment), but learnt that the inheritors were resident in Athens and didn't care. An approach to the Bishopric was met by a shrug, and the comment: 'There are so many of these private chapels, we don't have the resources to fix them.' Even though the Church is about the richest institution in Greece!

'But surely this is a special case! For one thing, the setting is truly amazing, the chapel being located exactly on the edge of the great wall of the Mt. Pantokrator Massif as it drops to the sea. The whole coastline is laid bare below, and on a clear day you think you can see forever. Historically, the chapel must be significant, even only as waymark on the pilgrims' route to the Mt. Pantokrator Monastery. Before roads were constructed in the mountain zone, pilgrims came on foot from all over the island, through the cool of the night, to take part in the Monastery's great *Paneyiri* (fiesta) on 6th August, following the old stone footpath from Pyrgi to Spartilas (now mostly wiped out by the road).

'The Taxiarchis chapel marked the end of the steepest climb, and from here on the way was easier. They would have rested here, thanking the Archangels with a candle, in a place where only seasoned hikers now go. But the Mt. Pantokrator Monastery is built on the site of an ancient temple dedicated to Zeus, so who knows how long worshippers have been stopping at this strategic spot?

'In Greek Orthodoxy, the Archangels are the great heralds

of good news. They reveal prophecies, knowledge and understanding of God's will. Archangels strengthen people in the holy faith, enlightening their minds with the light of knowledge of the holy gospel, and revealing the mysteries of devout faith. The name Taxiarchis is specifically given to Michael or Gabriel. The word literally means 'commander (archis) of a squadron (taxis)'.'

I have mixed feelings about the chapels which dot the island. On our first day we had seen the ruins of the Monastery of our Blessed Virgin above Arkoudilas beach. The chapel in the grounds of Mon Repos is also derelict. Yet on a pinnacle high above Gastouri is the chapel of Agia Kiriaki. A couple of years ago, Jannie and I clambered up like goats to this beautiful little building, in order to celebrate the saint's day with the villagers. Its roof had been restored by Nick Chadwick (aka Technick), fixer of all problems on the island. At the crossroads in Poulades there is another success: the villagers there have, over the years, built a little chapel, funding the materials from the proceeds of the annual *paneyiri* in August.

We three 'seasoned hikers' now follow the Pilgrim's Way back to the car. In the distance the clouds have cleared the masts on the summit of Mt. Pantokrator. Given time we could have carefully followed the yellow waymarks in a direct line of the peak, but today we rumble back along the fire track.

Mt. Pantokrator monastery has seen a number of changes since our first visit forty years ago, when its chapel lay in poor condition and the handful of monks meditated in rooms off the cloister at the very summit. Now the few that remain are housed in the restored building on the road up from the plateau. Originally this was just a rough track, but a few years ago it was concreted over. At first, on the final hairpin bend, there was just a radio mast used by the military. Corfu was a strategic point overlooking Albania and the communist world. Over time a pylon was added within the cloisters, first to aid air traffic control and then to host a multitude of mobile phone disks. After the fall of the Berlin Wall, many of our Albanian neighbours moved onto the island, some setting up a café-bar just outside the cloisters and starting to charge tourists for the loan of skirts to cover their naked knees. The final change and the most rewarding was when the chapel was beautifully restored. Today, it is an easy drive to reach the summit and sample a glass of wine as the sun sets over the Diapontian islands to the west, and the moon rises over the mountains of the mainland.

Soon after midday, our final guest-walker for the spring arrives. Patricia Cookson is an attractive and exciting person, one of just a few foreigners who could claim honorary citizenship for her work in putting Corfu on the modern tourist map. In 1972, she founded Corfu Villas, which more recently became CV Travel.

"It was the right place at the right time," she explains modestly as we set off down towards the High Col around the north of the summit of Mt. Pantokrator. "Corfu Villas transformed the north-east coastline, their clients becoming owners of the many beautiful houses on the coast. The villa renters also put money into the local economy by hiring boats and cars to visit local tavernas, while their teenage children would congregate in Kassiopi and St. Stephano to meet friends, drink their beer and enjoy the night life. The income the area received enabled the locals to make the north-east coast, and the village of Kassiopi, the fashionable area it has since become."

I smile and compare the similar origins but different end-product of Kassiopi and Kavos.

"Many of those teenagers succeeded in their careers and have come back to buy property. Today the villas along the coast are a preferred destination for the more well-heeled Brits."

I have been an admirer of CV Travel from the early days

and still respect an organisation offering a top class service under the new ownership of Kuoni, but under the same management including Debbie Marshall, its M.D. It offers nearly 100 beautiful villas for rent including 13 on the Rou Estate, a conversion of a two-hundred-year-old stone village which we will see from above as we descend towards the sea. It is the brainchild of Dominic Skinner, an architect who trained under Norman Foster.

The CV Travel brochure paints a rosy picture: 'The north-east has so much to offer: an area of incredible natural beauty where bays and coves of clean white pebbles nestle between rocky promontories. Visitors potter along the coastline, stopping off for leisurely lunches at tavernas on the edge of the water.'

Patricia suggests there should be a minor amendment. "There is, however, a danger of the tavernas becoming too expensive."

"Tell me, what changes do you see for tourism in the north-east?" I ask, genuinely interested in the future of the island's major income generator.

"First, I think more people will come to Corfu for walking. A new local walk has been opened between Avlaki, just south of Kassiopi, to St. Stephano. It would be wonderful if some of the guests could join Hilary's walks, and I also think she should promote taking private groups more. They would see that the island has more to offer than just this corner. Secondly, there is so much music on the island. The Corfu Festival in July and August is a must for music lovers. In the autumn, you and Jannie must come to the opera at the Ionian Academy. There is also a concert in one of the squares of the Old Town, arranged by Vivienne Pittendrigh who organises the Divertimenti Festival every year. But it is really time for the Tourist Promotion Board to co-ordinate the numerous cultural activities on the island and produce a single website to link them all together."

By now we are walking along the High Col in an easterly direction. To our right, the east face of Mt. Pantokrator falls into a deep valley, with ancient tracks taking the Corfu Trail down to Sinies.

To our left the final leg of the Corfu Trail drops down to Old Perithia in the foreground and to the north coast in the distance. The sun shines on a white all-inclusive hotel recently built beside the beautiful lagoon of Antinioti, one of Gerald Durrell's favourite haunts. In *My Family and Other Animals* he called it the 'lake of lilies' and wrote that 'it was a mile long, an elongated sheet of shallow water surrounded by a thick mane of cane and reed, and separated from the sea at one end by a wide, gently curving dune of white sand. . . It was the only place on the island where these sand lilies grew, strange misshapen bulbs buried in the sand, that once a year sent up thick green leaves and white flowers above the surface, so that the dune became a glacier of flowers.' I wonder what he would have thought of the new development.

To the east, almost within touching distance in the clear air that has followed the storm, is Albania, a mysterious land no more. "Tell me, Patricia, do you ever go over?"

"Of course. It is so easy now: after clearing customs we take a ferry from Corfu Town to Saranda, it takes about three hours. There is talk of letting small private boats go straight from Kassiopi. We then go down to Butrint, an enchanting World Heritage Site, which is a must for all visitors to the north-east."

"And for me!" I confess, "I have never been."

"Then you must use Demir, my marvellous private guide, who speaks perfect English; he'll look after you."

"What other changes do you see in tourism?"

"EasyJet has changed the face of the island. They have created a new market for visits on any day of the week, over the weekend and of any duration. There is a need for simple bed-

and-breakfast accommodation and for one good Boutique hotel, not tied up with tour operators. There is just one B & B in the north-east, the Bella Mare, at Avlaki. It is charming and now very popular with independent travellers. EasyJet have also enabled villa owners to rent independently and offer just their villa. Renters then organise their own flights and car rental."

"And how will that affect the traditional rental companies like CV Travel?" I ask.

"They will continue to offer charter flights, full and excellent service, and will still provide standard top-quality 7/14 night holidays. They will be able to be very competitive during peak season when they have flight capacity. But the big tour operators who compete only on price and give little back into the community will face tough competition."

At this moment, Patricia's mobile phone rings. With the masts of Mt. Pantokrator still in view, the reception could not be better. I overhear a technical discussion with words such as 'cropping' 'font' and 'text change' being thrown across the ether.

"Just trying to finalise an advertisement for a magazine," announces Patricia. "Modern science is wonderful, isn't it? I can work whilst walking along a fabulous, scenic path just under the clouds." At that point the sun comes out.

Sydney has been more interested in the flora lining our way. Every crack in the white rocks beside the track hosts a little gem, whilst the verges are an abundance of green grasses and yellow, red, white, pink and blue flowers. As Charles and Patricia stride on ahead of us, I'm called upon to photograph varieties which he will have to identify when we get home.

"Patricia," I call out. "Look what I've found; it's a beetle."

Charles on his own wouldn't have fallen for this trick. They return to watch this black monster clambering over a foot-high clump of dense vetch. In the world of the insect, this seemingly impassable forest is not the problem that we humans would face in a scaled-up jungle.

Charles and Patricia march on again laughing and chatting. My photography has progressed from nature's tiny wonders to the big picture. I am determined to capture the immense vista of the coast below, Butrint across the Corfu Channel and the mountains in the distance, now silver snow-topped from the storm overnight.

Around every corner, there is an even better view; then suddenly the wild land below turns into what at first I take to be a quarry but on further inspection turns out to be the new development at Rou. Already trees are greening the site, and I am told the planting of indigenous shrubs and flowers is creating an Eden of calm in this idyllic spot high above the sea.

My next distraction is a stunning old stone building at the hamlet of Mengoulas. I remember walking this way with our friends Peter and Pam; they had considered buying this magnificent property. The house and the view from it are unequalled, but its location high on the mountain could have made access in the winter extremely difficult.

After an inspection of this mansion and the new boundary walls of *siniotiki* stone (from Sinies), I realise that Sydney is already 300 metres ahead; Patricia and Charles are probably a similar distance further on and now out of sight round a corner. I call out to Sydney to stop the others as the shortest way down to Agni is down the road to Porta from Mengoulas. My message is relayed to the vanguard, who return in a grumpy mood.

"John, let's look at your map," suggests Charles. "Look, we were following the Corfu Trail to Santa."

"No, Charles, you are still on the track going right round the mountain."

Paticia is looking puzzled. "I thought that was an odd way we were going, Charles. I could see where I live next to Kassiopi."

We all agree that we must carry on down to Porta. At the next junction, Charles proposes a left turn on the road to Santa and then cross-country to Porta, following the official Corfu Trail in reverse.

"Charles, the off-road leg is though a forest, through unkempt olive groves down into a gulley and on through a forest; it's a very beautiful walk with loads of flowers. Hilary took us that way one Saturday. However, as it is getting late, I propose the direct route to Porta along the road."

"Sydney, which way?" asks Charles, seeing a supporter of his plan. Sydney hesitates: flowers or food?

"Well, I'm for John's way; we promised the tavernas we would be there by three," concludes Patricia.

As we set off, we see the bay of Agni way below us. I had started from Kavos aiming just to get to the end; Sydney had been happy to see flowers; and Charles had hoped to follow the Corfu Trail as closely as possible. I think we are all well satisfied with our journey, so I phone Jannie to pick us up once we reach Gimari on the main Kassiopi road. Whilst it is important 'to plan the walk, and then walk the plan', the best plans are the flexible ones.

Our delightful guest walker, Patricia, is as happy as her three boys. We are now re-entering civilisation. To complete strangers she calls out "*Kalo mina*" ('Have a nice month'), for sure enough it is the first of May. Whilst we are waiting for our transport to arrive, she has the last word which sums up our day. "So many of the visitors to the north-east have driven their jeeps along the route we took, but so few have walked it. I hope your book, John, will encourage more people to experience the lovely day I've had."

Agni is a jewel. This little bay is set in a ring of hills falling straight into the sea. 72 years ago, almost to the day, Lawrence Durrell wrote: 'We have taken an old fisherman's house in the extreme north of the island – Kalami. Ten sea-miles from town, and some thirty kilometres by road, it offers all the charms of seclusion. A white house set like a dice on a rock already venerable with the scars of wind and water. The hill runs clean up into the sky behind it, so the cypresses and olives overhang this room in which I write. We are upon a bare promontory with its beautiful clean surface of metamorphic stone covered in olive and ilex: in the shape of a *mons pubis*. This is become our unregretted home.' Kalami is the next bay up the coast and is linked by a small boat to Agni for visiting diners.

'Seclusion' Agni doesn't have. From all along the coast, boats of all sizes head for her piers and, above all, the three wonderful tavernas which sit beside the pebble beach. But we are right at the start of the season and just a single boat is moored off shore.

Today we have a dilemma. To choose one place to celebrate our walk would be unfair on the other two. All three are excellent in their own right. Looking out to sea, on the right there is Nicholas, the people's place, always full and friendly. On the left, Agni caters for the celebrities. In the centre is Toula, perhaps a favourite for the Greeks.

"So which one do we go to, Patricia?" I enquire.

"All three," she replies. Patricia is a very organised person and knows that this little bit of diplomacy is the only possible solution to our dilemma.

"Oh!" I exclaim. "Three meals?"

She notes my concern and adds "Starters at Nicholas, mains at Toulas and afters at Agni. And today, it's on the house. After so many years, they all know me well, and I would only suggest this to them if I thought it would be good PR for them." I'm even more impressed.

Pericles, moustachioed and friendly, welcomes us; we have done business before. He has rooms to let in Koukouli, the village in Zagori where Roy and Effie Hounsell have lived for nearly 20 years. Each spring Pericles buys a box of Roy's book

The Papas and the Englishman, which his guests find amusing and informative. Nicholas Taverna has a large covered but open area right on the beach. It is very popular with British tourists.

Greek starters are usually standard fare, but today Pericles is out to impress us. I think he secretly hopes that if he can stuff us full of wonderful food, then we will cancel our later engagements. Though each plate is mouth-watering, he underestimates the appetite generated by such a long walk in the mountains and the capacity of our trencherman Sydney.

We start with fried prawn balls.

"My favourite," says Jannie. "Pericles, how do you make them?

He smiles a secretive smile. "It's my secret."

Even before we have finished, a plate of prawn *saganaki* arrives, with an explanation this time.

"Fry the prawns for 5 to 10 minutes and then put them in a sauce of onions, herbs, tomatoes and feta." It all sounds so easy.

Stifado is an island favourite. Usually rabbit or beef is stewed with caramelized shallots, red wine and cinnamon. Today it is based on octopus. Each dish excels its predecessor.

Skordalia, puréed potato and garlic, is Corfu's very special accompaniment for fried fish. Pericles proudly presents us with it on a plate of small red mullet. The way they have been presented make me think the fillets could be kissing. Or is the cool wine the way I see them?

Finally, for any vegetarians, and also to push us over the limit, a plate of *gigantes*, or giant butter beans in a tomato sauce, arrives. We do them justice.

After thanking our host, we make our way along the beach to Toula's. Toula, herself, is in the kitchen, the control centre of another excellent restaurant. Though a book of her recipes has been published, she is today not so interested in discussing food. She is now a busy, doting grandmother, so we must look at her photographs instead. For Greeks, family comes first, and food after. We are summarily introduced to Thanasis her husband and then Nikos her son. Today we sit under a veranda at a reserved table with a red geranium displayed in the centre of a real tablecloth. As can be seen in the photo on the back cover, the other tables are taken by Greek families. Patricia's welcome completes the text for the sub-title of my book: 'Friends, Flowers and Food' – and what food!

We move on to a couple of carafes of red wine, excellent again. I forget who chose what main course, but this doesn't matter as I am a great believer in sharing.

By now readers will have enjoyed two recipes for *bourdetto*. Toula's is in its traditional form.

"I fry finely cut onions and a little garlic, add tomato paste, lots of red pepper and a little lemon. Then I add the *scorpio*," explains our hostess.

"I told Toula it was your favourite meal," says Patricia with a knowing smile.

Someone chooses grilled octopus, simple but delicious. A plate of *keftedakia* is put on the table. These small meat balls have a crunchy outside and tender, herb-laden interior. Meat balls must be one of the dishes the English do worst: large and soggy – and of course hamburgers are just squashed meat balls. Today, as we relax at Agni, it feels as if Greece is on another planet.

Jannie is consistent in her tastes, so for her it's Toula's fried prawns and rice, the speciality of the house. We are all allowed a sample of the rice: it is sublime, almost a meal in itself. Jannie is ecstatic.

Toula joins us and our praise rings out.

"The recipe for the prawns?" asks Jannie hopefully.

"Sorry it's a secret!" Toula replies.

It is now nearly five o'clock, which is late even for a Greek marathon lunch. It is time to move on. Eleni of Agni Taverna is waiting patiently. She is one of the taverna owners, and vies with Toula for the title of the best chef and taverna as well as being the Greek wife of an extremely energetic Englishman, Nathan. He has progressed from being the driving force behind the taverna, together with Eleni, to running a very successful tourist company with a large number of villas to rent.

"Eleni, I am sorry we are so late," says Patricia. "Could we have some coffee?"

"Of course, but you must also have Eleni's famous Lemon Yoghurt Crunch."

She joins us and we discuss her family.

"As the author of a new book, I can honestly say that every time we have come here the food has been wonderful. I will also mention the fact you are usually very full. So what's the secret?"

"I believe I give a very personal service. I am very proud of 'my clients' who come back every year."

This is surely the reason why the Greeks have made a success of tourism. By nature, they are a hospitable nation and they are proud of their culture.

Eleni continues. "They all have their favourite tables, but the most favourite of all is under that tree. They will book a table one week before they arrive on the island!"

Having never seen such a tree though it reminded me of a willow, I ask the obvious. "What is it called?"

"Agnos," she answers. "The bay is named after it. In the old days, baskets were made from the branches of the Agnos. I think you call it 'chaste tree' in English."

As we say our goodbyes and then make for the Land Rover to take the drivers back up to the top of the mountain to pick up their cars, I think 'chaste' might be the tree, but 'chaste' are not the tourists.

* * * * *

In the autumn, Patricia is as good as her word and we meet at the beautiful Ionian Academy for an opera recital organised by the Corfu Chamber Opera. The international Israeli soprano Idit Arad is performing Spanish songs and operatic arias by Verdi, Bizet and Boito.

In the interval, we are introduced to Keith Miller, an NBC News senior foreign correspondent who lives in London and Corfu. He was in Iran in 1979 and witnessed the fall of the Shah. He returned to report on the takeover of the US Embassy, seen by many as the turning point in American-Iranian relationships. (Having personally received the hate of the people on the street in 1962 during my hitch-hike through Iran to India, I see the 1953 US coup which toppled Mohammed Mossadegh as the turning point.)

"I've read a couple of your books," he claims.

I immediately like him. "And Patricia says you are an expert on olives," I reply with genuine interest. "We should meet up and you can tell me how I could start harvesting mine."

With a grin and a conspiratorial wink, he proposes a coffee at the Hotel Constantinopolis, a fine establishment overlooking the old port. "Can you make it at ten tomorrow morning before I return to my villa – and can you bring a dozen *Corfu Sketches*? They'll make perfect Christmas presents."

That is an offer Jannie and I canot refuse. Next morning after the signing ceremony, we get down to business.

"So what did you think of the opera?" Jannie asks.

"Didn't you miss me in the second half?" he laughs. "That's your answer."

I'm glad I was not alone, but opera is not really my scene; except when we stopped off with our ten-year old grandson at Verona and heard Verdi's Nabucco. It was a night I shall never forget: the Arena on a balmy evening, lit up by thousands of candles, with sublime music raising us to a higher level of happiness.

"Can we talk about olive oil production? On our walk, Patricia was very complimentary about your oil."

"And she enjoyed your walk and said how beautiful it was looking down from so high." He laughs again, "But she suffered and was hobbling for a few days afterwards. She claimed she needed long hot baths to recover."

"First can I ask you about the fruit fly? Do you spray your trees, because the *Dakos* take a likening to our trees."

"We spray with Bordeaux mixture."

"That was used in Ireland against the potato blight. In those days, it was a solution of copper-sulphate mixed with a solution of quicklime. My father introduced a colloidal preparation which was easier to use," I add. It was the cause of my father having to leave Ireland. ICI had the monopoly on the old chemicals and circulated a leaflet warning the farmers not to use his *Bouisol*. He went broke.

"I have never sprayed with *Lebaycid* which was used by the locals for years," explains Keith. "In some villages in the north of the island, up to half of the men have contracted lung cancer. They used to pump the toxic chemical with neither mask nor special clothing. Back in California it was banned many years ago."

"As we might harvest our olives, tell me how you started?"

"I sent a sample of olives to Cambridge for analysis. They came back with bad news. The acidity was 8% – only 2% less than industrial oil."

"And what should it be?"

He smiles at the memory. "For extra virgin up to 1%, virgin to 1.5% and table oil up to 5%."

"So how do you reduce the acidity?" I ask innocently, having rejected adding a little bit of alkali.

"As you know, the three million olive trees on the island are mostly very large, as they are so old. In other countries where the trees are small, the olives can be shaken or picked directly off the tree. Here we let the olives fall, but then the oil immediately starts to oxidise," Keith explains expertly. "In the old days, each olive was picked off the ground by hand every day. Now they fall into nets and are collected within two days. The longer the time they are left the higher the acidity."

"Whoops!" I interject with a laugh, "I've just loaded a bin liner with the olives that have been dropping on our terrace for two weeks. I was planning to take them back to England and marinate them. The tree, one of six huge ones we have on the property, has branches stretching six metres from the trunk."

"Sorry, John, they'll be inedible. We are starting our harvest now and will continue for a month to the end of November. We pray for wind which makes the olives fall so we can pick them immediately. The oil content is low at the start of the season, but the rain we've had is great as it is transferred from the roots to the fruit as fluid."

"Keith, could you solve a mystery for me," says Jannie. "Whenever there's been a fire on the island, the olive trees regrow after a couple of years. Is that because the roots are deep?"

"No it's because they are shallow. Olive trees are drought resistant and have horizontal roots to collect the moisture. They even gather liquid when the humidity is high."

"How much oil do you expect to get?" I ask, envisaging my future as an oil producer.

"Last year we gathered 428 kilo of fruit from six trees. This made 40 litres of the highest quality extra virgin oil, enough for ourselves and our guests to take home as presents. Milos oil is famed all over the world," Keith adds with a chuckle.

"Patricia said you had a large property, so why pick only from six trees?"

"That's because, John, you and your friends haven't joined us in the harvest! We have in fact over 100 trees."

I think for a moment. "We have a little diesel Toyota Aygo.

If it were converted to run on olive oil you could produce enough fuel to drive 10,000 miles each year; that's five round trips to Corfu."

"At about 50 cents per litre, the cost of pressing the olives," Keith adds, sharing my fantasy. He pauses and scribbles on a napkin some numbers. "That means that 30,000 cars could be driven on Corfu oil. I think I prefer what happens today: the best oil is for consumption and the oil from the pulp is used for soap and cosmetics and then the waste is burnt to heat greenhouses and the like."

"We could squash the waste into 'brickettes' as the Irish do with peat. When the price of oil increases, we might have to go back to Venetian times and use the oil for lamps."

"We will have to do something about alternative energy. I looked at solar panels but they are expensive in Greece. We are at about the same latitude as Northern California. There, a $2,000 solar panel system gets a 50% rebate from the state making it cost $1,000 and then we get a further 20% subsidy from the federal government, so we pay only $800. I regret installing electric under-floor heating; I thought engineers in Greece might have problems with a hot water system. If it gets a leak, one is in real trouble. Now I burn olive wood. We should copy the Germans: they drill down 100 metres and get geo-thermal power. The advantage is that water is cool in the summer and equivalent to a hot water bottle in the winter."

"Keith you have been reporting from the Middle East for many years. What is your estimate for when oil will run out?"

"2050," Keith replies. "I'll be dead by then."

"But my grandson will be only 50 years old. I agree with your forecast. If we are right, then our generation should feel incredibly guilty about the way we have wasted millions of years of nature's work. Perhaps the solution is to accept that our insatiable demand for oil and gas must stop," I conclude.

"If it is not too late," Keith replies.

It is time for this delightful American to return to his olive grove – or should I say oil well.

Autumn – from Ano Pavliana to Stavros and Sinarades

Flowers 6, Scenery 6, Underdeveloped 5, Challenge 4
See map on page 36.

October in Corfu is magical. Great storms drive in from the west as we sit on our veranda stranded at home by the forces of nature. From out to sea whirlwinds walk towards land and surf drives white foam across the bay, with thunder, echoing around the mountains, and lightning illuminating the evening sky, like the forewarning of an apocalyptic happening. Next morning the nightmare is over and a crystal clear blue sky invites walkers to boot up and make for the mountains, to stare at the far reaching vistas in every direction or wander through olive groves covered in purple cyclamen.

"Good morning, Jim," I start. "Our walk is off, I'm afraid."

"You can't make it today?" enquires my first guest of the autumn. "Let's make it another day."

"Sorry, I have Plantar Fasciitis."

"What ever is that in English?"

"Policeman's Heel. The plantar fascia is the ligament connecting the heel to the middle foot bones; it has been pulled away from the heel bone."

"That sounds awful?"

"It's absolute agony."

"Whatever has caused that?" Jim asks sympathetically.

"Too much walking, whilst unfit! I think our trek up the Corfu Trail started it. Then too much standing! I spent four weeks this summer watching my grandson train at Chelsea. And, oh yes, bad footwear: I always wear deck shoes."

"In which case let's be armchair walkers and meet over a beer," concludes Jim.

The plan for our excursion was to walk around and then to the top of Agii Deka, at 576 metres the highest mountain in the middle of the island. In the spring we had missed out this loop in the Corfu Trail by taking a short cut across our bay of Agios Gordis.

Hilary suggests it takes one day to get from the west coast at Paramonas, via Ano Pavliana, to Stavros above the east coast, where walkers stop for the night and a second day to climb up to the top of Agii Deka and walk across its northern slopes to Sinarades, my local village, to meet up with our short cut at Aerostato and then go on to Pelekas.

I had planned to walk the loop in two shortened days of about four hours each. On our first walk from Ano Pavliana, where we had finished on our third day, to Stavros we would have been accompanied by Jim Potts. On the second day we would have walked from Stavros to Sinarades, where our good friends Peter and Pam Jenkins live, and would have provided an excellent meal! During this second day, Jannie and Pam would have joined Peter and me at the village of Agii Deka after the boys had climbed the mountain and then we would all have ambled through a fabulous cypress forest at Kamara.

On our first day the Corfu Trail drops down from Ano (Upper) Pavliana on the west coast mountains to Kato (Lower) Pavliana and then across the bowl of the Messongi River Valley via the picturesque village of Vouniatades to Strongili and Stavros on the east coast mountains. Though badly damaged by a fire which swept across the valley about ten years ago, the olive trees have re-grown and the route is pretty if not dramatic.

Let Edward Lear describe the journey he made in the reverse direction: 'Across the olive woods [from Strongili] – wonderful scenes of long-armed light-foliaged trees – to Vouniatades, apparently a dreary village and then up to Ano Pavliana up a difficult track, & one so slushy & steep I could hardly manage. The view over Lefkimi to Paxos is beautiful. We came down to

Kato Pavliana to a high road to Vouniatades again'.

In March 1862, he walked from Corfu Town to Agii Deka. He wrote:

'I walked straight up, but slowly, to Ag. Deka. What unsurpassable beauty of distance & of foreground!'

In May 1862 he continued on to Stavros and to Strongili. He wrote: 'Walked on from [Ag. Deka], some of the most beautiful views of Corfu, & under the most beautiful phases of light & shade . . . to be seen. After the turning to Stavros, there were some novel & fine views of Ag. Mathaios & other places – but at the 10th mile from Corfu the land grew weary & wildernessy, & at the 12th mile, when we were told that the few dirty ruined houses above was Strongili horror arose.'

Another letter back to England was more positive: 'A pleasant shadeful walk . . . the olives are wonderful, the interminable perspective of the silver light-catching trunks contrasting with the deep shades on the green & fern below. Soon at Stavros, where a perlite villager showed us to the place where all the English were wont to go; & no lovelier view can be seen, so much so that I rank it first of all the distant Corfu views, as regard the seeing all & everything.'

The 'distant Corfu views' he refers to are down to Benitses on the east coast and across to the, probably snow-covered, mountains of the mainland and Albania behind.

At the top of the mountain of Agii Deka there is yet another abandoned monastery, a perfect spot to rest after a very steep climb up from Ano Garouna. For those whose Greek is minimal I should explain that the word *Agios*, which appears in many place-names, means 'saint'; whilst *Agii* is the plural form. Agii Deka is said to refer to the ten saints that came to Corfu many centuries ago, leaving another forty behind in *Agii Saranda*, across the Corfu Channel in Albania!

It is time to take to my armchair, order a beer and talk with my good friend Jim Potts.

All the friends in this book are united by their love for Corfu. In the main, they have been practical people, such as engineers. We have discussed a variety of issues, but there has often been the common theme of energy. For this I do not apologise: to me, it is one of the two most important issues of the day; the other being our presence in Iraq and Afghanistan.

My armchair companion is someone different: he could be described as a multi-talented intellectual. For me, one word defines an intellectual; it is 'poetry'. I am sure many people love poetry, but how many actually write it? And how many have had a book of poems published? Well, Jim Potts has. His Greek 'limerick-style' humour, which appropriately connects Jim, Corfu and Lear comes from his book *Corfu Blues*:

Alexander the Great

It's a pity the fella from Pella
Didn't listen to Aristotle,
He would have conquered the rest of the world,
If he hadn't kept hitting the bottle.

With the new European President writing haikus, let Jim offer his Greek version:

Byron Haiku

'Twas the bleeding doctors
Did him in,
Not the Bloody Revolution.

This delightful book, published by Ars Interpres of Stockholm in 2006, also contains some excellent prose. The following essay topics interested the politician and historian in me: Americans, Communists, Colonels; Sisi's and the Kaiser's beds; Zagori – War and Civil War; Cyprus, Durrell and propaganda; a Greek-American playwright; Byron and the

Greeks; Greek self-esteem; Paxos; Cocoyiannis and Zorba the Greek; Greek Music.

The title of the book and the last essay give a hint of another side of Jim Potts. He is a blues guitarist, and a good one as well judging by his latest joint CD with John Lee Hooker, which is awaiting release. In July 2004, Jim recorded a CD 'On the Memphis Road' at the Sun Studio, Memphis, interpreting rockabilly and blues music by Elvis, Johnny Cash, Jerry Lee Lewis and Carl Perkins and some of the Sun blues greats.

But we disagree on a minor issue: a couple of years ago we went with Jim and Maria to *Platopigatho* and he said the music was too loud. I have barely forgiven him, for he then got up and suggested to Angelis that the loudspeakers should be turned down. Of course, Greeks don't do quiet. Jim loves bouzouki music and *rembetika*, but on that evening he wanted to talk as well as listen.

To further my musical education, Maria invited Jannie and me to a concert of 'Old Greek Music'. In trepidation we joined them in a man-made amphitheatre at Mon Repos Palace which, though not as dramatic as the ancient amphitheatre of Epidavros, was a truly romantic setting on a balmy September evening. For two hours an orchestra from Corfu enchanted us with classics by Theodorakis and Hadjidakis, tunes from the 60s and 70s, powerful political songs against the Colonels. 'Old Greek' the organisers called it; so this must mean I'm old as well!

Corfu is famous for its musical traditions, and throughout the summer there are musical festivals all over the island. These vary from 1960s and 70s music at Ag. Ioannis to concerts in the Achilleion Palace where the eighteen-year-old Corfiot Dionysios Grammenos, winner of the Eurovision Young Musician Award in Vienna, played last year.

There is a regular avant-garde concert at the Triklino Vineyard and evenings at the Arena in Paleokastritsa. In Corfu

Town you can spend an elegant evening at the *son et lumière* at the Old Fort, or drink coffee whilst listening to wind-band concerts on the *Plateia* and in the many squares in town. Visiting international musicians such as the Volante Strings play in a number of large old historic houses, including Roger and Pat's, throughout the island. There is also a classical music festival in Paxos every May.

When the mood takes him, Jim himself has been known to play with a number of local musicians, including Raul Scacchi from Sinarades, a fine composer and member of Blues Refugees, and he enjoys listening to Roy Kendle of Blues Latitude in Kontokali, Lenno and friends at his place '@home' in Gouvia and guitarist Chris Holmes, son of the island's renowned painter of flowers, Lady Holmes.

Jim's new book *The Ionian Islands and Epirus, a Cultural History* has just been published. It is in the *Landscapes of the Imagination* series (Signal Books, Oxford, 2010). Jim says it covers around two thousand years and everything from Homer to Waller and beyond!

In 1967, after coming down from Oxford University, Jim took up the post of a teacher of English in Corfu because it sounded exotic; which it was in those days! He arrived on the island, taught for a year and met and married Maria Stráni, whose mother came from Paxos.

Despite a nomadic working life of 35 years with the British Council, Jim and Maria returned to Corfu whenever possible. In the 1980s, after Prague and Stockholm, Ethiopia and Kenya and seven years as British Council Director in Australia, for which he was awarded the OBE, Jim became British Council representative for Northern Greece and they lived in Thessaloniki for five years. On a journey to Corfu in 1982, they "turned right" at Metsovo and found the mountainous region of Zagori with its 42 villages.

"It was love at first sight," Jim tells me. "In particular, I fell for the stone architecture and the views of the Vikos gorge from the village of Vitsa. Families had left Zagori after the civil war, going to the cities or abroad. The arrival of Albanian stone masons (many Greeks seemed to have lost the art), and EU funding helped the owners to restore the massive mansions, many of which had been abandoned."

"Jim, there's another of the valuable features of the EU," I quip, remembering the Euro-scepticism that is rife.

He laughs. "The EU still seems to believe that Zagori has poverty: they once donated a large bag of rice to each inhabitant, who then gave it to the animals for fodder. Sadly, there is not much local industry and some people may be poor, but individual home-owners are not. Many have been able to access Regional Development Funds to convert their homes into guesthouses. These must stay open for five years to get the 60% funding, I believe."

I agree with him, as the villages beside the Vikos Gorge are truly gorgeous and have improved over the last few years.

In March, Jannie and I visited Roy Hounsell with some boxes of his book, *The Papas and the Englishman*. In the two years since we became his publisher, we noted how Koukouli had progressed, although it's sad to report that the church was robbed of all its precious icons and relics just before Christmas 2009.

Jannie tells our story. "We went on along the new motorway and turned up to Kastoria on the lake. Now, there's another fabulous place with the old Macedonian mansions restored."

"Jannie, you must one day follow the road on into Albania," suggests Jim. "Berat has beautiful stone castles and Agyrokastro has the same stone buildings and culture as Zagori. But Albanian beaches are already being spoilt by mass tourism. Then you should go on to Ohrid in the Former Yugoslav Republic of Macedonia with its wonderful big monastery."

"So, if you love the mountains so much, why also have a

base in Corfu?"

"Because we both came back to write and we love swimming. In the old days we went all over the island, particularly to Barbati in the north-east and St. George's Bay in the north-west."

"That's exactly what we did in our early days."

"But around a hundred two-storey holiday homes have been built on Barbati, destroying much of that beautiful olive-grove-lined bay in the process," he complains bitterly.

"Jannie is boycotting the owner's supermarket chain in protest!" I say proudly.

Jim continues. "Suprisingly we now enjoy going to Mon Repos beach, even with its beds of poseidonia seaweed, which some swimmers dislike, but which is in fact a good sign of a healthy environment. Oddly enough the sea there seems cleaner than in the 1960s."

"Jim, how is Maria's novel *The Cat of Portovecchio – Corfu Tales*, doing? I found the manuscript very amusing at times, as well as tragic-comic, but all my reading, writing and publishing is non-fiction. That a cat is the main character, and what a character, must be unique in a novel. Being set in the fifties, soon after the Greek Civil War, it also gave me food for thought."

"It has been doing very well with fantastic reviews," says Jim. "It was published in Australia by the distinguished publishers Brandl & Schlesinger. She's also had a novella published, in Greek this time. It's called *To Poulima tis Panoreas (The Pimping of Panorea)*. As the blurb says, it is set 'Somewhere in the Eastern Mediterranean, where the East joins the West, where Christianity walks in parallel with Islam and the deep blue sea is full of grey froth, oil and sewage.'"

"You mean Corfu? Though that's not how I would describe Agios Gordis, which Jannie and I came to in 1966. We still love the 'wild' west coast of our youth," I counter.

"It's a passionate cry of anger, and an allegory about greed and the harm done to the environment of islands like Corfu," Jim explains.

"There must be something about the Ionian islands that gives writers such inspiration: Louis de Bernières in Kefalonia and Emma Tennant and James Chatto here in Corfu." I suggest. "Everyone talks about how much Corfu has changed. Tell me instead: what is unchanged on the island?"

Jim thinks a while and then smiles "The countryside. Walks with Hilary have re-awakened the love of Corfu I had when we drove our Austin A35 along the lanes of the island back in 1967-1968, before we were married. Hilary's fellow walkers are a delight, such diverse nationalities. In spring some of the views are fantastic. I still love Corfu villages even though some have crumbling houses and often ugly new buildings. But sadly, Kassiopi, so beautiful in the 70s, is no longer the same." He pauses and adds "But sometimes we still visit Nissaki, where I lived like a hermit for a month in the summer of 1967."

"Walking through the olive groves is one of the great pleasures of the island. But even they have changed in the last forty years," I suggest sadly.

"For centuries, the trees have never been pruned, unlike in other countries. However, the oil they produced was amongst the best in Greece."

"Which is the best in the world," I boast.

"David Bellamy doesn't agree. He claims his oil from Tuscany is better. You know the derelict building with the tall chimney in Mandouki?"

"The one with AEBEK at the top?"

"That's the one. AEBEK was the name of the company when it closed down in the 1980s. It was founded in 1924 as *Elaiougia Kerkyas AE*. It employed 127 people making oil and soap and was one of the biggest factories in Greece. Sadly, its archives are left rotting in what's left of the place."

"There's still a small olive-oil-soap factory in San Rocco though. But how things have changed," I reminisce sadly. "I remember dozens of girls being brought over from the mainland to join the villagers in picking the olives one by one off the ground after it had been cleared in the autumn."

"Now nets are laid, after the ground has been cleared with chemicals," adds Jim with some regret.

"Jim, you and Marie are obviously very happy in Greece but how do you see your future?"

"You know I could have settled in many of the countries where we were posted such as Sweden and Australia, but I always felt that Corfu was my 'natural home' as well as Maria's real home and birthplace. We couldn't give up Corfu. But I believe one needs a more practical base as one gets older, so we have bought a house in Dorset, in the UK, as we both love the countryside and coastal walks there. So John, it seems we both have the best of both worlds, England and Greece."

My second armchair guests who Jannie and I were to walk with may not have arrived in the 1960s as had Jim, but they have taken the trouble to find out more about the island than almost anyone I know. They have swum off almost every beach, from Lefkimmi in the south-east round to Arillas in the north-west. They have never met any pollution, though on just one occasion Pam was attacked by a shoal of jelly fish.

Peter and Pam Jenkins' story starts in a railway tunnel near Redhill. Having visited many of the Greek islands, they decided to go to Corfu. During the night of the 15th/16th October 1987, with the hurricane flattening the trees of southern England, the train to Gatwick was trapped under the North Downs. The passengers all bedded down on the floor for the night. Eventually the line was cleared, but when they arrived at Gatwick, their plane had already left. Many other holiday makers just gave up and returned home; but not Peter and Pam. Thirty hours later they heard that there were eighteen spare seats on the next flight to Corfu. All the delayed passengers ran for the plane, and Peter and Pam were near the front of the race. They were off to a new life.

They fell in love with the island. Every year they returned, often more than once. They would book the cheapest deal on offer and then stay independently wherever their fancy took them: often in the unspoilt north-west. With Peter driving a hire car and Pam reading the map, they soon knew every lane, beach and village on the island. Interestingly, they avoided the Town; they are country people with a lovely house in the wilds of East Anglia.

A few years ago we met them on one of Hilary's Saturday walks. They said they were looking for a place to make into a holiday home. On arrival, they would buy the *Corfiot* magazine and view the properties on its list. But then they hit a problem: a major difference of opinion.

Pam, the romantic one, had just seen a village house which was just what she wanted. She said that the old lady next door was really friendly and gave her a bunch of grapes.

Peter, the practical one, asked her who would do it up, as it needed a new roof. He preferred a new house in an olive grove which they could just walk into.

She was sure they could get the local builder to build a new roof and that would bring money into the village and make them new friends.

In the end they agreed to defer the decision for another year. After a few such conversations on our walks, I offered to help them. I turned to my good friend, George Grammenos, who owns our local petrol station. In every village there is someone who knows all the local gossip such as land for sale and property on the market. George is just such a person. He knew of a Swedish lady who had beautifully renovated a four-bedroom, two-bathroom village house built in 1831 on the edge of Sinarades, overlooking the countryside yet close to the centre of the village. It was within their budget though too expensive for a local who would anyway prefer to build a new house on a plot outside the village. It was probably not grand enough for an Athenian, who wanted to spend the summer away from the heat of the capital. It was perfect for Peter and Pam.

Pam was happy. With her very limited Greek, she made friends with her neighbours, with their non-existent English. Peter was happy. At breakfast he could sit on the balcony and look over the olive groves towards the neighbouring villages nearby, with the mountains in the distance.

After a few years as villagers, do they still like their house? Pam says that every morning, when she wakes up, she thinks of me! "Buying our house in Sinarades was the best thing I ever did!"

Her neighbours are as friendly as ever: she is now playing cards with them and her poor Greek (or lack of it) has not created barriers. When the neighbours' children arrive from Athens they all go down to the beach together. In fact, Pam and Peter feel almost part of a new family. She phones them from Portugal, where they spend the winter months. There are roars of laughter from the Greek end of the phone. On 23rd June, on one of many festivals celebrated in the village, their neighbours light bonfires and Peter and Pam are invited to jump over them with rest of the family.

A day barely goes by without someone popping in with a little gift: some figs, a few spring onions, a bunch of *horta*, the wild vegetables picked on the road side. They now have several friends in the village, including the taxi driver who picks them up at the airport and always waits for delayed flights. One elderly man explained that Peter and Pam are his friends: "I speak to them every day."

As everyone has accepted them, they don't feel like outsiders. Recently when Pam had to go home for treatment, all the neighbours came to wish her well. When they are away, their garden is watered and their house is looked after; the neighbours have keys.

One could argue that they have been very lucky, but they have made their own luck by being so friendly. Villagers are perhaps more welcoming than in some resorts, where a few locals like the Brits just for their money. Life cannot be easy for the young Greeks, who are often qualified and want jobs. They wait in vain for employment for five or six years then go off to the USA or Australia to get work.

And how is Peter? Not unexpectedly, he has found that even a restored old house can have roof problems. As their old builder has gone back to Albania, he borrowed a long ladder and climbed up to investigate. Following his inspection, the roof now has more broken tiles than ever before; he has never been the best roofer! But he really loves the house and is adding more books to his library, which is a good definition of where he sees his true home. As the years go by, I can see them spending more and more time in Sinarades, as it is ideally placed mid-way up the island, next to some of the best beaches on the island and just fifteen minutes into town and the airport. They still go on picnics to their favourite places, but they now have a home to return to each evening, and a base for their family and friends to visit.

Sinarades is a flourishing village with its own primary school, a successful 80-strong philharmonic orchestra founded in 1960, glorious old alleyways and well-preserved Venetian buildings, plus two fine campaniles.

It is also the destination of tourists including those on an excursion from the many cruise ships that come to Corfu. They visit the 'Historical and Folkloric Museum of Central Corfu', which is housed, on two floors, in a beautiful traditional house right in the centre of the village. Entrance is via a *bodzos*, the uniquely Corfiot small veranda on the first floor accessed up an outside stone stairway.

A pamphlet describes the museum: 'The first floor is a reproduction of a middle-class village home similar to those found between the years 1860-1960 in the villages of Central Corfu. It consists of a porch, the kitchen, dining-room, corridor and bedroom. These have been furnished with the appropriate furniture, and household equipment, so realistically set up that one expects "the mistress of the house" to appear at any moment, and the entire family to welcome you in and offer you refreshments such as coffee with cognac, fig pie with ouzo or a semi-sweet wine, according to the time of day!

'On the second floor there is a study with books and ancient documents. Two steps further up there is a large room where the following are on display: Corfiot holiday costumes and musical instruments, farming tools, hand-grinders and olive measures, lamps and other lighting equipment, weights and scales, Corfiot ceramics, fishing equipment and a children's corner.'

Much of Corfu's musical tradition is built on the village philharmonic orchestras. No words can fully describe the moving Easter procession from Sinarades to our neighbouring village of Kouramades. The photograph on page 44 illustrates the black and yellow bandsmen marching behind the banner showing the miracle of Saint Kassiopias healing a blind boy. On the ground are strewn handfuls of bay leaves. Behind the Philharmonic, the priests are bearing the remains of the saint of the village and leading the villagers. In the background is one of the village's wonderful old houses.

Lovers of tourist destinations, such as Corfu, often have special secrets unknown by visitors. Jannie and I have a particular walk which we will never divulge as it is the most beautiful on the island. Our other, less well-kept secret is *Platopigatho*, a taverna only frequented by locals. Other than Jim Potts, who thought the music was too loud, all our friends have loved this slightly eccentric establishment. There was the evening when we could only have a table in the entrance hallway as the restaurant was technically closed! A party was being held to celebrate the christening of two Albanian children, and what a party it was!

I have great misgivings passing on the location of this wonderful place – it is on the road into the village from Pelekas – but the family want to be host to others than the locals: times are hard in Greece. To get there follow the road from Pelekas to Sinarades and, after the vineyards which are either side of the road, bear right towards the village where the bypass continues straight on. After 100 metres, you will find *Platopigatho* on the right.

Angelis, the 60-year-old owner, director of the Sinarades Philharmonic for 25 years, his wife Eleni, and their children Yiannis and Alexandra are true friends. I hope I am doing the right thing.

Angelis, originally a student of the piano, has been teaching different instruments and theory for most of his life. Alexandra plays the flute in the band. Yiannis, aged 27, has played in the Sinarades Philharmonic since he was 8. He was taught by his father and played cornet in the Navy band during his national service. He loves funk, jazz and classical and is a big fan of Miles Davis. He also plays bassoon. As a pig-tailed student at Larissa College of Music, he also studied botany. In the summer he would swim off the west coast of Corfu to the island of Kiradikaïa, a huge rock with a chapel on top of sheer cliffs. On his head was his camera with which he took photos of unique flowers.

Charles, Rachel and Sydney join us at the taverna on Sydney's last night on the island. Charles, a clarinettist, and Rachel, who plays the viola, are engrossed by the bouzouki player and his instrument. The success of *Platopigatho* is based on the music, which starts at 10.30 p.m. with Angelis playing keyboard, the local villagers who begin dancing at midnight and

Eleni's home-made food. Her starters are delicious: *Spetsofai* from Volos – hot sausage, thinly cut across, in a peppery onion sauce; pork and mushrooms; oven-baked aubergine with gouda; and fried peppers. The main course is grilled meat, with a lamb on the spit standard fare in the summer when we eat outside. An example of the eccentricity of *Platopigatho* is that when the barbecue caught fire, the man in charge simply shrugged his shoulders and opened another beer. The wine is a blend of the excellent local red wine *petrokoritho* and *kakotrygis* or 'hard-to-pick', the standard amber-white of the west coast vineyards.

"*Yiamas*, Sydney. You have been an excellent companion. Come back again. *Kalo taxidi*." And a good journey he has.

Charles and Rachel stay another day. Rachel's patience thoughout the holiday has been exemplary. Now she can be driven round the island and see some of the sights that the boys have. I hope thay will also come back to Corfu.

Autumn – from Agni via Old Perithia to the Trail's end

Flowers 5, Scenery 8, Underdeveloped 4, Challenge 8, Bus 4
See map on page 39.

For those trekking the Corfu Trail, the last day of the official route is gruelling, taking eight hours to walk from the east coast, up Mt. Pantokrator and down to the northernmost point on the island at the lagoon at Agios Spiridon. Starting at Kaminaki they follow along the coast to Agni, where we finished our journey on May 1st. In the *Companion Guide* Hilary describes this in great detail: 'through the pool bar and across the facade of the hotel', 'behind new villas', and so on. The land between the main Kassiopi road and the sea is, indeed, well developed. However, a comparison of photographs taken in 1970 and today suggests it has a long way to go before the north-east looks like Spain! (See page 47.) Walkers then climb up to the High Col of Mt. Pantokrator along the route which we descended. From now on it is mainly down-hill, via the semi-ruined Byzantine village of Old Perithia to which locals and tourists flock to eat excellent food in an almost alpine setting.

Our trusty guide, Edward Lear, recounts his late April 1855 walk: 'After a latish breakfast we set out [from Serpa?] to go to the top of San Salvador (Mt. Pantocrator). The first part of the way was truly lovely from the wild flowers, so fresh after the rain, but the ascent of the mountain, the highest in Corfu, was tiresome, & did not repay the trouble, though the view is very extensive, & towards Albania beautiful. We got down to another harbour . . . called Kassiopi, the scenery about which is delightful'.

Serpa is a place-name no longer used. It is however the name of the rock in the middle of the Corfu Channel. Lear implies it is a harbour, therefore it was probably San Stephanos. His walk right to the top of the Mt. Pantokrator and down again offers a challenge to tourists staying in this lovely secluded bay but it should be undertaken 'after a latish breakfast', not after a latish night before!

In May 1862, Lear wrote about the north-east of the island: 'How gladly one would linger in the beautiful calm & opal colour of that coast, & yet to pass months in it would seem hardly to compensate for the pain of weary island prison life'.

Flower lovers will find *sternbergia* on the mountain in the autumn. This golden-yellow flower looks like a crocus but is a member of the daffodil family.

My plan for the autumn was to divide the final day of the official Corfu Trail into two sections. The first, taking two and a half hours, would be from Tritsi, one kilometre from Porta, up to the High Col and then descending to Old Perithia for an extremely long lunch with dear friends Judy Mackrel and Mitzi. The second day a walk of three hours would be after another excellent lunch at Old Perithia to the end of the Trail.

Today, as my heel is still playing up, we miss out all the hard part, the walk, so Jannie and I meet Judy and Mitzi at the Taverna Ognistra, the first on the left of four excellent tavernas as one enters Old Perithia. The weather is perfect, which is often the case in October, so we eat out in the sun with lovely views all round. In winter we retreat inside and snuggle up in front of a beautiful fireplace.

The length of lunch in Corfu is usually related to the company and the ambience rather than the quantity of food. Let me describe our wonderful meal before introducing my 'armchair walkers'.

To reach Old Perithia we have had to drive north to the far side of Mt. Pantokrator, either via Kassiopi or Acharavi, as the only access to the village is from the north coast. As a result, we are late. Judy and Mitzi are already enjoying a half-litre of the excellent local red wine and nibbling slices of *nouboulo*, which is a slightly salty and smoky loin of pork. After our arrival, this is accompanied by *neratzosalata*, a salad of tart oranges, dressed with salt, sugar, paprika and oil.

We share a couple of plates of *tsigarelli*, which can taste hot or extremely hot. Two portions of *sofrito*, a delicious veal stew slowly cooked in a thick sauce of white wine and loads of garlic, follow.

To finish, our host produces a dessert plate of *Sikopita* (fig pie made with ouzo and honey), *Karidopita* (walnut pie) and strawberry pie plus a delicious yoghurt, honey and cherry concoction.

Jannie and I have been good friends with Judy since 1970 when she ran the Avis car rental for George Manessis, who more than anyone else maintained our love for the island through good and bad times.

Judy recalls George asking her on her first day at work in Town, "Can you manage?"

"George," she replied, "if I can manage 500 cars at Heathrow Airport, I can manage 40 cars in Corfu."

After five years she joined Gerald Durrell at his Zoo in Jersey. "The zoo was already well established," Judy tells us. "I was particularly fascinated by the primates: the Western Lowland gorillas from Central Africa had been at the zoo since its opening in 1959 and an orang-utan family had arrived from Sumatra a number of years before I joined. Gerald was also working with the Macaques or 'Black Apes' from the Celebes in Indonesia. All of these are critically endangered species."

"And his love for animals started on Corfu!" I muse.

"The highlight of my time in Jersey was when the Spectacle Bear became pregnant. These are the only bears that live in the southern hemisphere, coming from the Andes. With white fur around their eyes, they are called Spectacle because they look as though they are wearing glasses. Anyway, Gerald locates a handsome male, who proceeds to do his job. Our lady now disappears for four months to everyone's concern. At the critical moment, I was there when she gave birth. Absolutely amazing!"

"We remember you back in Corfu at the end of the 1970s, Judy," says Jannie happily. "You used to come to our rundown summer-house and we would all swim at Agios Gordis."

"Soon after that, probably in 1983, I obtained a Travel Agents Licence. I rented out ten apartments in Nissaki."

"Happy days! We first went there in 1966 with George. What a spot, a little shingle strip in the harbour. We used to order lunch, go for a swim and then be called in when the food was served." I have fond memories of this idyllic bay surrounded by hills covered in olive groves.

"In our early days there," Judy continues, "it was so busy that tourists would book their table at the taverna on the quay in advance. In 1979, I bought my first little house at Tritsi, my insurance policy you might say; I thought of calling it Pension Cottage! I bought a second house in 1983 and then Mitzi bought one in 1987. We let these throughout the summer and we were always full; probably 80% were returns and new clients always came by word-of-mouth."

"So what was your secret?" I ask.

"Tritsi is high up from the coast between St. Stephano and Agni, where there are now many expensive villas. It's a perfect place to chill-out. Our clients would organise their own flights but our local taxi driver met them at the airport. There was a hamper in the fridge when they arrived."

Jannie laughs. "It sounds like Australia. John, do you remember the Vineyard Motel in Chardonnay Road?"

"With a bottle of Chardonnay in the fridge."

"I'm not sure one could build up such a successful business these days," Judy continues, with concern. "Now ex-pats buy a bar, open for business, but they are not registered so they fall flat on their faces. My advice is to know the ropes before starting on a commercial venture in Corfu."

"It's pretty tough now that cheap all-inclusives have opened up and their clients stay in their hotel," I suggest.

"It's bad for employment as well," agrees Judy. "Top-class waiters are just handing out drinks; they no longer have time to chat with their clients. They are proud; so they just pack up and their job is taken by someone from Bulgaria or elsewhere in the Balkans who will work for less. It's like the early days of Butlins: happy campers and announcements over the tannoy. Just look at St. Spyridon where a beautiful beach has been destroyed and the tavernas at each end of the bay are empty."

"So what does your taxi driver think of proposals that the airport should be moved to Lefkimmi right down in the south?"

"The taxi costs would be astronomical. It would be absolutely disastrous for the north-east. But I can't see it happening, though the airport probably doesn't meet international standards as it is."

"Tell me, Judy, what is the best place that your clients can go to when they are here?"

"To Albania. Butrint is absolutely wonderful. I have been taking groups from the Durrell School there. Everyone is fascinated by their day. Its urbanisation is a bit out-of-control though. Saranda, which is the main coastal town in the Greek-speaking south of the country, used to be ten socialist-era blocks of apartments. Now there are vast numbers of unfinished blocks. It is an example of how Corfu has not developed. The old town of Cukë, just south of Saranda, is really worth visiting."

It's sad that people are more inclined to take a boat to Albania than explore the lovely island they live on!

"The Club Med has pulled out of a project just across from Corfu," I point out.

"They've had a five year battle and there are still disputes over land ownership, so they've packed in the project," says Judy. "It seems that everyone was claiming bits of land!"

At that moment some friends of Judy pass by and tell us that their walk over from Porta took just an hour and a half. They were on their way back after a good lunch! Their description of the trip was even better than Edward Lear's.

"She's the wife of the silversmith and sculptor in the town's old Jewish Quarter. Visitors don't realise what wonderful silver-working skills are here on the island. It is the same with lace. Old ladies still make it in Kassiopi for shops in Campielo," Judy explains with great enthusiasm.

Judy and Mitzi will soon be retiring.

"What will retirement be like in Corfu?" I ask.

"Thank goodness we still have our flat in London. You know, John, there is a tragedy building up: elderly ex-pats on diminishing pensions are finding it difficult to live here. The main problem has been the collapse of the pound against the euro. Medical treatment, however, is very reasonable. A consultant cardiologist in a clinic charges just €80 for an ultra-sound and an ECG. The Paleokastritsa clinic recently gave a friend three ultra-sounds; it cost only €200. We have some wonderful doctors in the hospitals but there are too few nurses. Greek patients rely on their family."

Retirement can be tough but it has its advantages: Judy and Mitzi will have more time, and they promise to come and stay with us on the west coast.

The final guest walker on this wonderful journey was to be Hilary's co-founder of the Corfu Trail, Fried Aumann. The original plan was to meet at Old Perithia for lunch and then stagger in celebration down to the north coast. Last year, Fried, Hilary, Dierk, Christine and a large contingent of local hikers had enjoyed a Saturday walk down the Corfu Trail for about an hour towards Krinias, and then across wild country to Loutses, where some of our cars had been left so that we could return by the main road. Fried had been scathing as the first kilometre of our walk had been widened by the local *Dimos* to become a 'tourist trail'. Our yellow waymarks had been replaced by rather hideous signs, and a portaloo had been erected at the end of their trail. He doubted, probably with some justification, whether the path would be maintained. Hilary's party continued down a very narrow path beside a gully through dense forest. After crossing the Parigori River, we set off to the right through deep jungle. I secretly questioned whether I preferred the widened path or this tough trail, which should not be attempted without a guide or excellent instructions. Along the route, blue waymarks had been painted; this was one of many local walks Fried had created and maintained in the spectacular countryside behind his base at Acharavi.

At the end of our walk, the Saturday walkers drove back to Old Perithia for the relaxed meal which follows Hilary's expeditions. The less able walkers had spent their couple of hours inspecting the derelict village of Old Perithia, having a coffee or two and ambling along sensible tracks. We all met up at Foros Taverna, which makes superb traditional Greek pies. Hilary always finds somewhere special to eat: on one occasion, in Porta, we had gorged ourselves on thick bean soup into which we put chunks of raw onion! After a tough walk, this tasted much better than it sounds,

In late October, at the end of the tourist season, with now no excuse for another lunch at Old Perithia, Jannie and I drive to meet Fried at his St. George's Bay Country Club (and home of the Rotary Club of North Corfu). This two-storey development of traditional Corfiot architecture surrounds mature gardens with a large pool set amongst palm trees. Free-range bantam chickens wander in the bushes. It is located at the Almiros end of Acharavi, the commercial centre of north Corfu, mid-way along a seven-kilometre shallow golden sand beach. The views are staggering: to the north-east are the Albanian mountains and to the north-west are Erikousa and Othoni.

Inside the main building there is an open-plan luxury lounge with an automatic grand piano playing. The well-stocked library has many books in German, with fewer in English, as only 10% of Fried's guests are from the UK. The complex consists of 86 spacious and elegant rooms and suites for 2–4 persons, with many overlooking the sea. He offers either bed and breakfast or half-board as he hopes his guests will explore the island and local tavernas.

A separate spa complex contains a half-Olympic-length 25m salt-water infinity pool and nearby saunas, showers and resting rooms. The pool has a retracting roof for all-year-round use. Next year he plans to open the hotel for weekends out of season. I can see a combined walking and spa winter holiday becoming a favourite.

The facilities he provides include a large Jacuzzi, biosauna, nordic sauna, steam grotto (for asthma and bronchitis) and tepidarium (at 45C for arthritis and rheumatism).

The treatments offered include Western and Eastern massage, Shiatsu, Ayurveda, Kneipp (to improve blood circulation), Schiele, thalasso, mud, beauty treatments, manicure, pedicure, hamam and rasul.

The sea-water pool is heated to 28C geo-thermally and chemicals are kept to a minimum. Fried has justified the cost of the installation on the grounds that electricity will become more expensive. It is heavily subsidised in Greece and he suggests the EU will eventually stop this subsidy.

Fried Aumann first came to Corfu from Rhodesia in the 1950s. He bought a large beach-side property in 1969, when hotels were either A class or De Luxe, that is 4 and 5 star. Up-market tourists used to come for May and June and then September and October, staying away in July and August as the hotels were not air-conditioned. Teachers and others who were less wealthy and who were prepared to bear the heat would come in July and August. In those days, passengers from cruise ships would be taken along olive-tree-lined country roads which, he pointed out, have now been widened, and become industrial zones. He was repeating the point made by the President of Corfu Travel Agents, Dimitris Charitos, in my interview after Day 2 of our spring journey.

Fried started building in 1978 and opened in 1980. Slowly, he has developed a very high quality country club and last year he launched the Spa which is open all year round.

"Jannie and I have just had a look at the Spa. It is fantastic and during the winter when the sea is cold, I reckon we would occasionally make the trip north for a long swim in the heated pool," I tell him enthusiastically.

"But will you get enough locals coming?" queries Jannie in her sensible way.

"I hope so. We already offer a deal on Saturdays and Sundays in partnership with the Invisible Kitchen," Fried replies. "But I am planning for the long term. In the future I see the tourist season being extended; we will then be popular in the late and early season with our heated pool and spa. It is also the best time of year for walkers. Our current clients are very keen on the many trails I have marked in the area."

"Your problem will be the total lack of direct flights out of season," I argue.

"That's true, yet in the winter, 15 German airports fly direct to Majorca and pensioners can fly from the UK direct to Portugal and Spain."

"The result has been overdevelopment. Maybe in Corfu we should be concentrating on harvesting the olives in winter!" I argue.

"I don't see package holidays to Corfu in the winter; too much is closed. But we still need direct flights for independent travellers. Back in the 1970s, the BEA/Olympic partnership flew on Sundays from Athens to Heathrow via Corfu, all year round. Last year there were four charters over Christmas; now there will be only one. EasyJet promised to fly year-round but they say that since the economic downturn they cannot afford to do so. German Greeks from Ipiros used to fly to Corfu from Dusseldorf which had a low budget connection with Luton. Now they take the ferries from Venice or Ancona. Then there were to be flights from Milan's Bergamo Airport, with air connections from northern Europe and easy access by car from Switzerland. It took only an hour to fly to Corfu, but the airline went bust. At least Aegean now flies twice daily from Heathrow to Athens with luggage checked through."

"Fried, it's worse than you suggest. The season is getting shorter each year. Tour operators have cut out April altogether, and the season down in Kavos is now only just four months long."

"But tour operators still go to Dodecanese and Crete seven months of the year. Maybe the answer for Corfu is to get rid of cheap tourism as it leaves so little money on the island. We should be encouraging new tourism, such as walkers. You must see the new Avlaki to St. Stephano walk; that's what we must offer." Fried laughs. "But the Corfiots have yet to get the message. I know that for the average walker I am expensive, so I have told other hotels they could be picking up some new clients. Do you know what they say? 'If they walk, it's because they can't afford a car!'"

It's not really funny, but Jannie does giggle at this suggestion.

"Future tourists will be young: they book direct by internet, but the Greeks do not look at their emails or reply to fax enquiries once the season is over! I deal with small tour operators like Sunvil; they email me special instructions and I always reply. The quality villa rental companies such as CV and Meon do the same. Nathan of Agni Travel has built himself a niche market and also gives an excellent service. But

Simply Ionian has been bought by First Choice and has become a mass-market operation."

"And what are your views on the all-inclusives?" I ask, remembering Dimitris Charitos' comments about those in the Acharavi area.

"Take a small family hotel which offers cheap holidays. Their prices are based on taverna prices, that is, dinner at €15, breakfast at €8 and bed for €25. They are sold by tour operators, after their mark-up, for €65. An all-inclusive charges €27 and they are sold for €50. The small hotels can agree a lower price to compete with the major all-inclusive, but then they go bust. Sadly, all small hotels in Acharavi are either empty or occupied by Albanians. However, the best all-inclusives will be taken over by Aquis and moved up-market with more realistic prices."

"So what work do the Albanians get?"

"Albanians are excellent gardeners as they work non-stop for long hours. And then there are the Bulgarians who as ex-communists were trained to be proper waiters. The hotels don't want Greek waiters any more as they give the customers a card for the family taverna and they are not as well trained."

"Fried, you paint a very depressing picture. Where did it start to go wrong?"

"In the early days of charters they always included bed and breakfast, which was good for the small places and good for the local tavernas. Then the EU said operators must offer flight only, which of course was good for independent travellers. This cut the prices so low that only the big companies like Thomson benefited as they could buy flights and accommodation in bulk, and sell flight-only deals as well. This moved the tourists business down market. The poor hotels were also at their mercy as the big companies could cancel their contract if other destinations, such as Turkey, became cheaper."

"So, tell me, what is the solution for Corfu?" I ask,

beginning to doubt whether there was one.

"I believe the Ministry of Tourism, now Tourism and Culture, must develop a long-term plan for tourism. So far each new government announces new goals for tourism. There is no continuity. They announce over and over again that the aim is for 5-star tourists and 5-star hotels in 5-star resorts. But in a country with 1-star infrastructure this is impossible and demanding customers are not happy. There should be destinations earmarked for western tourists and others for Russians and locals. In Corfu we must move the market up again. We must sell the island's assets: the countryside, the Corfu Trail and the fabulous Old Town. Sooner or later aircraft fuel will be fully taxed. This will benefit short-haul holidays to the Med, and make sense environmentally."

Fried is now talking my language. "This brings us to my favourite subject: your energy efficient establishment."

"Let me explain. The sea-water spa pool uses geo-thermal heat. Two wells were dug into the sea-water strata at 161 m. It now seeps higher and we pump from 60m and possibly 40m in the future. In Crete, it is only 25m. The water, which is always at 16C, enters the heat pump which works like an air-condition unit in reverse, reducing the heat from the seawater in order to increase the temperature of the pool to a constant 28C. It then returns the now colder seawater into the ground. We also get warm water for the laundry and central heating in winter."

"Is this cheaper than using gas or electricity?" I ask, making copious notes of all the figures.

"Electricity prices in Greece are relatively low, as we import it from Albania and from atomic powered stations in Bulgaria. We also get cheap Russian gas, because of a deal to allow gas pipes through Northern Greece. One of the results of cheap electricity is waste. Locally in the winter there is a community with two residents which has 200 street lights, 20 metres apart, whereas in Athens they would be 50 metres apart. The shops here are closed for the winter but still have their neon signs on."

"What about wind-turbines to generate electricity?" Fried is really firing me up!

"Wind energy has been a disaster because of the politicians. They are scared of the 'not in my back yard' types. However, a Hamburg-trained engineer, with a German manufacturer's sponsorship, is providing, with help from the navy, turbines for 'remote islands'. Then we are implementing the law from Brussels which forces electricity companies to buy wind power. A German company has long been testing the potential for wind-turbines on the Mt. Pantokrator range, but it cannot get turbines blades through the narrow streets in the villages. I've asked them why they don't lift them by helicopter from Barbati? There is so much red tape in Greece: perhaps younger ministers will tackle the problems. Italy needs electricity and hopes for solar power from North Africa, which we will be able to plug into. But this is 30 years away."

"Finally, what are your views on the Lefkimmi airport?" I ask.

"I don't think it will ever be built. Under present conditions, its effect on the north of the island would be catastrophic. Therefore lately they talk about a double-pack of a new airport in the Lefkimmi area and an express highway from there to the north. It will take 20 minutes from the new airport to Corfu Town and another 20 minutes from Town to Acharavi. But who is expected to pay for this? Corfu is too small for a toll-highway and airport that are financed and run privately. Just the expropriation of the land needed would take decades. And hopefully the EU will not waste more taxpayers' money. Now that the cheap traffic is moving to destinations outside Euroland the existing airport would suffice, provided it is privately run and automatic landing facilities are installed."

Fried Aumann has delivered a lot for our lovely island,

which he cherishes. Thanks to his hard work, in conjunction with Hilary, the Corfu Trail will be very much enjoyed by future walkers. I hope these walkers will also visit his fabulous spa, which deserves all our support.

The British legacy:
orchids, cricket and Mon Repos

In this chapter, there are three walks with connections to the British rule of the Ionian Islands from 1814 to 1864. Our presence was unlike many others in our imperial past – we left without a fight. In 1797, Napoleon defeated the Venetian Republic and annexed the islands. In November 1815, the Treaty of Paris was signed whereby the Ionian Islands became 'a single, free and independent state under the protection of His Britannic Majesty'. In 1859, William Gladstone, who was a philhellene and at that moment out of office, became Lord High Commissioner but failed to persuade the islanders that a reform programme was the solution to the problems which had built up in the islands. They demanded union with Greece. On June 2nd 1864 the British departed.

The first walk is to the British Cemetery, home to memories of the British who ruled the islands and to the many who fell in love with and then settled in Corfu. It is also home to the most remarkable collection of orchids, growing wild amongst the tombstones.

Starting at San Rocco Square, one should walk south-west along Mitropoleos Methediou, a busy one-way street with traffic moving very slowly towards the square. After 300 metres, at the end of the road, turn hard left along Kolokotoni towards the prison. The British cemetery is 100 metres on the left.

Much of the following information comes from George Psailas who, born in the gatehouse of the cemetery in 1927, became its gardener in 1944 and is now the caretaker. Interestingly, he holds a British passport as his family was from Gozo in Malta; the Maltese were excellent stonemasons and built the fountains on the Esplanade. They also grew vegetables in the area to the west of the airport and were good jewellers.

For his services he has been awarded the British Empire Medal.

The British cemetery is on the site of the Nekropolis of Paleopolis, the Old Town in which graves date back to the 7th century BC. In 1946, aged just 19, George had to deal with the aftermath of the Corfu Channel Incident, in which 46 British sailors died when two Royal Navy destroyers hit mines off the coast of Albania. Twelve of the sailors are buried in the Cemetery, whilst the names of others whose bodies were never recovered are inscribed on a memorial.

In his *The Foreigners' Garden* George wrote:

'If all people loved flowers, we would never have wars. It may seem incredible, but it is very true. For 67 years I have been living, night and day, in a piece of land where our beloved persons rest for ever in peace, without disturbing anyone, without claiming anything. However, the nature, "mother earth" offers them its best jewel, the various flowers of the seasons: spring with its windflowers orchids, little daisies and iris; and autumn with its cyclamen, saffrons, snowdrops, and many others.

'Therefore I decided to leave a souvenir celebrating the anniversary of my 50 years of service, dedicating this little booklet to a small and neglected flower: the wild orchid.

'It is really wonderful to live, winter through summer, in the country and walk on the mountains, in the valleys and vales, to see the green changing with the seasons.

'It is wonderful to admire the natural colours changing in the leaves of the trees in autumn and becoming red, yellow or brown, and in spring the variety of little wild flowers with their live colours, etc.

'The loveliest thing in the world is the flower. I spent my 67 years of life in an earthly green paradise, in a peaceful corner very close to the town of Corfu.

'Don't look for beauty anywhere else. Go around this island of Corfu and there it is. Corfu has everything. Unfortunately, due to the great development of the island, we unwillingly destroy and make many wild flowers species disappear, especially the wonderful and rare wild orchids.

'Out of 200 orchid species found in Europe, 90 or 100 can be found in Greece (book *Anast. Alkimos*) 50 species can be found in Corfu (book, *Dirk Kapteyn den Boumeester u E. Willing*) out of which 30 are in the British Cemetery Corfu. Moreover, there are some more species deriving from cross-breeding. The wild orchids are not as big as the tropical ones and their flowers are not as large. However, they can fascinate you with their colour, the variety of forms and their natural scent.

'The wild orchids which can be found in the British Cemetery of Corfu blossom approximately by the end of February with *barlia robertiana* and end by the beginning of June with *anacamptis pyramidilis v. brachystachys.*'

'Though it is for the orchids that naturalists will make the journey, it is for the peace of this little corner of England that all should come. It is hidden throughout the year in its extraordinary vegetation: its extremely tall cypresses, some more than 150 years old: the beautiful and rare Californian Sequoias; arroquarias, Jacarandas and various cactus. The glades contain a mass of flowers such as seasonal hyacinths, tulips, amaryllis, agapanthus, anemones, Easter lilies, cyclamens and finely-scented snowdrops.'

In the chapter on flowers there is a full list of the orchids to be found in the cemetery.

On your return to the centre of the town, cross over San Rocco Square and turn left 120 metres along G. Theotoki, the main shopping street, where it becomes semi-pedestrianised, into the street to the market. Almost immediately on your right is Rouvas, the place where the locals go for lunch. Rick Stein in *Mediterranean Escapes* refers to this excellent little restaurant where he chose the rabbit *stifado* and *pastitsio* for his recipe book. The team, between a visit to the British

Cemetery and a coffee on the Liston before a cricket match on the Esplanade, enjoyed cuttlefish, *soupia*, slowly cooked in tomato and onion sauce; *pastitsio*, a beef and macaroni pie with cinnamon, red wine and *kefalotiri* cheese; large meatballs; and a typical vegetable dish made by adding artichokes, peas, a few small carrots and dill to fried finely chopped onions and garlic.

Our second walk is to watch the cricket. One could take the direct route along the pedestrianised part of the main shopping street, through Voulgareos in the Old Town to the Liston, a distance of 400 metres. Alternatively walk in a northerly direction through the market for 200 metres and turn right under the walls of the New Fort and enter the Old Town at Solomos Street. Walk to the Liston either from the Old Port around *Mourayia* and through the British Palace of St. Michael and St. Peter; or via the Orthodox Cathedral and the Church of the island's patron saint Agios Spiridon; or directly via the main tourist street Nikiforou Theotoki, and M. Tourmougolou, the best bookseller in town. This cannot be missed as it is on the north side of the street at number 47, under the arches and sculpted heads of the keystones of the House of Daniel Cobici which was built in 1680. George has in stock most books on Corfu including *Corfu Sketches*, which describes five walks through the historic centre of the town showing where Theresa Nicholas made her beautiful watercolours and sketches.

These days, cricket is rarely played on the Esplanade in front of the Liston, as much of it has been turned into a carpark, though traditionally Wednesday afternoon, a half-day as in the UK, was the time for a match. Matches started at 3 p.m. and were for 33 overs per side. The photo on page 48 shows Lib-Dem Lord Tim Razzall bowling from the Palace end against Gymnastikos, the Corfiot equivalent to 'Gentlemen' on May 2nd 2009. The result was a tie.

The first recorded match was in 1823 and the game would have been played throughout the British Protectorate by members of the garrison. It has been played ever since by Corfiot and visiting teams. Within minutes of our arrival in Corfu in 1966, we were taken for breakfast on the Liston. In my book *Greek Walls* I wrote:

'Here (on the Esplanade) we parked.

"This is where we play cricket and over there is where we'll have breakfast," said Theodore.

"The ground looks too rough to play cricket on," I said.

"That's how we like it," he said with a huge laugh. "There are always small stones under the matting. We have very accurate bowlers; they know where the stones are."

Seeing my surprise he continued with a wicked grin. "If we bat first, we take it very slowly, *siga siga* as we say in Greek. Then when the other team bats, it gets dark and the lights of cars sometimes dazzle our opponents."

The Corfiots were clearly a cunning race.'

In John Forte's book *Play's The Thing* (Darf Publishers, 1988), he translates a few common cricket expressions into Greek:

Bails	*Rollinia* (from the Italian)
Batsman	*Batsman*
Batting side	*Pano* (from the Greek 'up')
Bowler	*Bollerr*
Caught	*Apo Psila* (literally ' from on high')
Not out	*Ochi* (Greek 'no') *sotto* (Italian 'under')
Out	*Ow'dat* (applied both to the appeal and the umpire's response to it)
Stump	*Xylo* (Greek 'wood')
Wide	*Wide*

In recent years, the state of the outfield has progressed from lethal to extremely slow as winter rain and summer watering has turned the field into a meadow. If you are lucky enough to witness this English pastime, sit in front of the Liston, order a *tsintsibirra,* a ginger beer, close your eyes, and listen to the sound of ball hitting willow and sometimes ball hitting parked car.

The third walk, at the end of an energetic day, is to the Mon Repos Palace. Walk south from the cricket past the fountains, the Victorian bandstand and the recently refurbished memorial to Sir Thomas Maitland, the first Lord High Commissioner of the Ionian Islands. Follow Garitsa Bay until the complex set of traffic lights, which are so complicated that they have only flashed amber since they were installed, and then walk straight on along the one-way street towards Kanoni. The entrance to Mon Repos is across the junction where the Kanoni road comes in from the right and leaves as a one-way street towards the Mon Repos Beach to the left.

The grounds of the Palace overlook the sea and are worth wandering through to the southern end and the Spring of Kardakis, whose waters, when drunk, are said to guarantee that the visitor will return to the island. In the first chapter there was mention of the *Guardian* article which claimed that the Palace had 'been allowed to fall into disrepair'. It has now been restored to its original beauty. A little trip into Greek history explains how this misunderstanding could have arisen.

In 1828, the second Lord High Commissioner, Sir Frederick Adams, built this perfectly-proportioned neo-classical Regency summer palace for his Greek wife. In 1864, after the cession of Corfu to Greece, it was given to the Danish King George 1st of Greece and was used as the Royal Summer Palace – Prince Philip, Duke of Edinburgh, was born there in 1921 – until King Constantine was forced to abdicate by the Colonels in 1967 after initially collaborating with them. The 1974 referendum, which changed Greece to a republic, left Mon Repos in limbo, a relic of the *ancien régime*, and over the years it fell into serious decay.

In 2001, the Palace was renovated at the cost of €1 million, partly funded by the EU. Perhaps the *Guardian* was writing about the Palace pre-2001 and failed to check on how it is now.

A better explanation is that they based their story on a BBC interview with the leader of the Corfu Independence Party who was showing the world a little chapel in the grounds of the Palace which indeed has fallen into disrepair – like the Taxiarchis chapel on Mount Mt. Pantokrator. In both cases, their congregations no longer exist: the King and Queen have been exiled abroad; the pilgrims to the Mt. Pantokrator Monastery, who stopped off at Taxiarchis, now go by car. For lovers of church architecture, the good news is that the Ministry of Culture is preparing the necessary studies for the restoration of the chapel.

In conclusion, dear reader, please visit the restored Palace and enjoy the museum which presents a view of the time when the house was built and also shows how Corfu has developed from antiquity – the Palace is on an archaeological site – to the present.

Past the entrance to Mon Repos is the road to Analipsis, from where Edward Lear sketched the olive groves descending to the sea, with Garitsa Bay and the Old Fort beyond. Today, from north-facing common land, one can still savour his delight, particularly in the winter when the mountains of Albania and the Greek mainland are snow-capped in the far distance. In May 1862 he wrote: 'Then to the hill of Analipsis: the view is the most pleasing hereabouts, & were there well-drawn figures, it would be beautiful, at sunset especially, when the mountains, by many detail-shadows, lose much of their wall-like form'. Sadly 'that beautiful village of Analipsis with its little cottages' no longer has 'its scattered sheep, with kids and calfs round the door'. Instead it has modern four-storey apartment blocks.

I think I can agree with him when he writes: 'After such evenings in Corfu what is left as to beauty of outer life?' I also endorse his description of 'rose & crimson evenings; lilac & silver mornings'.

To experience such an evening, return from the Mon Repos Palace along the one-way street past the Mon Repos Beach and relax at *Nautilus* on the southern tip of Garitsa Bay, whilst the sun sinks behind the town across the bay.

aceras anthropophorum
Man Orchid

ophrys apifera
Bee Orchid

ophrys ferrum equinum
Horseshoe Orchid

ophrys lutea minor

241

orchis italica
Italian Man Orchid

orchis laxiflora
Jersey or Lax-coloured Orchid

orchis morio
Green Winged Orchid

orchis provincialis
Provence Orchid

orchis quadripunctata
Four Spotted Orchid

serapias vomeracea
Long Lipped Serapias

ophrys bombyliflora
Bumble Bee Orchid

ophrys tenthredinifera
Sawfly Orchid

calystegia soldanella
Sea Bindweed

convolvulus altheoides
Mallow-leaved Bindweed

alkanna tinctoria
Alkanet

anchusa azurea
Large-blue Alkanet

orobanche arenaria
Sand Broomrape

orobanche lavandulacea
Lavender Broomrape

orobanche crenata
Bean Broomrape

smyrnium rotundifolium

pallenis spinosa

galactites tomentosa
Galactites

tragopogon porrifolius
Salsify

crepis rubra
Pink Hawksbeard

scrophularia perigrina
Nettle-leaved Figwort

bellardia trixago
Bellardia

geranium asphodeloides

geranium pyrenaicum
Pyrennean Cranesbill

iris germanica florentina
Tall Bearded Iris, German Iris

gladiolus illyricus

ephedra fragilis
Joint Pine

fritillaria graeca thesala

muscari comosum
Tassel Hyacinth

allium trifoliatum

lamium bifidum

stachys triloba

249

quercus ilex
Holm Oak

cercis siliquastrum
Judas Tree

vicia benghalensis
Reddish Tufted Vetch

pisum sativum
Garden Pea

medicago marina
Sea Medick

lychnis viscaria
Red German Catchfly

saponaria calabrica
Calabrian Soapwort

glaucium flavum
Yellow Horned Poppy

cistus monspeliensis
Narrow-leaved Cistus

valeriana tuberosa

lunaria annua
Honesty

Unidentified orchid

Day 3 – Korission sand dunes

Day 3 – cliffs north of Alonaki Bay

Day 3 – inland towards Mt. Ag. Mattheos

Day 5 – Marmaro Hills

Day 5 – Marmaro Hills on sunny day

Day 8 – karst plateau

Day 8 – High Col below Mt. Pantokrator

Day 8 – above Mengoulas

Flowers

Today Jannie and I are in a valley in the Cotswolds. It is early February, when all sane gardeners are resting. From beside the stream which runs through his garden, Sydney appears in his Wellington boots with a hand-trowel in one hand and a basket full of weeds in the other. Well, I think they are weeds. He is already preparing for the weekend in June when he opens his garden to the public.

Over a strong cup of tea, he tells me how he has analysed, then sorted into family order, over 700 photos of flowers I had taken in Corfu. He has then selected the best photo for each of 150 different flowers into 'Best of Breed'. Finally he has chosen the best 48 to appear in the book including an orchid on page 252 which he would like a reader to identify!!

I ask him to sum up his thoughts about Corfu flowers.

"They are magnificently abundant," he claims. "I was expecting less profusion."

"Have you any complaints?" I ask jokingly.

There is a very long pause. "Yes, I was expecting more species not found in England!" There is no response to that.

The topology of the island of Corfu can be simplified to a high mountain ridge across the north and a lower range down the west coast and hilly country on the east.

Mt. Pantokrator, at 911 metres, is at the east end of the ridge. It is surrounded on its west side by a karst plateau and falls steeply to the sea on its south-east side. The west end of the ridge is no higher than 500 metres.

The west coast range of mountains rises to between 350 and 450 metres and falls quickly into the sea. Under the top soil is a layer of clay, which is slippery when wet and can cause landslides. In the south west a stretch of coastal sand dunes is followed by sandstone cliffs rising to 130 metres.

Olive groves cover the island up to 500 metres. Therefore the terrain is not very varied, with exceptions being the karst plateau in the north-east and the sand-dunes in the south-west. The same flowers can be found in abundance across the island with different species and varieties also to be found on the plateau and in the dunes.

Flowers are mainly in bloom from March to early June, and again in September and October.

The flowers are listed below in family order with orchids first. This is because they abound all over the island. Of special interest is the British Cemetery which contains over 30 different orchids which are marked * and are indexed 901+. Images of these are available on the internet. Seven photos of orchids were taken by Professor Rob Kesseler in the centre of the island near his home. These are numbered 990+. His books include *The Bizarre and Incredible World of Plants*; *Pollen – the Hidden Sexuality of Flowers*; *Seeds – Time Capsules of Life*; *Fruit – Edible, Inedible, Incredible* (published by Papadakis Publishers). Columns are:

W the index to the flower in www.corfuflowers.com.

D the day we saw the flower. (C cemetery, K Kesseler)

P the page number in the book's photograph section.

W	D	P	ORCHID FAMILY
694	8	241	*aceras anthropophorum* (Man Orchid) *
901			*anacamptis pyramidalis* (Pyramidal Orchid) *
			anacamptis pyramidalis var. brachystachys *
902			*barlia robertiana* (Giant Orchid) *
903			*cephalanthera longifolia* (Narrow Leaved Helleborine) *
904			*dactylorhiza romana* (Roman Orchid) *
			dactylorhiza sulphurea.s.pseudosambucina *
905			*epipactis helleborine* (Broad Leaved Helleborine) *
906			*limodorum abortivum* (Violet Bird's Nest Orchid) *

907			*neotinea maculata* (Dense Flowered Orchid) *
795	C	241	*ophrys apifera* (Bee Orchid) *
703	8		*ophrys argolica*
908			*ophrys bertolonii* (Bertolini's Bee Orchid) *
991	K	243	*ophrys bombyliflora* (Bumble Bee Orchid) *
909			*ophrys carmeli ssp attica* *
154	K	241	*ophrys ferrum equinum* (Horseshoe Orchid) *
			ophrys ferrum equinum ssp gottfriediana *
			ophrys ferrum equinum Monstrosity *
910			*ophrys fusca* (Sombre Bee Orchid) *
911			*ophrys helenae* *
707	8		*ophrys lutea* (Yellow Bee Orchid) *
700	8		*ophrys lutea ssp. melena* *
			ophrys lutea ssp. lallilea sup. murbeckii *
139	K	241	*ophrys lutea minor*
924			*ophrys reinholdii* (Reinhold's Bee Orchid) *
912			*ophrys scolopax* (Woodcock Orchid) *
			ophrys scolopax ssp attica *
			ophrys scolopax ssp cornuta *
777	C		*ophrys scolopax heldreichi*
913			*ophrys sphegodes* (Early Spider Orchid) *
80	5		*ophrys sphegodes mammosa*
			ophrys sphegodes ssp mammosa Bastard *
			ophrys sphegodes spruneri (Grecian Spider Orchid) *
			ophrys sphegodes S. epirotica *
993	K	243	*ophrys tenthredinifera* (Sawfly Orchid) *
914			*orchis albanica* *
			orchis coriophora ssp fragrans (Bug Orchid) *
			orchis coriophora x morio *
160	K	242	*orchis italica* (Italian Man Orchid) *
915			*orchis lactea* (Milky Orchid) *

782	C	242	*orchis laxiflora* (Jersey or Lax-coloured Orchid) *
645	6	242	*orchis morio* (Green Winged Orchid) *
			orchis morio ssp picta *
916			*orchis papilionacea* (Pink Butterfly Orchid) *
			orchis papilionacea x morio *
136	8	242	*orchis provincialis* (Provence Orchid) *
923			*orchis provincialis ssp pauciflora* *
693	8	243	*orchis quadripunctata* (Four Spotted Orchid) *
917			*orchis saccata* (Fan Lipped Orchid) *
491	3		*orchis simia* (Monkey Orchid) *
918			*orchis tridentate* (Toothed Orchid) *
919			*orchis ustulata* (Burnt Orchid) *
920			*plantanthera bifolia* (Lesser Butterfly Orchid) *
698	8		*platanthera chlorantha* (Greater Butterfly Orchid)
921			*serapias cordigera* (Heart Flowered Orchid) *
500	3		*serapias lingua* (Tongue Orchid) *
749	8		*serapias neglecta* (Scarce Serapias) *
922			*serapias parviflora* (Small Flowered Tongue Orchid) *
150	K	243	*serapias vomeracea* (Long Lipped Serapias) *
996	K		*spiranthes spiralis* (Autumn Lady's Tresses)
			AIZOON FAMILY
461	3		*carpobrotus acinaciformis* (Red Hottentot Fig)
			ARUM FAMILY
671	7		*arum italicum* (Large Cuckoo Pint)
			BEDSTRAW FAMILY
689	7		*cruciata laevipes* (Crosswort)
			BELLFLOWER FAMILY
592	5		*campanula bononiensis*
473	3		*campanula ramosissima* (Pale Bellflower)
			BINDWEED FAMILY
441	3	244	*calystegia soldanella* (Sea Bindweed)

499	3	244	*convolvulus althaeoides* (Mallow-leaved Bindweed)
			BORAGE FAMILY
503	1	244	*alkanna tinctoria* (Alkanet)
479	3		*echium plantagineum* (Purple Bugloss)
626	6		*symphytum bulbosum* (Tuberous Comfrey)
475	3		*borago officinalis* (Borage)
726	8	244	*anchusa azurea* (Large-blue Alkanet)
746	8		*anchusa arvensis* (Bugloss)
			BROOMRAPE FAMILY
593	5	245	*orobanche arenaria* (Sand Broomrape)
774	C	245	*orobanche lavandulacea* (Lavender Broomrape)
763	8		*orobanche cernua*
687	7		*orobanche amethystea* (Amethyst Broomrape)
417	3	245	*orobanche crenata* (Bean Broomrape)
			BUTTERCUP FAMILY
414	3		*anemone coronia (Crown Anemone)*
576	5		*anemone hortensis (Broad-leaved Anemone)*
617	6		*nigella damascena (Love-in-a-mist)*
			CARROT FAMILY
606	5	245	*smyrnium rotundifolium*
452	3		*ferula communis* (Giant Fennel)
748	8		*orlaya grandiflora* (Orlaya)
			CABBAGE FAMILY
467	3		*aubrieta deltoidea* (Aubrieta)
440	3		*cardaminopsis arenosa* (Sand Rock Cress)
610	5		*cardamine pratensis* (Lady's Smock)
661	6		*crambe tataria*
468	3	252	*lunaria annua* (Honesty)
623	6		*malcolmia angulifolia*
628	6		*matthiola incana* (Hoary Stock)
564	4		*matthiola tricuspidata* (Three Horned Stock)

756	8		*rorippa amphibia* (Great Yellow Cress)
			DAISY FAMILY
566	4		*helichrysum leontodon*
566	4		*helichrysum stoechas* (Stinking Everlasting)
556	4	246	*pallenis spinosa*
453	3		*chrysanthemum segetum* (Corn Marigold)
605	5		*chrysanthemum segetum* (Corn Marigold)
591	5		*calendula arvensis* (Field Marigold)
511	1	246	*galactites tomentosa* (Galactites)
561	4		*centaurea nemoralis* (Lesser Knapweed)
755	8		*centaurea cyanus* (Cornflower)
629	6	246	*tragopogon porrifolius* (Salsify)
595	5	246	*crepis rubra* (Pink Hawksbeard)
621	6		*Chrysanthemum coronarium incl. var. discolour* (Crown Daisy including bi-coloured variety)
			FIGWORT FAMILY
635	6	247	*scrophularia peregrina* (Nettle-leaved Figwort)
442	3		*verbascum blatteria* (Moth Mullein)
631	6		*verbascum graecum* (Greek Mullein)
611	5		*verbascum phoeniceum* (Purple Mullein)
439	3	247	*bellardia trixago* (Bellardia)
			FLAX FAMILY
403	3		*linum leucanthum*
			FUMITORY FAMILY
476	3		*fumaria capreolata* (Ramping Fumitory)
485	3		*fumaria officinalis* (Common Fumitory)
			GERANIUM FAMILY
688	7	247	*geranium asphodeloides*
679	7	247	*geranium pyrenaicum* (Pyrennean Cranesbill)
567	4		*erodium malacoides* (Soft or Mallow-leaved Stork's-Bill)
679	7		*erodium cicutarium* (Common Stork's Bill)

			HEATH FAMILY
514	1		*arbutus unedo* (Strawberry Tree)
			HONEYSUCKLE FAMILY
586	5		*lonicera caprifolium* (Perfoliate Honeysuckle)
			ST. JOHN'S WORT FAMILY
579	5		*hypericum annulatum*
			IRIS FAMILY
482	3	248	*iris germanica florentina* (Tall Bearded Iris, German Iris)
580	5		*iris germanica* (Tall Bearded Iris, German Iris)
550	4		*iris albicans*
526	1		*gladiolus italicus* (Field Gladiolus)
655	6	248	*gladiolus illyricus*
			JOINT PINE FAMILY
630	6	248	*ephedra fragilis* (Joint Pine)
			LILY FAMILY
728	8		*asphodelus ramosus* (Asphodel)
733	8		*asphodeline lutea* (Yellow Asphodel)
126	8	248	*fritillaria graeca thesala*
478	3		*ornithogalum ubellatum* (Star of Bethlehem)
710	8		*hyacinthella leucophaea* (Hyacinthella)
711	8		*hyacinthella leucophaea* (Hyacinthella)
612	5		*muscari botryoides* (Small Grape Hyacinth)
427	3	249	*muscari comosum* (Tassel Hyacinth)
718	8		*muscari armeniacum* (Armenium Grape Hyacinth)
670	7		*allium roseum* (Rose Garlic)
658	6	249	*allium trifoliatum*
			MALLOW FAMILY
652	6		*Malva* (Mallow)
			MINT FAMILY
697	8		*ajuga orientalis* (Oriental Bugle)
674	7		*ajuga genevensis* (Blue Bugle)

263

501	1		*ajuga reptans* (Bugle)
420	3		*prasium majus* (Prasium)
486	3		*phlomis fruticosa* (Jerusalem Sage)
722	8	249	*lamium bifidum*
558	4		*stachys scardica*
551	4	249	*stachys triloba*
438	3		*salvia triloba* (Greek Sage)
			BEECH FAMILY
677	7		*quercus coccifera* (Kermes or Holly Oak)
519	1	250	*quercus ilex* (Holm Oak)
			PEA FAMILY
125	4	250	*cercis siliquastrum* (Judas Tree)
413	3		*lupinus angustifolius* (Narrow Leafed Lupin)
470	3		*lupinus varius*
515	1		*psoralea bitumenosa* (Pitch Trefoil)
450	3	250	*vicia benghalensis* (Reddish Tufted Vetch)
463	3		*lathyrus ochrus* (Winged Vetchling)
614	5	250	*pisum sativum* (Garden Pea)
395	3	251	*medicago marina* (Sea Medick)
739	8		*dorycnium pentaphyllum*
445	3		*tetrgonolubus maritimus* (Winged Pea)
740	8		*tetragonolo purpureus* (Asparagus Pea)
435	3		*anthyllis vulneria praepropera* (Mediterraneum Kidney Vetch)
513	1		*coronilla emerus* (Scorpion Vetch or False Senna)
633	6		*securigera securidaca*
			PINK FAMILY
457	3	251	*lychnis viscaria* (Red German Catchfly)
570	4	251	*saponaria calabrica* (Calabrian Soapwort)
736	8		*saponaria ocymoides* (Rock Soapwort)
397	3		*silene colorata* (Mediterranean Catchfly)

608	5		*silene frivaldskyana*
451	3		*silene vulgaris* (Bladder Campion)
466	3		*stellaria holostea* (Greater Stitchwort)
			POPPY FAMILY
627	6		*papaver somniferum* (Opium Poppy)
456	3		*papaver rhoeas* (Common Poppy)
663	6	251	*glaucium flavum* (Yellow Horned Poppy)
			PRIMROSE FAMILY
469	3		*glaux maritima* (Silk Milkwort)
424	3		*anagallis arvensis* (Scarlet Pimpernel)
			ROCKROSE FAMILY
411	3		*cistus incanus ssp creticus* (Cretan Cistus)
507	1		*cistus incanus* (Large Pink Cistus)
408	3		*cistus salvifolius* (Sage-leaved Cistus)
436	3	252	*cistus monspeliensis* (Narrow-leaved Cistus)
455	3		*helianthemum nummularia* (Common Rockrose)
587	5		*helianthemum salicifolium* (Willow-leaved Rockrose)
			SAXIFRAGE FAMILY
724	8		*saxifraga rotundifolia* (Round-Leaved Saxifrage)
			WOOD SORREL FAMILY
995	K		*oxalis enneaphylla*
779	C		*oxalis stricta* (Upright Yellow Sorrel)
			SPURGE FAMILY
727	8		*euphorbia helioscopa* (Sun Spurge)
705	8		*euphorbia myrsinitis* (Broad-leaved Glaucous Spurge)
			VALERIAN FAMILY
643	6		*valeriana officinalis* (Valerian)
405	3	252	*valeriana tuberosa*

Food

Here are the tried and tested recipes of the Greek dishes we cook in the UK with English ingredients. Most are for six people but my *Kleftiko* needs a shoulder of lamb, which may mean that there will be meat left over for a few mouth-watering sandwiches.

Greek food is generally served *ola mazi*, with a plate in the centre of the table shared by 'all together'.

Jannie's Taramasalata
(Smoked cod's roe dip)

Moisten 175g pieces of crustless stale white bread with milk and mix with 2 crushed garlic cloves and 180g of smoked cod's roe, dug out of its skin. With electric hand mixer gradually add 5 tablespoons of extra virgin oil and 1 tablespoon of lemon juice, tasting all the time. Add finely chopped parsley.

Horta
(Boiled vegetables in lemon & oil)

Corfu is blessed with wonderful fresh vegetables, which can be bought from local stalls along the roadside and the markets.

Drop the vegetables in lots of boiling water and cook until *al dente*. Immediately drain off all the water and allow to cool slightly, adding olive oil and a little lemon juice when still warm. (Only very little salt needs to be added.) Try little courgettes, broccoli (including the stems sliced into 1cm cylinders) or French beans; always cut into mouth-size pieces before dropping into boiling water. For country dwellers, try dandelion leaves (which can be used in a salad), charlock or mustard, wild asparagus and edible weeds.

Tsigarelli
(Spicy spinach)

Boiled mixed greens (spinach, Swiss chard etc.) are added to spring onions browned in oil, tomato paste, cayenne pepper and garlic stems, both the cultivated and milder wild versions, and finally seasoned with chopped parsley, dill, fennel and mint to taste.

Potates Keftedes
(Potato croquettes)

Boil and mash six potatoes with butter; stir in two well-beaten eggs, 100g grated cheeses (e.g. cheddar and parmesan); form into round, not too thick, flat cakes; toss in plain flour and fry in very hot olive oil until golden brown.

Potates Fournou
(Roast potatoes)

Wash small new (Charlotte) potatoes; bake on an oven tray with olive oil, whole garlic cloves, plenty of dry oregano, lemon juice, salt and pepper until just soft. Turn frequently.

Imam
(Baked aubergine)

Slice aubergine in half and bake until soft, then pour over a mix of chopped red onions and tomato purée, rebake and finally sprinkle with feta (at *O Yiannis*) or gouda (at *Platopigatho*) and return to oven until cheese is soft.

Salata Horiatiki
(Village salad)

'Village' or rustic salad consists of bite-size chunks of tomato, green pepper, cucumber (sliced in half lengthways and then across) and feta, with thinly sliced red onion and black olives (ideally Kalamata) folded on a plate or bowl. Sprinkle with oregano and four parts extra virgin oil to one part red wine vinegar.

Neratzosalata
(Orange salad)

Peel and slice tart oranges into thick slices. Sprinkle on pinches of salt, sugar and paprika and drizzle on oil.

Bourtheto
(Red fish stew)

Fishermen used whatever they had left over after selling their fish: e.g. minnows, boney *scorpio* or glorious grouper. *Kokkino pipero*, hot red pepper bought in sacks in the market, gave the stew its heat and its colour without the need for tomatoes. Finely chop and fry 3 large onions and 5 cloves of garlic in a saucepan until soft; add 1 tablespoon of both sweet paprika and cayenne pepper and water and simmer for 15 minutes. Cover with water and add 1.5 kg cod steaks, 1 tablespoon of tomato paste and salt and cook for 30 minutes. Pour on juice from one lemon and serve. This recipe is similar to *Toula's*. *O Yiannis* adds mashed sun-dried tomatoes.

Bianco
(White fish stew)

Boil 500g peeled potatoes, 6 thinly sliced garlic cloves, salt and pepper, and ½ cup oil for 10 minutes in shallow uncovered pan. Add 1kg grey mullet steaks and cook for 20 minutes. Pour in juice from 1 lemon and serve.

John's *Kleftiko*
(Roast lamb)

Kleftiko is named after the Klefts, who were the heroes in Greek history and the main fighters in the War of Independence. They lived in the mountains and would put whatever meat they caught in a pot and take it to the village baker, who would put it into the cooling oven after the bread had been baked.

My version, which I cook frequently in England, tries to emulate the Kleftic way. Cut each clove of a whole head of garlic lengthways into 3. Wash and dry a 2-2.5 kg shoulder of lamb, then make deep incisions with a sharp pointed knife and insert a sliver of garlic into each until all the garlic is used. Pat grated sea salt onto both sides, put on a large piece of foil and pour the juice of 2 lemons equally over both sides of the shoulder. Wrap up the foil and leave for 3 hours or over night in the fridge. Rub 2 tablespoons of dried oregano evenly onto the shoulder, seal again in the foil and put in the (fan) oven heated to 170C. After 10 minutes turn oven down until indicator changes from 'roast' to 'warming' at 150C and cook for 4/5 hours, by which time the meat will fall off the bone.

Roger's *Stifado Kouneli*
(Rabbit stew)

This wonderful warm winter stew can use chopped beef steak, which we buy already prepared from a supermarket, or rabbit, which our marvellous fishmonger in Twickenham segments for us.

Heat 3 tablespoons of oil in a casserole; dust rabbit pieces with flour and fry until brown. Add 5 garlic cloves, 50ml red wine vinegar, 600ml red wine, 400g can chopped tomatoes, 5cm cinnamon stick, 6 cloves, 2 fresh bay leaves, 50g currants, 6 ground allspice berries, 1 teaspoon salt and ½ teaspoon ground peppercorns; bring to boil and simmer for 55 minutes.

Caramelize for 10 minutes 450g pickling onions or shallots in a pan with 15g melted butter, ½ teaspoon sugar and 2 tablespoons of water. Stir into rabbit when cooked and simmer for further 5 minutes.

Spanakopita
(Spinach pies)

Spanakopitakia are little triangular shaped mouth-watering morsels made from *filo* pastry which is available at most UK supermarkets.

Softly brown half a finely chopped small onion in a tablespoon of oil and add 500g finely shredded spinach leaves until they wilt down. Drain, press out excess liquid and return to pan with 2 finely chopped spring onions and cook for a minute, then cool.

Crumble 100g feta cheese into a bowl and mix in 1 egg, 1 tablespoon of grated of *kefalotiri* or parmesan, pinch of freshly grated nutmeg, 2 tablespoons of chopped fresh mint and salt and pepper.

5cm from the bottom of a 7.5cm wide, full-length strip of *filo* pastry, place 1 heaped teaspoon of mixture. Then fold the bottom 5cm of pastry across to left to form a triangle; carry on folding the parcel over straight, then right, then straight, then left, until the pastry strip ends, keeping the triangular shape. Brush with butter and bake in hot oven. Eat whilst hot and crisp.

Baklava
(Sweet pastries)

Heat 100g unsalted butter with 1 cup of sugar and 1 cup of hot water and add 2 cups of chopped walnuts. From 450g of *filo* pastry, lay three or fours sheets on a well-buttered baking-tin and brush with melted butter. Spread on a thin layer of the filling and lightly sprinkle with cinnamon. Repeat the layers of *filo* and nuts; tuck in ends and sides to contain filling; brush top with butter and score into squares with sharp knife. Bake in moderate oven until crisp and golden.

Boil 1 cup sugar, 1 cup of honey, 1 cup of water and juice of 1 lemon and pour over *baklava*. Cool before serving.

Conclusions

In 1966, Jannie and I discovered the empty beaches of the wild west coast. Accessed by tracks dating back a hundred years to British rule, they were one of the reasons why we fell in love with the island. The locals were the other reason for our romance: they would never pass without a greeting; and they often gave us a little gift.

Our walk along the Corfu Trail took us along some of the same tracks, and the locals were as friendly as ever. However, over the eight days, I discovered parts of the island I did not know existed. The agricultural south-west offered us a vision of years gone by; the dunes beside Lake Korission released the secret of its juniper forest and its floral glades; the west coast ridge provided us with sensational vistas; the northern slopes proved how undeveloped parts of Corfu are still; and the karst plateau of Mt. Pantocrator opened my eyes to ancient fields covered in orchids.

I enjoyed an amazing holiday with my two friends: Sydney introduced me to his world of flowers; and Charles was throughout the complete diplomat though at times a poor route finder. Each evening Rachel and Jannie joined us for excellent dinners and to hear the amusing stories from the day's walk.

Perhaps the best part of our journey was the company of our guest-walkers; they had interesting stories to tell and I learnt a lot from them.

The one conclusion I could not have forecast was how so many of our guest-walkers on our journey along the Corfu Trail are actually doing something *now* about a world short of energy: Nikos and his insulation; Mitch with his solar energy; Dierk, who is energy self-sufficient; and Fried with his geo-thermal energy.

Jannie and I also do our little bit: our house is over insulated and we now drive a Toyota diesel Aygo, which last summer in Denmark, where everyone drives slowly, achieved 78 mpg. Toyota claim I can get 83 mpg; we are still trying!

My Danish sister-in-law has also made her contribution to a greener world. Her wind turbine has been generating electricity since 1984; it is an essential source of income for her. Unlike Britain which talks a lot, Europeans are actually tackling the energy issue. Right across Northern Germany and Denmark wind turbines are turning in the wind and saving fossil fuels. Photovoltaic solar panels cover numerous roofs in Southern Germany and line the Italian autostrada.

NBC's Keith Miller, whom I interviewed in the Day 8 chapter, said that he thought oil would run out by 2050.

I replied "My grandson will be exactly 50 years old. If you are right, then our generation should feel incredibly guilty about the way we have wasted millions of years of nature's work."

Our guests have provided food for thought on how we can reduce our dependency on fossil fuels. Unless we do so, the elderly and poor will face a cold future as prices escalate.

My two good friends and I had a wonderful holiday. We say: "Please come to Corfu and walk the Corfu Trail; enjoy the flowers in the spring; feast on the Corfiot cuisine; and forget all the troubles we face in the world today."

Bus times and walking organisers

Buses leave Green Bus Station near port or (*) Blue Bus Station, San Rocco Square; weekend buses less frequent; phone 2661028927 or see http://www. allcorfu.com/ou-buses.html for latest times.

Day	To/from	From town	To town	Min	nb
1	Kavos	8.15, 10.00		90	6
1	Lefkimmi		18.15	75	
2	Lefkimmi bypass	8.15, 10.00		75	6
2	Argirades		17.30, 19.30	60	1,6
2	St. George		16.30	60	1
3	St. George	9.00		60	1
3	Milia	8.15, 10.00		60	1,6
3	A Pavliana		15.00	45	2
3	Ag Gordis		18.15	40	2
4	A Pavliana	6.00		45	2
4	Ag Gordis	8.15		40	2
4	Pelekas *		18.30	30	*
5	Pelekas *	10.00		30	*
5	Paleokastritsa		16.45	45	
6	Paleokastritsa	8.30		45	
6	Agros		17.00	75	3
7	Agros	9.00		75	3
7	Spartilas		16:30	60	4
8	Spartilas	5.00		60	4
8	Kentroma		16.15	75	5

1. Summer time bus goes to St. George
2. Pentati bus. Summer time bus goes to Agios Gordis
3. Sidari bus (Time at Sidari)
4. Prinila bus (Time at Prinila)
5. Kassiopi bus (Time at Kassiopi)
6. Bus to/from Kavos

For walking holidays, contact Ramblers World Wide (01707331133) and Aperghi Travel (00302661048713)

YIANNIS BOOKS

John Waller trained as an engineer, founded a computer company and invented software. He was a Liberal councillor in the London Borough of Richmond for 17 years and three times parliamentary candidate for Twickenham

Other books published by Yiannis Books are:

2004 ***Greek Walls – an Odyssey in Corfu*** by John Waller
2005 ***Corfu Sunset – Avrio never comes*** by John Waller
2006 ***Irish Flames*** – Peter Waller's true story of the Black and Tans by John Waller
2007 ***The Papas and the Englishman – From Corfu to Zagoria*** by Roy Hounsell, introduced by John Waller
2008 ***Corfu Sketches – A Thirty-year Journey*** with sketches by Theresa Nicholas and text by John Waller
2009 ***Corfu Town Walks*** – 8 pages laminated A5 walks

In 2007 John wrote the play ***Flames of Freedom*** based on the book, *Irish Flames*.

"A tightly plotted historical drama, with plenty of twists and turns in the action to keep the audience interested. The factor of truth in the story also adds another dimension of interest." *Abbey Theatre, Dublin*

He hopes for a production in Ireland or England in the near future.

Details are on www.yiannisbooks.com.

Greek Walls

an odyssey in Corfu

John Waller

illustrated by John Chipperfield

John Waller, engineer and
ex-politician, when given a
punt for his 60th birthday,
started his writing journey:
2004 *Greek Walls*
2005 *Corfu Sunset*
2006 His first novel
200? *3 persons in a punt*
(From source to sea
down the Thames!)

You've been to Greece? "Wallow in nostalgia" with *Greek Walls*
You've never been to Corfu? Read *Greek Walls* and you'll go!

In 1966, John Waller and
his Danish wife fall in love
with Corfu, 'a heaven on
earth'. On the wild west
coast, they build a small
summer house, which
nearly slides down the
mountain. Their neighbour
pumps sewage onto their
land …

**"Often funny, always
informative"**
*Hilary Whitton Paipeti,
The Corfiot*

"Most enjoyable read"
Lesley Toll, Daily Mail

"Wildly entertaining"
*Tom Teodorczuk,
Evening Standard*

yiannisbooks@aol.com

Front cover 'View from the villa'
by kesselerob@aol.com

UK   £7.99
EU   12 euro
US $15

ISBN 0-9547887-0-2

9 780954 788704 >

Corfu Sunset
Avrio Never Comes

John Waller

Illustrated by John Chipperfield

John Waller, engineer
and ex-politician, when
given a punt for his 60th
birthday, started his
writing journey:
2004 *Greek Walls*
2005 *Corfu Sunset*
2006 His first novel
200? *3 persons in a*

You love Greece? How about the Greek workmen?
Fancy living in the sun? Read *Corfu Sunset* first

Just retired John Waller
and his Danish wife
decide to renovate their
near-derelict holiday
home. They gain control
from their neighbour
who has pumped sewage
on their land.

In a frenetic summer
they build a road up the
mountain and a pool,
veranda and new roof
for their villa. A party is
held to celebrate a great
Greek victory.

Delightful episodes and characters emerge from the pages of *Corfu Sunset*.
A highly amusing account of the highs and lows of property ownership
abroad with attention to detail that puts most travel authors in the shade.
*Tom Teodorczuk, **Evening Standard***

Corfu Sunset is essential reading for anyone thinking of moving abroad to a
place in the sun, revealing with panache and passion the rewards and drawbacks
of buying property in a remote but warm outpost of southern Europe.
*Nigel Lewis, **Daily Mail***

yiannisbooks@aol.com

Front cover by Helena Hutchinson
'Sunset through the olive tree'.

ISBN 0-9547887-1-0

UK	£7.99
EU	Euro 12
US	$15

9 780954 788711

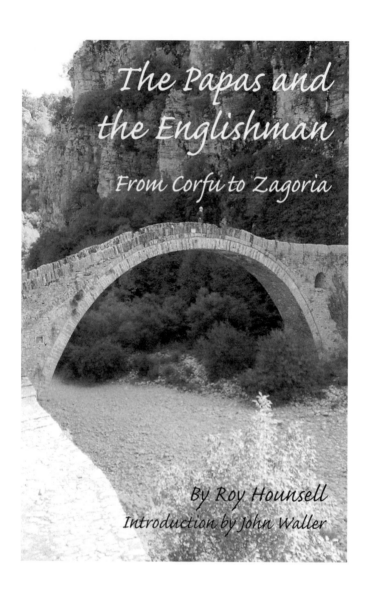

The Papas and the Englishman

From Corfu to Zagoria

By Roy Hounsell

Introduction by John Waller

In 1991 Patrick Leigh Fermor was asked, "If you wanted to go somewhere – somewhere right off the map, with no tourists or modern developments – where would you go?"

He replied: "Epirus – the north, the mountains. You might have a chance of finding places there." It was in 1991 that Roy and Effie Hounsell moved into their place in Zagoria.

In 1980, having been made redundant, Roy and his wife left England to try their hand at establishing themselves in Corfu. They visited mountainous Zagoria in Northern Mainland Greece and were captivated by its magnificent, rugged beauty and its mouldering, unspoiled stone villages. All desire to move there was dashed by their poor ability to speak Greek. Eventually they bought a tumble-down property in Koukouli. They struggled with the rebuilding, helped by the village priest, Papa Kostas, created a garden out of the jungle and joined in with the villagers to become regarded as locals.

"What makes this different from other "No Going Back" sagas is how the authors have engaged with their neighbours and helped keep an isolated community alive." *Marc Dubin, co-author, Rough Guide to Greece*

"Charting the progress of the author's transformation from 'outsider' into genuine local, this book sets standards for the relocation genre. Roy Hounsell writes lovingly about the beautiful location, and unpatronizingly about the people he meets and befriends along the way." *Hilary Whitton-Paipeti, Editor, The Corfiot*

"Many of us dream of buying and renovating a house in the mountains – but Roy Hounsell's unusual tale of his Greek adventure is a useful and well-paced read." *Nigel Lewis, Managing. Editor, A Place in the Sun Magazine*

yiannisbooks@aol.com

UK	£ 7.99
EU	Euro 12
US	$ 15

ISBN 978-0-9547887-3-5

9 780954 788735 >

Corfu sketches *A thirty-year journey*

Sketches by Theresa Nicholas   Text by John Waller

Over 200
sketches

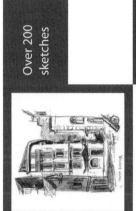

UK £19.95

EU €29

US $39

www.yiannisbooks.com

Corfu sketches – A thirty-year journey shows you Corfu, the World Heritage Site and its villages, as seen through the eyes of an artist who has lived on the island since 1961. Enjoy five walks: along the Tourist Trail; through the Venetian Old Town to the Mourayia, the sea walls; to the Jewish Quarter and its synagogue; up the hill to the smart end of town and via the Old Port to the market. Then join in the Easter parade. Visit 30 villages, meet their people and see the work they do. **Look carefully, *little has changed.*** This will be a journey you will always treasure.

283

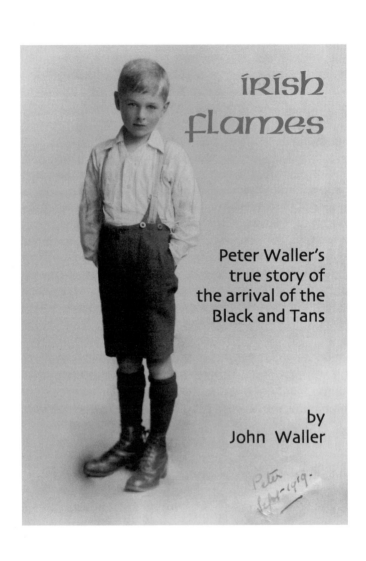

íRísh flames

Peter Waller's true story of the arrival of the Black and Tans

by
John Waller

Before Peter Waller died – he is pictured on the front cover aged eight – he gave a partial manuscript to the author, his half-brother. Here is Peter's story.

"IRELAND in 1920. The Black and Tans have just arrived to crush the growing Irish Revolution and one boy watches as his country is torn apart by flames of freedom, hate and love.

Irish Flames is a thriller based on the intimate memories of Peter Waller – a boy growing up during those troubled times.

Stories of the brutality of The Black and Tans have been passed down through generations of families but now the words of an eyewitness can show us what it was really like.

Anybody with even a little Irish blood in his or her veins will find this story a remarkable account of the end of British Rule."

The Irish Post (April 22)

ISBN 0954788729

£8.99   €12.99

www.yiannisbooks.com

ISBN 0-9547887-2-9

9 780954 788728 >

Walk Corfu Town with John Waller
1. Along the Tourist Trail

From the carpark (X) in the centre of the Cricket ground.

1. Visit the Old Fort built in 1546 during Venetian rule (1386-1797). Go under the Venetian Lion and past the church to reach the summit. The view is from the Garitsa Bay (Y).

2. Visit the Palace of SS Michael and George, built during British rule (1814-1864).

3. Walk to the Liston (arches), built during French rule (1807-1814) in the style of Rue de Rivoli.

4. Go through the centre of the Liston into Nikiforou Theotoki St. On the right, is the Square of the Saints.

5. 100m further on is the centre point of the World Heritage Site (WHS). On the right is the House of Daniel Cobici, built in 1680.

6. Above the arches are the sculpted keystones; underneath the book shop.

7. On the left, 100 metres further on, are more faces.

8. Return to 5, turn left, then right into Ag. Spiridonas and pass the Church of Ag. Spiridon, the island's patron saint, built in 1589.

9. Finish on the Liston for a cup of Greek coffee and baklava!

286

Flames of Freedom

The play **Flames of Freedom** is based on the book *Irish Flames – The Arrival of the Black and Tans*. British history (e.g. Retreat from Kabul, Bombing of Afghans in 1919, Reprisal of Balbrigan and the Destruction of Cork) forms a background to the play and asks the question 'Are we seeing a repeat today?' The play focuses on the relationship between Robbie (my half-brother) and Conn (the innocent gardener who becomes a militant).

In Act One, we see rural Ireland in April 1920 before the Tans arrive and Conn's transition from hearing about 'Freedom' and wanting to be as 'free as a swallow', to joining the Volunteers, who burn down the Barracks. The final scene in Act One is the famous speech by RIC Colonel Smyth at Listowel when he announces the **SURGE**.

We also meet Martin, leader of the Volunteers and headman at the neighbouring estate owned by ex-Indian Army Colonel Kernahan. Robbie's mother Meli lends Martin plays e.g. Cathleen Ni Houlihan.

My father Alec arrives back from Palestine and is welcomed by elderly Mrs Murphy, the family cook and mentor for three generations of the family. Meli and Alec discuss Palestine and promises made (as in Ireland), Mesopotamia, needed to safeguard oil in Persia, and British bombing of the Kurds, the Marsh Arabs and the Afghans.

In Act Two, the Tans gate-crash the New Year's Eve (1920/1) party at the Big House and are ambushed on leaving. Their leader is killed and Martin is wounded. Meli saves Martin's life; Conn is beaten up at the Tan's HQ and vows to kill the 'traitor' Kernahan; the Tans return to torch the Big House with possibly Robbie, Con or Martin inside.

The final scene is set in a Boston Bar in 1932. Martin, a reporter on the *Globe*, Robbie, visiting Harvard, and Conn, a militant brawler, meet again. Robbie, 'a posh Englishman' in Conn's eyes, argues with Conn, a 'murderer' in Robbie's eyes, who concludes: "Martin, write that war will never end until occupiers leave and men are free."

Great gifts

For further copies of our books, please send a cheque, payable to Yiannis Books, for the cover price to:

John Waller
Yiannis Books
101 Strawberry Vale
TWICKENHAM
TW1 4SJ

We will return, postage paid, signed books as requested PLUS a FREE pack of 4 Corfu Town Walks, priced £4.99.

Please indicate to whom you wish the book to be inscribed.

For bulk purchase we can offer a discount. Please email john@yiannisbooks.com.

More Corfu flowers

We are building a database of Corfu flowers based on the 150 identified on our walk and the orchids in the British cemetery. Please send an image of the flower, its Latin name and English name, the date photographed and where it was seen to info@corfuflowers.com.

Your name will appear against the photograph if you so wish.